D1204508

The Salmon

MICHAEL WIGAN

The Salmon

WILLIAM
COLLINS

William Collins
An imprint of HarperCollins*Publishers*
77–85 Fulham Palace Road,
Hammersmith, London W6 8JB
www.williamcollinsbooks.com

First published in Great Britain by William Collins 2013

1 3 5 7 9 10 8 6 4 2

A catalogue record for this book is
available from the British Library.

ISBN 978-0-00-748764-6 (hardback)
ISBN 987-0-00-748765-3 (eBook)

Printed and bound in Great Britain by
Clays Ltd, St Ives plc

To Robert Pointon and Hugh Ardagh, my two teachers at Sussex Tutors in Brighton, England, who taught me how to appreciate literature and write clean English. I hope I have not let them down. Neither, as far as I know, had any interest in fish. The desire to communicate precedes having anything useful to say, as anyone in the pub before closing knows.

Contents

The Journey

The night is overcast and promising. I packed a large spot-lamp, reserve mini-torch and windcheater into the truck and chugged 5 miles through the blackness up a track to a high tributary of Sutherland's River Helmsdale, in the north high-lands of Scotland. My destination is an isolated spot, several miles from any road or house. I could only feel a light wind, which is good for salmon-watching because wind-ruffled water obscures the fish-action.

Painstakingly I checked a stretch of river, as I do every year, for numbers of paired salmon preparing to spawn. This section of the river has excellent pebbly expanses of small gravel in which salmon like to make their nests or 'redds', and year after year I have found salmon in couples side by side in the riffly bits behind large boulders, facing upriver. They are unworried by the bright light, instead focused on the act which ensures that their genetics pass down and that their own progeny will one autumn occupy that same riffle and reproduce there too.

In the spotlight you can see everything; the markings on their backs and their rich tartan bodies – which by this time of year are red and black and magenta – the heads of the cocks in luridly contrasting colours, and you see their tails gently finning in the current, steady as metronomes.

But tonight there was nothing there. The pools were empty. It was easy to see because the water was low, lower than I had seen it before in November – which is a wet month hereabouts.

Then I heard what sounded like hooves crashing through water. I thought I had winded stags, for some of the red stags come to the river's edge at this intersection and they run from human scent. I thought a small party had crossed the river below, so I walked down the bank.

In the radiance of the powerful spot-light was a striking spectacle. A salmon on its side was arcing in a shallow pool, its body bent like a bow. The sound I had heard was the smacking of its body back against the water. I looked closer. There were two, a cock and a hen, small-sized. They had swum up the river this far to find suitable redds, prompted by the echo of their own birth in this tributary, maybe in the self-same stretch, in an earlier time. But the pair was marooned. They had got this far and the frost had driven the water level down as they waited to reproduce, while below them the riffly water was even slower. When salmon swim through low water the mucilaginous slime can be scraped from their bodies, exposing them to infections. It was hard to go down and impossible to go up. This pair had traded on rain and been let down.

Undeterred, they were spawning anyway, and she was busy laying eggs with her shuddering body ejaculating the pink globes into a groove in the pebbles. I was watching a heroic act of self-replication.

Presumably the rest of the normal number, maybe a dozen pairs in a three-hundred-yard stretch, had dropped back as water had shallowed. Indeed, that appeared to be so because in the main stem of the river there were salmon pairs all around. Some sections were a maelstrom of spawners, cramped for space, elbowing and shoving each other to get at the good clean gravels.

The air was chilling down. I clambered back into my truck and thought. This was a new event; sometimes the river was too high to see the fish pairs well, sometimes the wind shook up the surface too much to get a clear view, but in the best years you could look down on the spawners as if in an aquarium. You know if the fish have already spawned and buried their eggs in the gravel because when hit by the light they run and squiggle downstream. Un-spawned, they face the light. It is one of Nature's great spectacles.

For the salmon is natural royalty – no other fish has excited human interest to the extent that *Salmo salar* does. Let's tease out the mystique which has resulted in salmon-fixated anglers, in salmon-bewitched writers, in salmon biologists and random salmon-dreamers.

This is the fish that connects land and sea, it is our bridge with the maritime, and the sea is twenty-first-century man's largest getaway. Anyone can find a boat and go out there, un-harassed, free to turn left or right or go straight on. The salmon is an emissary from this vast fecund zone, where the occupants are out of sight beneath the waves. This is the place where salmon accumulate their fat and gain body weight. It is where they feed to become some of the fastest swimmers anywhere. This is the place salmon acquire the condition that allows them to leap waterfalls, moving up rivers to re-visit their birthplace.

I have just seen the highest waterfall in Scotland which they can ascend in one mighty leap; it is 12 feet high and vertical. To help their passage the local fishery managers dam up the water in the pool below, raising its level by four feet, so that the homing salmon has a mere 8 feet to leap. Olympic athletes would balk.

I was told that the fish poke their heads out of the water and inspect the situation before assaying a leap that must cost them their last ounce of energy and strength. Then they use the upthrust from the deep boiling of the falling water to kick with their tails and twist their bodies, arrowing through spray over the lip of the ledge above. No wonder people marvel – a fish that flies!

What these fish are conveying to the upper reaches of natal rivers is a food-load accumulated in or near the Arctic Ocean. Many salmon from the American and Canadian north-east, nearby to an older class of European salmon, winter close to the shore of western Greenland. Here they gorge on krill and shrimp and capelin, small fish packed with nutrients that can be converted into body weight and condition.

It is known now that to find the food supply salmon use temperature bands as trackers. The presence of salmon is dictated by the food supply, and that is determined by seawater temperature. Lower temperatures mean slower growth rates, smaller egg sizes and later development, and smaller size can expose them more to predation. In the 1990s scientists found that capelin off Newfoundland spawned a whole month late owing to very low temperatures in spring, which would have had a knock-on effect for salmon. In this way a seasonal shift in the behaviour of prey can be critical for the body condition of salmon needing to bulk up for the journey home.

Salmon eat molluscs, worms and other fish at sea – even insects which land on the surface when they are near coasts and winds are offshore. It was always reckoned that salmon were opportunistic omnivores, and recently it has been found that their wide-ranging diet embraces lanternfish. These strange-looking denizens of the deep rise to the surface at night to prey on larvae and other floating titbits only to be intercepted by any foraging salmon as they come up.

Researchers were surprised to discover that this hunt was prosecuted even at considerable depths. Previously thought only to happen near the sea-surface layer, it transpires that salmon dive, and dive far. How they detect prey in the lightless deeps is unknown, but presumably they use echolocation or other senses so far unidentified. The behavioural picture gets more complex. Not only do they travel thousands of miles between feeding and breeding grounds, but they go downwards too. They touch our planet at its extremities.

Some of this adventurism helps explain their mighty grip on our imaginations.

The range of the fish is one of the factors. Not only does it span the north hemisphere from top to bottom but its potential larder is three-dimensional. Many animals can only find food to left and right, but salmon do so in all directions. Like birds in the air, they are free on all sides, yet often they end their breeding cycle in streams that a person could step over – so narrow they can barely turn their bodies round. Instead of turning, having spawned the fish still face upstream and drift down backwards with the current, often patched with fungus, half-alive, half-decaying. Using their salty environment as any rotational wild grazer uses its range, meeting appointments with feeding opportunities at different points, the fish climaxes in cramped confinement. Tackling lanternfish at depth, they reproduce in shallow stream-water often only half-submerged, usually under cover of darkness.

It is the transport of sea protein to the headwaters of rivers deep inland that completes the bridging of maritime and terrestrial. For the bodies of the deceased salmon that expired after spawning are deposited into an environment often starved of protein enrichment since the movement of glaciers down to the coast thousands of years ago. The residues of those shrimps, molluscs, fish and worms which have built our silver wanderer fall from its decaying carcase, seeping into the impoverished soils of the headwaters.

This is more strikingly so with the cousins of Atlantic salmon, the species inhabiting the Pacific and the American West. The largest of the seven species, kings or Chinooks, are physically bigger, but all Pacific species lay more eggs and are in greater abundance than Atlantics. Crucially, none of the Pacific species makes it back to sea; they all die after spawning inside the river-system. So when millions of these fish expire in the forested headwaters of British Columbia, Alaska, or the other states of the seaboard USA, it is equivalent to fertiliser dumping along river-banks on landscape scale.

Certainly, bears and eagles, wolverines and carrion-eating birds all feast on salmon remains in the spawned-out cemeteries where their lives ended, but for these species too this is body-building prior to the onset of harsh winters, with protein originally gleaned from the sea. A neat protein transfer has hitched a ride on salmon.

People conjecture whether the original runs of Atlantic salmon into the rivers of Western Europe and Scandinavia may have equalled in mass what still occurs in the western Americas.

Not only were the numbers of Atlantic salmon on a different scale to those of today, but so too were their dimensions. In 1885, near Rotterdam on the Rhine, 69,500 salmon were netted with an average weight of 18 pounds – a size approximating more to that of a Chinook than a modern-day Atlantic. We will never be sure what the volume of primeval runs into Europe were, except that they were spread over all of the western coastline and in infinitely greater numbers. But in 2010 I gleaned an idea of what the scene must have resembled at the foot of a lake called Meziadin in British Columbia in late July.

I had been fishing for steelhead, a sea-running trout, with Walter Faetz on the Bell Irving, a wilderness tributary of the major far north river-system named the Naas. Walter said he wanted to show something to my fellow angler and me. We drove an hour, drew up on a lakeside and launched a small boat. First, Walter motored up-lake awhile and we saw restless sockeye salmon packed in the outflow of a small river waiting for rain to allow them to run it. Then we chugged down the placid un-peopled lake to the outflow.

Here was a stretch of tumbling water, then a small circular lake maybe two hundred yards across, debouching through more rocks at the corner. Gaunt pines surrounded a scene of primitive energy. Vaulting into the air at the top end were vast fish appearing like polychrome Zeppelins out of the burbling water, to land again where they had lifted off. In their dying livery of magenta, crimson and mottled sick-yellow, king salmon lunged from the flowing river, lying down on it again and gradually submerging as if in slow motion.

In our small inflatable we paddled over where they lay. White fungus was growing on their fin-edges and backs and also on their heads. They were disintegrating whilst alive. Underneath the boat and to either side, they were flopping and swishing, listlessly lunging at each other, indifferent to our presence just feet away.

Across the current played out another enactment. Here was a long ridge of freshly churned gravel, and from its whiteness and lack of algal covering it was clear the gravel had been recently ploughed. Gently finning in the few feet of water above it were hundreds of bright crimson sockeye salmon – another, smaller species of salmon from the Pacific. The fish were stacked in layers, like wine bottles in an invisible rack. If I had got out and stood on that gravel-bank I would have surmounted millions of eggs promising the next generation of sockeye in this fecund river. Patiently awaiting our departure perched bald eagles looking huge in the spindly pines and gloomy light, preparing to compete with the patrolling grizzlies for the dying salmon. Compute the volume of fish-protein in that modest body of water and the mind boggles.

None of that protein richness would leave this environment; it formed part of the ecology – sea refreshing impoverished land far from the coast.

Out of interest I procured facts from the government website which records annual runs of salmon at a fish-pass just below Lake Meziadin. We drove there and saw salmon leaping in futility against the dam walls, others catching the faster water on the side where the fish-pass laddered its way up past the dam. The number of Chinooks that ran this branch of the Meziadin River was around 500, the number of sockeye around 200,000, and the coho run around 4,000. The River Meziadin is small – my fishing partner and I easily cast line across the central river-flow – yet the fish biomass on the redds in the autumn, acre for acre, must approximate to a beef feed-lot in the American Midwest.

What we witnessed was fish abundance from another epoch. It was part of a wider picture; that year, on the heels of scientific predictions of a diminished sockeye salmon run, in fact some 24 million fish showed up. Scientists sucked their thumbs. Fish are a jump ahead. It is tempting to wonder how close that scene with Pacific salmon in British Columbia paralleled in abundance what occurred in western Europe with their Atlantic cousins over 10,000 years ago, before human impact.

It may not only be the soil and avian predators that benefit from this transport of protein from the sea. In British Columbia, amply funded for fisheries research, it has been found that in their first year of life out of the egg, young steelhead a few inches long subsist largely on 'spawner-derived' feeding. After one year of age, 95 per cent of stomach content was proven to be from salmon eggs and carcases. This was discovered by tethering 400 dead salmon in a river and testing the stomach contents of young steelhead living downstream of them. In other words, they too were nourished on dead salmon at a critical development time. Related to salmon but not the same species, these migratory co-habitants would seemingly struggle if the big salmon runs disappeared.

Is this the case with Atlantics, our European species? Do their descendants subsist on their shredded flesh? No one knows.

The charm of the Atlantic's salmon is that a small percentage do not die; having spawned, some survive. It is thought that around one in twenty live to spawn twice, and they are mostly females. This simple fact changes their whole definition from that of their Pacific cousins. Their softened bodies roll with the current towards the sea. Able to move pigment around their bodies, they have changed colour throughout their lives – in sandy-bottomed streams parr colour up sandy; put a cock salmon in a dark tank and cover the top and it darkens, faster towards spawning, but take him out and he pales. Now the sea-seeking fish silver up, fresh-minted; their bodies carry a latent promise of recovery, return and procreation again. Ancient Egypt's Pharoahs would understand: they have an afterlife.

The passage to recovery is far from safe. Otters find them easy prey. Raucous gulls tug their barely sentient carcases from the shingle and devour them. Crows patrol the river edge for prey, squabbling over the rotten bodies. If any fortunate fish do manage to reach the ocean they run smack into hit-squads of patrolling sea mammals, in the form of grey and common seals. These far larger creatures can catch salmon by slashing them senseless with their flippers, and in a copy of sea-lion acts in the zoo, they flick them into the air, strip off the skins and swallow them as they fall.

The two seal species have protection in Europe, enjoying an almost complete prohibition on culling. Not consonant with the heavily managed catch quotas for all commercial fish, this status of sanctity and exclusion from management has its origin in the excesses of the whaling industry long ago. Whaling desecrated the populations of one of the world's largest and most miraculous beasts in a hell-for-leather (sic) war on natural resources that has no historic parallels for goriness and intemperance. In the case of the American buffalo, one species was hunted down; in the case of the whales, several species were decimated. For whales are ocean mammals which have to surface and can therefore be seen. The oceans were raked and re-raked until almost none of the species with value were left. The scars from that era have entered Western psyches and will be a long time healing.

Seals are the major predators of fish close to the coast. Commercial fishermen have shown that they eat far more of the fish in the North Sea than fishermen are catching. However, for the time being the images of whiskered recumbent lumps straddling offshore rocks, doe-eyed saltwater Labradors, is forceful: they are sacrosanct. The only shots they have to put up with are from cameras. There is no public appetite for the resumption of anything that could look remotely like whaling, with any sea mammal. No one wants to risk a repeat of those haunting consequences.

As in some other stories we will come to, the reason for selective management is the secrecy of the sea. Beneath the waves, all is hidden. If the waters were peeled back from coastal north Scotland and the hundreds of thousands of large seals were made visible, attitudes might change. The fish would look miniature and vulnerable by comparison, their attackers gross and greedy. But we see what we see, and what we see, we believe.

Seals have trouble catching fast-moving salmon in open seas, but weakened by reproduction and their starvation in freshwater the post-coital ghosts drifting from river-mouths make easy pickings in late winter. Early spring salmon in colder waters move slower, and they are easier prey too.

A few salmon survive. No one knows what predestines these few fish to survive their ordeals, but they do. Maybe they are just the fortunate ones. Many species cling to existence with only small numbers of breeders. They say the fecund rabbit can breed a million descendants in its own lifetime. Adult 'hen' salmon produce some 800 eggs for each pound of their body weight, so a good fish of fifteen pounds would squirt from her quivering flanks into the redds some 12,000 eggs. If she beat the odds and returned to spawn twice, she might have grown and be able to produce more eggs the second time. The egg output, though, depends on seasonal and physical factors and can vary widely.

The most times any salmon returned that I have heard of was a fish that negotiated survival for eight re-runs, which was netted off Newfoundland and aged by scale-reading – a cross-cut scale being interpreted like the rings of a tree. This one must have been up near the rabbit in terms of prolific genetic legacy! Similar return rates have been recorded in some of the glorious rivers of New Brunswick. On the eastern side of the Atlantic, a fish analysed in Wales had returned to the redds five times.

It is in the northern oceans that depleted salmon rebuild their condition. If you were to catch and eat these salmon before they had reconstituted themselves, they would be oily and disagreeable, like cod or mackerel after spawning.

For a long time pundits tried to work out where salmon winter; it was akin to the mystical quest for the end of the rainbow. Somewhere a fish as long as your finger grew exponentially to become a fish as long as your arm. Where was this fabulous larder? It is known now that a proportion of British salmon winter off western Greenland, where Greenlanders in small boats net them close to the coast. These salmon stay more than one winter. They are a minority here; many larger salmon from North America fatten off Greenland too. A little further north, the salmon of the Russian Kola Peninsular and the salmon connected to rivers on Norway's long coastline winter in the North Atlantic off Norway.

The salmon of eastern North America winter in the Labrador Sea and on the northern Grand Banks, as well as western

Greenland. It can be overlooked: the distance across the Davis Strait starting from northern Newfoundland is only 600 miles. Greenland's seas are a neighbourhood bouillabaisse. The fact of highly variable runs of east-coast salmon in North America is reckoned by scientists to be related to the environment, food supply and ocean temperature; so much is reasonably obvious. But unlike on the eastern side, where salmon-run prediction is not attempted, Canadian and American forecasts on fish runs are based on what is found in the sea off Newfoundland and Labrador when the water reaches four degrees. In the 1980s and 1990s, between Labrador and western Greenland sea temperatures were suppressed by Arctic waters pushing south. This in turn saw declining growth rates across species like capelin and cod, delayed spawning times and generally reduced salmon runs.

Not only are weather and climate unpredictable variables at sea, but living matter in the sea is infinitely complex. Any child at the seaside has noticed that if you bottle seawater the life seems to fade away. This is because the sea is a dynamic environment in a state of continuing flux. Filled with plankton, microscopic living particles of plants and animals, the sea is a bubbling broth. It has been calculated that the amount of organic material in an acre of sea equates to the vegetation on an acre of average land. Planktonic abundance fuels the vitality of seawater and is the foundation for a pyramid of creatures feeding from one predator level to the next.

Adult salmon are near the top of this pyramid. Fast swimmers, they evade other fish. Vulnerable to being cornered by seals and acrobatic sea mammals when in semi-confined areas like estuaries, they are generally too swift for capture. The rich soup of planktonic life becomes in turn the feed for krill, capelin, herring, shrimps and molluscs, which are all part of salmon's ocean diet.

Important elements like phosphorus and nitrogen determine marine productivity. These either wash onto the shelves that are the underwater extensions of landmasses, or are pushed from below in the deep ocean by upwellings as ocean currents mix, driven by the Earth's rotation. Areas of the ocean vary enormously in their productivity, the North Sea and the Grand Banks being shallow expanses and exceptionally fertile, as contrasted to vast parts of the mid-Pacific where the water, as you peer into it with the sun behind, is startlingly clear precisely because there is so little plankton and suspended material. It is as void as sterilised bottled drinking water. In other places millions of plant cells can occupy one cubic foot of seawater.

This partially explains what has been called the 'explosive growth' which salmon display after leaving their freshwater nurseries as six-inch smolts.

Marine biology and marine research have made quantum leaps in recent time. Two areas of rapidly advancing research concern life in the bathymetric deeps, where life-forms have been discovered way below depths at which it was formerly thought any life at all could exist, and secondly in the pelagic or surface skin of the ocean. Although we now know that salmon obtain food from depths of as much as 800 metres in the dimmed realms of the sperm whale, and can stay at 400–600 metres for as long as 24 hours, it is in the surface ocean layer that smolts have to survive when they leave rivers.

Their departure is called the smolt 'run'. The small fish leave their natal river for the great unknown when prompted by rising temperature. A government fisheries department in Scotland used infra-red images at night on a tributary of the River North Esk to watch smolts assembling for the 'run'. The technology was not perfect; rising water levels lost the images of fish, but the presence of smolt-traps further downriver showed that smolts did indeed continue running in high waters. For the bigger picture the technology served adequately. It showed that fish shoaled in small parties of three to six, they used the core of the current for propulsion, and they descended rivers pointing seaward.

Tagging with microchips has established another new finding. Smolts enter the sea in a mass to minimise predation. Having travelled downriver in small schools, they pack to go to sea, then closer to the sea becomes an assembly point. The reason is the same as why other small fish shoal – it enhances an individual's survival chance to be one of many congregated in a dense mass.

A salmon river is occasionally blessed with egg-bearing gravels all the way up its sinuous length. The Miramichi in Canada is an example of a spawning bed over a hundred miles long. Hen fish will sweep out redds and lay their eggs in them from the narrowest streams at the top to the wide, gravelly wash-out bars near the river-mouth. To coordinate the smolt runs, however, the development of eggs into fry and parr and then into smolts in the headwaters of the river must be earlier in the season, so that when these young shoals of salmon go seawards they do not miss the camouflage of other shoals of smolts which have matured later and which are waiting nearer the river-mouth.

Accordingly, in northern Scottish rivers parr begin to go silvery, and turn into smolts or 'smoltify', as early as March in the headwaters and as late as May lower down. To prepare them for ocean life, away from the shady corners and dark shadows of natal streams, they develop an ocean livery. Their skin grows a layer of silver guanine crystals. These crystals arranged in verticals rows act as mirrors, camouflaging the little fish by reflecting its surroundings.

The keen perception of Dr Richard Shelton, formerly head of the government's marine laboratory in Pitlochry in Scotland, noted that the only parts of the smolt to remain unaltered are the black edges to the fin and tail. He believes these are helpful visual aids to other smolts in keeping the pack together, whilst not giving too much definition away to predators.

To help the smolt register where it originated, and to find its own personal natal stream later as a fully grown fish, the hormone thyroxine is raised temporarily to allow the small brain to take in vital extra survival information.

The cohort of smolts journeys down the river, making the little flips and splashes familiar to springtime anglers, and reaches the sea to coincide with feeding opportunities. The oldest smolts reach the salt first and the youngest, maybe only a year old, go last, an order which is reversed when they return as adults. A critical feeding assignation is with the outburst of sand-eel larvae on the sandbanks.

The similar appearance of different smolts is deceptive. Those from the southern edge of range, France and Spain, are a fraction of the age of individuals from colder northern rivers. Whereas many southern European smolts are just over a year old, those from Arctic Norway, Greenland and Ungava Bay may be seven before they risk life at sea. From Iceland and Scotland smolts have dwelt from between two and five years in the river. The age difference reflects the length of the growing season, further north, less time.

It is an extraordinary thought that physically similar fish, at the same development stage, vary in age by so much. There are no obvious parallels in bird or mammal biology. Possibly there are comparable patterns in other fish, but none comes to mind. Salmon evolution is supreme adaptation.

What happens after the entry into seawater has recently been tracked in an internationally funded programme codenamed SALSEA-Merge. SALSEA is the most remarkable research on a fish at sea in recent time. The European Union, Canada, the USA, the Total Foundation in France, the Atlantic Salmon Trust in the UK and a variety of universities and agencies combined to fit out the RV Celtic Voyager and two other vessels with proper equipment, and then put the right people on board who knew what questions to ask and how to get answers.

The results fill in another corner of the lifestyle jigsaw.

The research boats spent three years catching around 27,000 juvenile salmon from 466 different locations in the North Sea, the Norwegian and Irish seas, and generally in the north-east Atlantic around the Faroe Islands and Iceland. Information from 284 out of Europe's 1,700 salmon rivers from nine countries was used in genetic sampling and analysis. The biggest sample came from Scotland, followed by Norway. By targeting the most productive and the largest rivers, the SALSEA team reckons that 80 per cent of Europe's productive salmon area was embraced by the research effort. The resulting picture then is a clear story about European salmon, including Russia and Scandinavia, up to 2011.

The novel side of the analysis was the use of genetics. Only recent science allows researchers to find out where a fish comes from. Work on Ireland's River Moy had already shown what a sprinkling of other rivers had found too – that inside their catchments salmon stocks can be divided up into genetically discrete populations. It was true of a minority of rivers, but demonstrated the impressive complexity of salmon adaptation.

The Atlantic salmon in some form or other has been occupying European and North American rivers for 60 million years. In that immense time it has developed local strains to adapt to local conditions. Then the last Ice Age ended, with a thaw that peeled back the ice-covered land over all Britain north of London. A mere 15,000 years separates us from the frigid conditions that dominated before. In cosmic terms it is a blink in time. Salmon saw pristine territory opening up in front of them, and occupied it.

Rivers in Scotland have plenty in common with other rivers in salmon range. They are spring-fed. These springs can come from hundreds of feet below ground and each one has a differing chemical composition. Also, the springs bubble from the ground loaded with different temperature readings, dependent on their depth.

Variations between springs account for differing populations of salmon. For the scent in each stream, and the mineral contents, differs from that of its neighbour. Salmon have brilliant olfactory senses, being able to pick out the most dilute odours from home-stream chemistry even through a fog of additives and man-made complexities. The fish's ancestors have used that water and over time adapted to it.

Sometimes that adaptation will translate into an identifiable genetic type. SALSEA went to sea armed in advance with the genetic map of many rivers. The researchers were hunting smolts, young salmon entering an alien saltwater world pregnant with feeding and with threat. What galvanised researchers to go to all this effort? The answer to that question is both simple and complex. At the simple level, it is because the salmon is important enough to justify it – it is a glittering symbol of environmental wellbeing. The complex answer backtracks in time.

In the 1960s European rivers had seen prodigious runs of salmon. The silver bonanza from the spring tides re-ran the programme of fresh shoals arriving through the year and it seemed as certain as the sun dropping in the west that from the start of spring these great leaping, wild, sparkling fish would go on and on revitalising rivers which had gone doggo for the winter.

Then a decline commenced. Fewer and fewer salmon came back in the 1980s, and then the 1990s. The canaries in the mine, or anglers, found their enticing presentations drifting across the stream undisturbed. Nothing jumped. Nothing swirled at the fly. The waters rolled to sea unruffled. The rivers missed their most dramatic occupant.

A few rivers had installed fish counters, usually consisting of electronic beams broken by an upstream-swimming fish, and these counters, logged by computer, were telling an alarming story which backed up the anglers' perceptions of fewer silver visitors.

It was estimated that in the 1960s and 1970s the population of salmon in the eastern Atlantic was around eight to ten million fish. In America and Canada, where many rivers had been dammed, where forest clearance in river-country had silted up river-beds and traumatised ecosystems, there is another story of dwindling fish, but we will revisit that side of the tale later.

The decline from abundance was giving rise to serious worry.

In places where smolt survival was being measured, such as at Scotland's North Esk government monitoring station, and the Bush and Burrishoole system in Ireland, young sea-going smolts had once returned as salmon in numbers approaching 15 per cent of the outgoing migration. This figure was falling and falling steadily. It fell to eight and then as low as five per cent. On the River Conon in the northern Scottish Highlands, where they can measure these things, the return rate of smolts in 2011 was four per cent. In some rivers the number will be even less.

For anadromous fish, which live at sea and breed in freshwater rivers, this figure was low – very low. It told scientists that ocean-wide changes were occurring. Somewhere out there a black hole was consuming the small silver fish that used to fatten in the larder of the north-east Atlantic, before returning to their birth-places in the pebbly streams. In some American rivers spawning pairs were down to a handful of pairs, a chilling brush with death equal to a doomed scenario.

The most obvious subtractions from salmon runs were then looked at and addressed. Salmon netting, which was recorded as having been prosecuted in some parts of the UK and Europe since the twelfth century, was an obvious target. Here was an industrial-scale subtraction, taking fish before they could breed. Furthermore, it violated one of the tenets of modern fisheries management – that you must know what stock of fish you are taking.

Netsmen took salmon offshore as they migrated past. No one had a clear idea which rivers they were due to swim into. A salmon in the net was a salmon in the net; they all looked much the same. They fetched the same price, too. Logic demanded that random salmon capture cease. On the back of the idea that netting was 'indiscriminate', harvesting individuals valuable to species survival alongside those from more numerous components of the migration, appeals were launched to save salmon by buying out or leasing netting stations. Many were laid off and mothballed and bought out. In Scotland alone the catch by nets was ratcheted down from around 100,000 salmon a year in 1990 to 13,000 twenty years later.

Salmon netting still exists in a few places in 2013. Norway remains unreconstructed about salmon netting. Scotland has a handful of active netting-stations, resistant to being bought off and encouraged by rising wild salmon prices, England even fewer. The Norwegian Saami people from the far north, with precious little to sustain them, still net salmon on the Arctic coast. In a conservation milestone for salmon, Iceland terminated netting at sea as far back as 1932. Pressed by the European Union, the west-coast Irish drift nets were outlawed in 2007.

The most important salmon-netting haul in modern times was taken off Greenland. It commenced in 1959 when gill-netters working the fjords were startled to find glittering salmon in the mesh. A boom in salmon commenced, which pulled in drift-net fishers close to Greenland's western shore from Denmark, the Faroes and Norway. The working season was August to October, with the winter iced over. Catches rocketed, peaking at 2,689 tons in 1971. All of a sudden salmon, which are a rare fish in the sea, were being caught like mother cod, which can lay millions of eggs. The International Council for the Exploration of the Sea (ICES) reckoned the Greenland operation in winter 1972 had removed a third of all the salmon locally present. As more attention was paid to what exactly was being caught the fish were traced to the east coast of America and Canada and, secondly, older female salmon from Scotland.

Something had to be done. The solution was devised by an Icelander called Orri Vigfusson, who is now a household name in salmon conservation. A partner in a herring fishing family that hit hard times when herring runs shifted, Vigfusson was familiar with the vagaries of fishing. Basically in sympathy with remote communities eking out precarious existences, Vigfusson saw that in order to endure the solution had to be fair. An international arm was needed to lend support and the quotas discussed at the negotiating table were assembled by the North Atlantic Salmon Conservation Organisation (NASCO), a multi-member body formed in 1984.

Encouraging alternative fisheries for the Greenlanders, and with striking success raising money all across salmon range, Vigfusson made his breakthrough leasing arrangement in 1993. The Greenlanders were not sold down the river – far from it. Their argument that the salmon fattened off their coast was accepted. The payment could be seen as a grazing fee. They were paid to abstain from their rightful fishery, beyond a small permitted tonnage for 'subsistence'. No salmon could be exported.

The agreements have had to be regularly renewed and reassessed, a lack of finality seen by their critics as a weakness. There have been teething troubles. Greenlanders with limited opportunities for economic activity have exceeded quotas. Annual payments have been withdrawn, and then reinstated when malpractices have been straightened out. The way may have been tortuous, but it has succeeded.

A similar arrangement was reached with the Faroe Islanders, who had been shown how to catch salmon on baited long lines by Danish fishermen from the island of Bornholm who had perfected this art in the Baltic. By 1991 Vigfusson had clinched an agreement with the Faroese, made easier because the Icelandic government already had fisheries access arrangements to their seas with their closest neighbours. The Faroese were the only foreign fishermen allowed to catch Icelandic fish.

Vigfusson had shown how to raise money for salmon protection and how to broker international agreements on a new basis. Tirelessly he had circuited the salmon world, flying from one event to the next, rattling in buses round the bumpy roads on the Greenland coast, meeting one fishing community after another, making addresses and hosting fund-raisers, coming up with ideas for alternative employment, patiently arguing and negotiating. People had faith in his integrity and un-deflected purpose. He crossed national divides and came from a neutral country carrying no historical baggage. Salmon conservation using his model took a mighty stride.

Today there are still anecdotal tales, usually involving Spanish trawlers playing fast and loose with everyone and everything, but in the main salmon netting has being progressively removed as a major factor in European salmon decline.

Anglers knew they had to join the effort to restore the bountiful fish. Inducted in its virtues by an American salmon community almost completely stripped of their iconic east-coast visitor, and championed by the charismatic Alaskan-born angler and conservationist, Lee Wulff, who coined the memorable phrase 'Gamefish are too valuable to be caught only once', 'catch and release' was introduced to UK anglers around 2005. Since that time it has taken off. The fish is brought to the landing-net as fast as possible, revived by allowing the lungs to re-fill with oxygen, and let go when the body is properly horizontal in the water and the tail-movement quickens.

Talked of and practised by individual anglers for at least a century, especially when the salmon was late-season and coloured, catch and release took a formal position in salmon management relatively lately. Now it applies to fresh salmon in mint condition, not only coloured flabby ones.

Scotland's Aberdeenshire Dee broke the mould and made catch and release compulsory all season in an unprecedented announcement that caused a mighty stir at the time. But it was done. Other rivers followed suit with milder variations on the theme. Some salmon were allowed to be killed 'for the pot' at times of year when runs were bountiful, and restrictions on numbers of fish allowed to be killed were applied to sensitive parts of the run, typically the early spring.

The result? Were there more shoals of salmon pushing the tide up the banks as they swarmed into those waiting river-mouths? Hell, there were! The decline persisted.

It was against this background of dwindling stocks that SALSEA girded its loins to find out what was happening in the part of the salmon zone that remained an almost total mystery – saltwater.

The background to this mystery was not only a fish that was doing a vanishing act, it was climate change. The north-eastern Atlantic, where many European salmon wintered, was warming. No thermometer was needed to discover this. Surf anglers on the north coast of Scotland's desolate extremities threw their spinning lines baited for cod and hooked sea bass. Previously sea bass had not been caught further north than The Wash in south-eastern England. Exotic fish were dragged up in trawlers all the way to Iceland. Red mullet and sea bream edged up the latitude line. Coral reefs crumbled in unfamiliarly warm waters.

Disc-shaped sunfish, previously only ever seen, and then rarely, off the south coast, were hauled onto boats far up the coast of Britain. From sardines to whales, fish moved northwards. Smolts were not immune; their pathways adapted too.

Oceanographers confirmed it: the North Atlantic was warming. For fisheries this presented challenges.

In 2011 there was a furious row in Europe's fishing states when Iceland, not hitherto invited to the meetings which allocated quotas amongst traditional fishing nations, and not an EU member, discovered big shoals of mackerel swarming around its north coast, and started catching them. The Faroe Islands found and did the same. Tempers flared. The two small states became overnight pariahs. These fish 'belonged' to fishing nations further south. Iceland and the Faroe Islanders argued that the mackerel in their waters were in prime condition with top-notch fat content, perfect for market. For countries further south to limit their new bonanza was bizarre; the fish belonged to whoever had possession of them. The argument sputtered on. National politics had run up against fluctuating natural cycles, a test for diplomacy.

Fish follow temperature bands which are the conveyor belts for food. The mackerel do not care whether they swim off Iceland or off Ireland, they register the volume of shrimp and squid and other high-octane titbits that can be gorged upon, and follow them. Mackerel are not anadromous like salmon, with both a freshwater phase and a saltwater one, but their extreme mobility tested the capacity of nation states to live in a changing world. There were parallels with salmon politics.

The background to the search for smolts from European rivers was the same warming North Atlantic. There was a simple distance factor: the smolts from the southern extremity of salmon range in rivers in northern Spain had a longer journey to reach the winter food supply; further to swim, in hostile territory. All along the journey were the enhanced risks of predation and starvation. Conversely, as freshwater temperatures were also rising, smolts were growing faster in natal streams, and were bigger and often younger when they reached the salt. Ratcheting up the pressure, survival rates of fast-growing smolts are lower.

Celtic Voyager and two other research vessels embarked on their exploratory fishing trips in a world being re-drawn by dynamic flux.

Anxiety about the Atlantic salmon was sufficiently syncopated and international to produce the SALSEA programme. Although salmon smolts were the tools, the programme, lasting over three years from 2008, was designed to advance the understanding of ocean ecology and fish genetics. The authors even talk about hopes that they have provided invaluable data for 'the future ecosystem-based management of the oceans'. Big aims.

To catch these very small fish in a large piece of sea they adapted a standard small trawl for smolt capture. A small-mesh net was pulled on two side ropes and kept on the surface by large floats on each side. At the 'cod-end', or last compartment in a narrowing cone-shaped net, was the fish 'box' accumulating smolts. The smolt trawl was towed in arcs at speeds of three to five knots, anything from 150 to 400 metres from the mother ship. It was 155 metres long with a mouth forty by ten metres. The main thing was – it worked.

Quantitative results varied by region. The report cites one case where 233 trawls netted 1,728 smolts and 53 adult salmon, at a rate of 3.4 fish per trawl. This trawl had hit a migration 'pathway'.

The long-awaited paper, which included data collection from as far back as 1999, was published in January 2012. Authors Jens Christian Holst and Ken Whelan warn that owing to cost no such programme is likely to be done again. So we should heed what they discovered.

The location of smolts was closely linked to ocean currents. Differences in temperature and salt content change the density of seawater, which in turn drives global ocean circulation through the medium of currents. The young salmon use currents as escalators. They ride them for propulsion and add to this their swimming power. Recovered tagged fish showed that smolts' swimming power was often equal to the speed of the ocean currents. They may be small but they are powerful.

Climate variability also affected where they went. Oceanic circulation round Scotland and the North Sea is anti-clockwise. It is also driven by winds, especially between March and May. As the climate alters, these winds have been strengthening and this affects marine growth and fish travelling in the upper layers, like smolts.

Smolts' growth rate, as measured by SALSEA, is prodigious, fairly justifying the description 'explosive'. Each day they might grow 0.6 per cent of their body length. At the southerly edge of Atlantic salmon range smolt survival is worst. Whether the young salmon were leaving the River Loire Allier in northern France and heading westwards round the Atlantic coast of Ireland to find feeding midway between Iceland and Norway in the Norwegian Sea, or leaving north-west Spain and negotiating the English Channel, southerly stocks struggled more. The impoverished Allier has only a bare-bones population of 500–1000 breeding salmon to start with, and the Spanish rivers are similar.

Norwegian and Russian young salmon, with less far to go, and feeding further north, do better.

When travelling off Norway Europe's little silver fish meticulously follow the shelf-edge between the shallow coastal ledge and the deeps. The shelves form shallow-water skirts off the landmasses all round the North Atlantic where salmon winter. They differ from deep drop-offs, more characteristic of volcanic landmasses. The salmon's landmasses have a glacial origin, shelving into the sea as glaciers turned to water. Why the smolts tracked the shelf-edge can be guessed at, how they followed an invisible fault-line underneath them is a mystery.

Richard Shelton was one of the scientists working on the early phases of research and he puzzled over this. How could the fish so accurately follow this shelf? Temperature, salinity and depth were tested for roles as routeing guides and none of them seemed to fit. In their lateral line, or the line running mid-body from end to end, salmon harbour the magnetic oxide of iron called magnetite. One possibility Shelton considered was that smolts were orienteering by the Earth's magnetic field. This remains conjectural. But stick to the shelf-edge they did. This edge lies about halfway to Iceland. Knowing where they are is a first step to protecting them.

When they reached a projecting seabed north of Iceland called the Voering Plateau, our smolts ceased linear movement and dispersed in big gyres. In the Norwegian Sea and west and east of Greenland they feed and grow at what Shelton describes as, 'rates rivalled by few other cold-blooded creatures'.

What was their pattern when moving? Trawling results suggested loose shoals of 100–700. There was no evidence of very large-scale shoaling behaviour, which was mildly surprising. So the canny scientists put closed-circuit cameras in the net-end at right angles to the direction of towing, to view better what was being caught.

The observers saw no huge fish agglomerations being gathered in the wings of the net, rather smolts 'sneaking about' as Shelton put it, in ones and twos. At night smolts were hard to find, and researchers reckoned that nocturnally they must dive deeper than the ten-metre-deep band they occupied by day. But why? Most fish rise in the so-called 'water-column' at night, as darkness affords safety from above. Behaving contrarily, diving smolts must do so for food. But what food? Or what improbable night-time threat are they escaping nearer the surface? Answers breed questions. The salmon's mysterious behaviour has caused it to be dubbed 'the oceanographer's fish'.

The northwards drift of prey species sticking to their northwards-shifting temperature bands influences smolt locations. The team found that the smolts which reached western Greenland seas and settled north-west of Iceland, staying longer at sea and returning to the UK as hugely bigger multi-sea winter fish, were faring well.

The ability to track both regional and river-specific stocks of smolts at sea is new. Because the experiment's focus was on fish from Europe's main salmon rivers, the great majority of net captures were successfully 'assigned' to their river of origin. It is part of a wider knowledge-picture, where the factual fog is clearing over all migratory routes and behaviour. Microchip and tagging technology, along with a technique involving bouncing signals off satellites, have revolutionised knowledge about migrating creatures. The migratory wading bird, the woodcock, is the next in line for a tracking research programme. Across the natural world years of speculation are being replaced with firmer data.

The salmon fishing writer Richard Waddington devoted many pages of his 1947 book *Salmon Fishing: A New Philosophy* to a laboriously articulated theory that wintering salmon positioned themselves in the mid-Atlantic in order to intercept common eels migrating as elvers or 'glass eels' from the Sargasso Sea off eastern central America. Salmon swam with these easterly migrations of juvenile common eels, he surmised, being sustained and fattened by them all the way back to their growing zones in the freshwaters of UK and Europe. It was somehow a beguiling idea.

The author died long ago, but depending on circumstances in his afterlife he may now have the chance to reconsider and chide himself for those errant thought processes. Knowledge is a grand corrective.

Knowledge was meant to be a defining feature too of the revered Scottish ecology writer, the late Frank Fraser Darling. But when it came to salmon he stumbled. Fraser Darling wrote that the fish that ascend rivers early spawn at the bottom end, and the late-season runners go to the top. In fact it is the other way round, which is why today's efforts to resuscitate the spring salmon, assuming that like breed like, take hatchery fish from the upper parts of rivers, not the bottom end. The top reaches are where the springers are.

He made another assumption which is fantasy: that east-coast salmon seldom come back from the sea more than once whereas west-coast salmon can breed four or five times. Scale-reading, which ages salmon, and should have put matters straight, had been around for over fifty years when he wrote this.

For some reason salmon seem to befuddle commentators. The director of Scotland's Marine Laboratory, therefore the senior government person in fisheries, portentously declared in a book on salmon published in 2000 that it was now well established that 'a large majority of the fish returning to spawn in a particular river originated from that river'. Wow, really? But that was what the Scottish Ecclesiastic Hector Boethius announced in the sixteenth century. SALSEA misroutes down this way too: 'Reducing man's impacts on our salmon stocks may be the key to ensuring their survival'. When can we move on, please? It may be a matter of debate whether the Atlantic salmon is the greatest of fish, but it is certainly the one that leads to most confusion.

Before SALSEA it was thought from examining pelagic trawls that smolts at sea ate blown insects to start with and moved deeper down the water column as they got bigger to find crustaceans and small fish. When the diet stepped up to embrace fish, growth accelerated. SALSEA saw that the diet of young salmon changes with ocean conditions. Researchers concluded that they ate almost anything. Capelin (found on the Canadian shelf and off west Greenland), young blue whiting, lanternfish, five-bearded rockling, sprats and sand eels all formed part of their sustenance. Smolts would consume eggs, larvae and young fish and zeroed in particularly onto a sort of bug-eyed shrimp called themisto.

Interestingly, the herring and mackerel which were moving in the same area, though themselves bigger, selected smaller food, mostly crustaceans called copepods. Smolts punch above their weight in the food chain.

Influences on salmon routeing included predator avoidance and their own growth. Uncircumscribed by physical limits, some young salmon migrate all the way not only to the Arctic ice-shelf, but under it. Presumably, beneath the ice-shelf at least one direction is guaranteed free from lethal attack, and there are no trawlers.

SALSEA leader, Norwegian scientist Jens Christian Holst, has written: 'From the very first scent of salt these fish are continuously hunted by marine predators.' They face different predator assemblages at different stages in their migration to the wintering grounds. Directly offshore, and whilst they are in the process of adapting their saltwater/freshwater balance for marine survival, sea trout, sea bass and cod feature. There are the salmon gourmands, seals. Further offshore those enemies are joined in the attack by saithe, pollack and more seals, and even rays and skates. North American Atlantic salmon face similar families of predators, but from local species.

Moving further out, coast-huggers like sea trout cease to be trouble. Diving seabirds such as gannets enter the fray. Minke whales and fin whales join the list of toothed adversaries. Even sharks, cephalopods (molluscs including cuttlefish) and tuna can eat smolts. Dr Holst says, 'the list could be continued at length'! He adds that fast growth is an obvious survival aim for smolts trying to prolong their lives at sea. One sees why.

In eastern Canada a survival peculiarity has been noted linking smolts with spent kelts. In the straits of Ben Isle kelts gathered outside the rivers they had descended until the smolts joined them. Both young salmon and older ones then moved northwards in convoy to the feeding grounds. What is happening? Are smolts being taught their passage by their elders? Is there any protective function in the presence of the kelts mixed with the next generation? Another chapter in the mystery of salmon migration opens up.

SALSEA also recorded what effects human actions were having on smolt runs. Escaped smolts from freshwater rearing cages in lakes and lochs run as nurseries for the salmon farm industry, or young feral salmon, were identified by their genetic markers and found in numbers. Their groups were looser in formation than those of wild smolts. Just how many feral smolts were found is a matter tenderly circuited.

For it is a potent finding. Salmon farm escapement is a highly political and controversial matter and now science can tear back the veil on the resulting profile of ocean fish populations. The relevance for salmon survival of the presence of farm-origin fish competing with wild ones in the sea for the same food is a question which needs answering.

Scale-reading using digital technology was another tool in SALSEA's knowledge review. Reading scales is nothing new and the Inspector of Fisheries in Scotland, Peter Malloch, based on the River Tay, developed basic scale-reading theories over a century ago. Wider spacing between rings told of richer feeding. From scales readers could say how well fish had fed and grown at sea, what smorgasbord of young fish, fish eggs and larvae had been eaten, prefaced by how these fish had fared in their freshwater phase.

Scales are like dentine in human teeth: they read like tree-rings and tell a story. The scales fall from our eyes: the biography of a fish is available in its scale history. In contrast to many fish population studies done for Europe's Common Fisheries Policy using predictive modelling by computers to allocate catch quotas (an innately unsatisfactory methodology), scales reveal what conditions were recently like. They offer real-time information, not academic projections for the formulation of shaky assumptions.

Long-time series of salmon scale histories existed in several places. The Copenhagen-based International Council for the Exploration of the Sea (ICES) made available its archive of thousands of tagged and recaptured salmon details based on scale-reading. SALSEA took this forward. New developments in digital analysis have added to the knowledge bank to be gleaned from scale readings.

Scales read on adult salmon when they came back to rivers are correlated genetically to young smolts caught in the smolt trawls. Some of these scales had been taken from the adult fish long ago. So young North-Atlantic smolts were being traced by their scales to fairly distant ancestors. In total, 23,000 scales from seven rivers in six countries were studied. From this sample smolts were mostly two years old, some one and three years old, and a few four years old. The further north the river of origin the older the smolt age; southernmost smolts were growing faster in their home rivers and undertaking the marine migration earlier. As it happens, they were often dying earlier too.

The research revealed that smolts preferred temperature bands of 9–12°C and salinities over 35 per cent. They avoided the shelf directly off western Norway, possibly because salinity is low, and aimed for the deeper, more saline water further west on the shelf-edge. The colder the water the faster their growth rates. This is the opposite of growth and temperature effects in freshwater natal streams where colder water arrests growth.

One of the triggers for the whole SALSEA programme was the fear amongst salmon managers that certain pelagic fisheries in the salmon-wintering seas were sweeping up shoals of young smolts as a by-catch whilst fishing for other pelagic species. In particular there was concern that surface-trawling for mackerel and herring on the Norwegian Shelf was netting little smolts along with the rest and, in the worst scenario, inadvertently massacring entire populations from single river catchments. British fishery scientists had found Norwegian fishermen picking salmon smolts out of their pelagic nets and making special suppers from them. Russia has 40–50 trawlers working this sea far from anyone's coast and therefore in international waters.

There is an internationally agreed fishery model run by the North East Atlantic Fisheries Commission, but it does not prohibit fishing on the surface. It has no smolt-protection aspect. This could be addressed. As Ken Whelan has said, the next phase is going to be political. Russia's recent admission to the club of salmon fishing countries, where international rod angling is a serious financial sector, rejoicing in faithfully returning visitors willing to spend money in remote zones, may help this negotiation. Whoever thought that visiting the Kola Peninsular in the Russian Arctic would be a visitor destination of significance before the advent of salmon fishing? Now important Russians know the optimum meaning of a salmon, and the fish is becoming an icon there too.

Fishing states using these northern seas do conduct large-scale surveys of the ecosystem. Now that SALSEA has identified where the smolts are likely to be it becomes theoretically feasible to design pelagic or surface-trawling operations to minimise impacts on young salmon. Already in Norway's wider fisheries regulations over too much of a particular by-catch triggers the closure of that sector until the unwanted non-target fish has moved on. The same might be possible in the herring fisheries of both Norway and Iceland to protect smolts there.

The other fisheries which may kill smolts are looking for blue whiting, capelin and horse-mackerel, termed 'industrial' fisheries because the lower-value fish are turned into fish-feed. It is a horrible irony that super-valuable young salmon are being enmeshed with large hauls of lower-grade fish used for conversion to fishmeal for aquaculture, quite possibly to end up in the stomachs of farmed Atlantic salmon. Valuable wild juveniles feed hordes of feedlot adults.

One improvement may be to alter the depth of pelagic fishing. If smolts occupy the surface of the sea down usually to six and at most ten metres in daylight, dropping lower at night, why not trawl lower still when the targets are herring and mackerel? When tried, this solution worked well. Whatever disciplines are adopted must produce an economic yield for the pelagic boats, and therein lies the challenge.

Ken Whelan is adamant that administrators in the EU fisheries division must be reminded that wise-use management of rare Atlantic salmon is now feasible. He talks of a future thinking in terms of protecting 'corridors in the sea' or 'sections of the ocean' for the smolt runs. Using known timings of smolt movement from the new migratory map it might be possible to abstain altogether from pelagic trawling where they are vulnerable and at the most sensitive periods. Such an aim sets the bar high.

Politics is never far from the marine resource scene. The impasse over the mackerel catch by Iceland and the Faroes, in an area not far away from the young salmon zone, is discouraging. Entering 2013 is the fourth year of the controversy and both the Icelandic and Faroese governments say they intend to continue harvesting their manna from heaven, though at lower levels. Iceland in 2012 was economically prostrate after a collapse of their banks; harvesting the valuable mackerel was an obvious recourse.

But time has shown that salmon protectionists are a powerful force too. SALSEA proves it, and it would be contrary to experience and history if the findings of this detailed study were simply to be buried and ignored. Iceland, for one, has a valuable sport fishery in salmon.

Development of the sport fishery has been transformational on Iceland's western coast. Professionalised presentation of rod angling for migratory salmon as a lucrative tourist sector has been an economic triumph. Where not long ago visitors to Iceland rode ponies across the volcanic tundra, marvelling at the lunar bleakness and subsisting on a diet of puffins and mutton, now fishermen from all over the world tumble out of Reykjavik airport jabbering into their mobiles and pop-eyed with excitement at participating in one of the most charismatic salmon sport fisheries anywhere.

The water coursing over volcanic rock in treeless moonscapes is gin-clear, requiring peculiarly focused angler skills. There is no industrial pollution, people are rarer than puffins, the sea is a familiar element and provides the nation's biggest income, and the newest landmass in Europe has an air of being truly virginal. Salmon-language is fully understood in this peculiar land of fumaroles and sulphur-belching hot springs. Agreements on salmon may form the basis for a new accord on other fish which colonise new territories, even mackerel.

Smolt stage is the black hole of salmon growth, and one reason why SALSEA ever happened. As fry and parr in rivers, the little salmon can be found and examined. Adult salmon are big enough to be tracked, at least some of the time. If they turn up on fishmonger's slabs somewhere, people notice. Protection at that stage is a practical possibility. Smolts, in contrast, are needles in the haystack of the ocean.

SALSEA makes a stride in knowledge about salmon's ocean phase. However, it did not satisfy all those awaiting its findings. Managers of salmon sport fisheries were looking for answers to their own pressing questions.

They complained that original promises on the development of the genetic map actually fell far short. Some tracking has limned in a few details, but the big picture remains largely unknown. They make the point that, interesting though genetics might be, the practical application of using the information on the average fishing river is limited. Say you discover there is a different genetic stock in one branch of the river – intriguing – but how can you manage the fishery, aside from keeping the tributaries in good health, to accommodate that information hidden in the DNA?

Most cogently, critics point to the report's failure to nail salmon farming as the destroyer of wild fisheries through its lethal by-product of proliferating parasitic sea lice. The million-strong swarms of sea lice created by salmon-cage aquaculture adhere to smolts as they leave fresh water and kill them, thereby throttling wild salmon survival. They say the report's equivocal and incomplete findings will leave politicians an escape route from firm and decisive action in favour of more time-consuming and inconclusive research, measures once sarcastically dubbed as designed, 'to maintain the momentum of procrastination'.

They have a point. Some of the more arcane disputes about discrete genetic stocks in different branches of one river, and efforts to keep them pure, are undermined by the historical fact that river stocks have been intermixed long ago. All over Britain salmon have been moved from hatcheries and tipped into rivers wherever owners of fisheries wanted to beef up fish numbers, or revive them. It has been going on for over a century. It is the same in other salmon countries, too. Genetic purity is a myth, which is surprising given that genetic purity of stocks is the new mission for salmon theorists.

In Scotland re-stocking only with stocks from that river, and even from a specified part of the system, is now official 'best practice', to the frustration of many wizened fishery managers. The new knowledge about discrete strains is not being used in the most intelligent way.

It has always been hard for the genetics messiahs to deal with the fact that on the British west coast river where the Beatles originated, the Mersey, the water has been re-populated with salmon entirely by the vagaries of Nature, its own native stock having been wiped out. The Mersey now has Creole salmon of mixed origin coming from at least thirty different rivers. Who can object? 'Nature hates a vacuum' is true for salmon as for all else. Genetic straying has re-populated a major river.

The Thames is another melting-pot culture. Its tentative existence as a salmon river once again owes its brilliant success to stocks from many different places. Reflecting its diverse human mix London's passing salmon population is polyglot too.

I saw a dramatic illustration of the basis for genetic straying whilst rafting in British Columbia late one summer. At day's end our three rafts headed for a tributary with a nice shelving sandbar to moor up on for the night. We crunched onto the beach and were stunned to find huge salmon lying dead on the water's edge.

There was a biologist aboard. He looked closely at the fish and saw that their gills were clogged. They were king salmon, the big boys, and there were around forty of them stranded down the river-edge for a few hundred yards, all just above the tributary's junction with the main river. The biologist said the fish were all within a day of spawning. So a valuable stock or 'year-class' of a rare and wondrous fish lay wasted about us never to breed, eradicated in the last moment of its evolutionary purpose. Why? The brown water was still silty from a landslide further upriver. A natural event had wiped out the big fish in this tributary for one breeding season.

What gave the event an added twist was the furious debate taking place in west Canada's media that summer about threats to king salmon, their precarious status, and the need for firmer protection laws. Nature had thrown a joker onto the gaming table and we were staring at it.

But it was also where genetic straying and fish unfaithful to their natal imperative step in. Suppose, as we know is possible, that one pair of king salmon had gone up a tributary close by. They bred there. That strain of salmon thereby dodges fate and escapes elimination. In due course some of the progeny from that union relocate themselves as adults in breeding livery back in the original natal stream, and re-populate it.

Straying is Nature's way of spreading risk. The same is true, surely, about the differing ages at which young salmon go to sea. If some 'smoltify' and migrate in their second spring, and some in their third, the risk of total elimination is spread. On big rivers in Scotland like the Tay, different grilse runs climb the system from early spring to the autumn. They are all fish which spent only one winter in the sea, the definition of grilse. Bookies call it hedging bets.

Peter Malloch might have had a lot to say on some of the purist preconceptions about river-stocking only with site-specific strains which have crept into modern management. It was Malloch who realised a century ago that salmon sometimes remained at sea a long time, and that not all fish were grilse as had been assumed before. He understood the salmon's admirable diversity. The migratory fish turn homewards to reproduce, swimming south. It is presumed, but only so far tentatively claimed, that they follow the same passage, but going the opposite way, as that which they used as teenagers – another neat theoretical twist made available by modern science which this aristocrat of salmon analysis long ago would have appreciated.

Left behind in the marine larder are the others, the non-movers, growing and growing. Or not growing: some salmon a long time at sea are not especially big. Maybe they too are hedging their bets, passive actors in an evolutionary insurance policy.

A salmon's eventual size is determined by its length; it can be fat or it can be thin, but without length it can never match the biggest. Girth is the feeding which beefs up the body length. Some of these wintering salmon spend two years in the vicinity of the Arctic, some three, some four, and some even prolong their Arctic sojourn to five years.

Turning southwards as the new year awakens, they ultimately acknowledge the ritual of reproduction, or so it is assumed.

Scale-reading shows that after January sea-feeding picks up again following the short winter check. Thus, the fish achieve peak condition prior to the demanding migration south.

Today's existence is tougher for salmon, for as the northern hemisphere has warmed, dragging the food supply northwards, the return journey south lengthens. Migrating salmon are starting further from home.

Krill may move, natal streams do not.

How long they take to swim home is unknown. Scale-reading differentiates between sea-time and freshwater-time, but we do not yet know in which sea, at what time. Could we? If scales were better able to track diet perhaps we could pin down more accurately how long the journeys take. Sand eels are on known sandbanks and capelin live in the north – the diet could position the predator.

However, there is another lateral-thinking way, a technique not yet fully developed for practical use. We need tags that could measure the angle of the sun at midday, then, as polarised sun filtered through the seawater, it would be possible to calculate latitude. Temperature and the intensity of the light are recordable now; the next step is a reader for polarised light. The tags used on smolts register temperature and depth, but so far they cannot measure the angle of the light. This tantalising technical advance may be not far off.

What is hard fact is that salmon are fast movers. When they do reach rivers they can travel incredible distances in a day's journey, proven by the presence on them of sea lice. These are saltwater parasites which can only remain attached in freshwater for up to two days. Sea-liced salmon have been found thirty miles up rivers, and more. Fresh from the marine, Atlantic salmon are true Formula One fish, as some sparkling-eyed anglers have cause to know.

They do not, though, just arrive at the mouth of their natal river and motor into it. They savour the moment of transition, whilst making a vital physical adaptation to their water-balance mechanism. In the sea a salmon has to cope with water that is chemically stronger than its own body tissue, making it lose its body liquids. To compensate, a salmon at sea actually drinks seawater, which then passes through its stomach and intestine. Its kidneys expel small amounts of the salt in concentrated urine, conserving some of the swallowed water to make up for the liquid losses.

In his 2009 treasure-trove about the Atlantic salmon, *To Sea and Back*, Richard Shelton refers mischievously to the 'uriniferous' smell of farmed salmon: he has sound physiological reasons to do so! So many fish excreting powerful body wastes in a basin of seawater, only lightly refreshed by the average tides, might well produce some fairly rank odours and taint the aroma of the imprisoned inhabitants.

Entering the milder environment of freshwater a salmon finds its fluids more concentrated, not less, than those of its surroundings. It starts to absorb water through the permeable linings of its mouth and gills. The excess is filtered as dilute urine through the kidneys. So fresh and salt water are quite different environments. Salmon biology has the sophistication to occupy both.

Sometimes for weeks the fish pregnant with breeding preoccupations ride the tides near the river-mouth, tasting the fresh water debouching from the estuary, sampling it, experiencing the reawakening of chemical memories from long ago when they were fish only inches long. The expectant river-runners can be spied from the cliffs above estuary mouths drifting on the tide, maybe fleeing a hungry seal.

The year 2011 was dry for a while in midsummer in Scotland when I was sailing with the life-boat crew along the coast of east Sutherland. On a bright day in a calm sea we approached the River Helmsdale where the boat was to tie up. There, offshore, were leaping salmon, throwing themselves into the air. Those who see this often say they do it prior to entering the river, usually when a freshet of rain has gushed into the sea, bringing oxygen and water particles to their sensory receptors, stirring fusty recollections. Then, often waiting for the moon, they hitch a lift in like any surf-rider, selecting the highest tides.

Just as salmon unerringly follow the shelf-edge off Norway, so they unerringly seem to know what lies up rivers in the hinterland. If a river has lochs and lakes feeding it, salmon swim it earlier, for they can progress to a safe haven up ahead in the expanse of the loch. Scotland's west coast has what are called 'spate' rivers, because they are shorter than eastern rivers, and salmon generally run into them during or after rain when water levels are higher. These fish know there is often no sanctuary or a loch; their only refuge is a deep pool, and it might already contain other occupants. On the River Helmsdale we know from the presence of sea lice on fish caught by anglers that many salmon run straight through the 24-mile system and forge on through the fish-pass into the chain of lochs at the top where they can safely bide their time until autumn spawning.

The river system made in heaven is perhaps the one with big headwater lochs providing a sanctuary for the salmon and an inducement to run the river to get to it, thereby presenting anglers with chances of an encounter. Even better, possibly, would be the system with a big loch in the middle, with salmon filtering into it from below and out of it from above, the loch also acting as a natural regulator of water levels.

Sometimes forgotten are landlocked salmon. They lack the mystique of the ocean rover, and they do not leap waterfalls to remind us of their grace and power. More importantly they do not have to worry about smolt losses to cetaceans, Russian trawlermen or any other conventional threat. Pike with backwards-curving teeth might be their toughest adversary. In addition they need none of the adaptive mutations for moving between saltwater and fresh.

The lines are not hard and fast. In anadromous salmon populations some parr never leave their rivers and behave as landlocked salmon, awaiting the return of gravid hen salmon for their sneaky off-chance at fertilising the next generation.

Perhaps it should not be surprising that populations of landlocked salmon comfortably survive today. In Norwegian, Swedish and Russian lakes there are landlocked salmon as well as in North American ones. These northerly receptacles of cold water never heat up too much for salmon's tolerance. Landlocked salmon could be compared to brown trout, happy not to migrate whilst some of their siblings run the gamut of the wilds to become sea trout.

Norway's huge Namsen River has a majestic and impassable waterfall. Whilst I was watching its awesome power and letting the physical reality of the cascading torrent sink in, the droll ghillie told me that only the week before a visitor angler playing a feisty salmon from a downstream-drifting boat above the fall had failed in his battle-concentration to notice the advancing roar of the crashing water. He went backwards over the top, attached with his fishing line to the fish of a lifetime, and was never seen again. The story was relayed with barely suppressed ghoulish relish. Did he get his kicks telling that story every week? At any rate, above the Aunfoss waterfall subsist the resident salmon which never migrate, cut off by a giant curtain of cascading water.

Landlocked salmon are not uncommon in North America. In Idaho I have seen the scarlet kokanee, which are Pacific-origin coho salmon, and I found the sight somehow disturbing. Here are these small shoals of highly coloured fish in the translucent shallow waters of rivers and lakes, looking nervous and wary. You sense they are trapped, freakish prisoners, despite their presence having been determined by ancient geology. Really, they are true and admirable survivors, but it does not feel like that. And their chromatic violence in the drab landscape adds to a sense of displacement.

In Lake Ontario the early settlers found landlocked salmon weighing up to forty pounds. So much for the sea only being able to build up weight; pike disprove that and the lake salmon underlined it. These monsters, however, are now gone. In Maine the landlubbers are called 'sebago', being the name of lake in which they were first identified, and in other Maine lakes there are different varieties of salmon non-migrants.

To an angler a salmon is in its natural place in a river. That is where an encounter can occur. A river is the proper mis-en-scene for connection with the fish by a wispy length of nylon on a bendy stick, and a hook maybe no bigger than a gnat. What salmon do in rivers is a subject upon which fishermen have ventured opinion in a veritable lexicon of viewpoints. Seldom has so much speculation been focused on one inhabitant of our environment. How many shelves could you fill with the books which have celebrated the mysteries and majesties of moles, rabbits or hedgehogs?

Long ago debate centred on whether salmon eat in rivers. It seemed impossible that a large creature could enter a river a year before undertaking the rigours of spawning and live off its reserves. Anyway, why did they take fishing flies if they were not eating?

Peter Malloch, as Scotland's Inspector of Fisheries, seemed to have nailed the matter way back. He and his team eviscerated thousands of salmon. They never found anything in the stomachs, no matter how long the fish had been in the river. Even if, as happens in a few places, salmon over-winter in a river and do not spawn till late the following year, they still do not feed. It is a stupendous fast. However, it failed to stop many subsequent armchair theorists raising spectres and postulating that salmon must eat, that sundry reasons existed for their stomachs being empty, that what was evident knowledge was as full of holes as a colander. The fact, amazing as it is, remains: salmon cease feeding in freshwater. Like snakes, which can live for months, even years, without eating, salmon subsist on their stored marine reserves. If they open their mouths to seize fishing flies in rivers, fishermen may claim they have been artful enough to override behavioural rules; angler achievement is all the greater. Not quite as great, though, as the biology of their quarry.

An area for debate between anglers and salmon professionals is whether the leaping salmon is moving upriver or not. So many times ghillies and anglers talk of 'fish running', meaning they are ascending the ladder of the river-system. But if you watch salmon from under a river at their level, as is possible in the riverbed salmon museum on Sweden's River Mörrum, you see that jumping salmon may move slightly forwards from where they took off but they drift downwards as they descend in the water-column, landing back on the launch pad. Salmon maintain their station more than some of their aerial antics would suggest.

Whereas anglers believe that salmon are running past them, and sometimes try to hasten upriver and get ahead of them, river counters using electronic beams show that salmon 'run' mostly at night. Summertime salmon almost invariably use the cloak of darkness to hide their journey. Some counters work with parallel sets of beams, interrupted beams signifying a fish swimming upriver. Counters can be calibrated so that only fish of a certain size register, excluding smaller ones and trout.

In Canada counting salmon in clear-water rivers can be unfussy: I have seen a wide placid river where the flow is channelled into a central funnel and a human counter perched on the platform end working a clicker to record every fish passing. These wilderness workers, operating in rotations, need good bug dope, a wide-awake buddy checking for bears tiptoeing down the platform, and extraordinary concentration. Happily the runs are often focused into just a few weeks, and, pressed for time, they move in the day.

More usual aids are military-type night-sights, which, focused against a light background, make salmon watchable as they swim upstream. Most of those fish leaping under the noses of anglers are not moving upriver but performing their acrobatics for other inscrutable reasons. Nineteenth-century writer William Scrope charmingly referred to them leaping because of 'excitement'.

Again, anglers talk of fish running in spates. They actually wait until the debris and clouds of suspended particles have ebbed and abated and then they run, in the cleaner flow. It is dangerous for salmon to get muck in their gills, and as birds constantly preen their feathers for efficient propulsion so salmon look after the efficiency of their highly tuned bodies. One or two days after the flood-crest is a likely running time – and they are slower to chase a melting snow spate than a rain-driven spate.

Where anglers are spot-on is in the commonplace assumption that salmon get interested in fishing flies after they have moved position. A salmon that has dwelt in one place for a month may have watched innumerable flies swinging over it and pays them no greater attention than the man on the park bench does who subconsciously watches buses looping their circuit. The same fish having shifted station will be activated and lunge at the fly, maybe attempting to purify its new location of annoying irritants.

Tagging has shown that salmon often enter a river, stay a while, and then leave it. During a long summer salmon may climb rivers, fall back to brackish estuaries, wait for another oxygen-rich freshet to stimulate a move upstream again, and then repeat the yo-yo procedure. Although Atlantic salmon are renowned for their generally faithful return not only to the river of origin but to the section of river from where they broke out of the egg, they can mess with the rules too.

A salmon has been tracked tasting the water on Scotland's west coast for a while, then moving to an east-coast river, and finally ascending the third river it had trialled in one year, where it spawned. This ranks as an extreme example of genetic straying. A salmon tagged on the Dee in Wales was re-captured in Denmark. I am unsure whether a salmon tagged in Europe has ever spawned in North America; reports vary, but betting against salmon's versatility and survivor-adherence would be a mistake.

I was on Russia's Kola Peninsular on a river called the Kharlovka in low-water/high-temperature conditions when it appeared to the anglers and the ghillies that the fish actually left the river, retreating to the refreshment and oxygen of the open sea. We could see them driving downriver. At this point the sea was only a mile or two distant. There would be a good enough reason: when wild salmon are closely confined fungal diseases spread fast. They can spread even faster amongst fish in low water and even disfigure a whole river population. Saltwater does the laundry.

Salmon fungus comes in more than one type, and can keep growing on fish that are already dead. The fungus is an external manifestation of a fast-spreading microbe. It is normal even in ordinary seasons to find pre-spawning salmon with white fungus starting on their heads and backs, and when spawning is done these mouldy discolorations accelerate to be abrupted only when the fish is cleansed by saltwater. Warm, low-water river conditions make matters worse.

Managers report that this occurred on the Tweed in Scotland late in 2011. It was not the potentially lethal condition called ulcerative dermal necrosis (UDN), in which lesions can penetrate into skeletal tissue, rather, as assessed by the river biologists, a more common fungal affliction broadly termed *Saprolengia*, caused by overcrowding.

The last time fungal diseases killed huge numbers of pre-spawners in Scotland was in the 1960s, when runs were prodigious. I remember walking down to look at the water in August with my grandmother, a dedicated angler who went to the river as others go to their office. White lethargic salmon with rot peeling from them cruised aimlessly in shallow water. I recall her sombre mood. Some see fungal outbreaks on a major scale as a response to over-population, and this distressing scene did indeed coincide with a heavy run of fish. Widespread fungal attack has not recurred on this river since.

Fishermen are the best monitors of a river-system. Their observations and speculations about this fish serve the species well. What salmon do in rivers will probably preoccupy anglers for as long as they persist in trying to catch the fish in what might be seen as an elaborate manner. Easiest perhaps then, sifting the options for evidence, to watch salmon in rivers.

I remember meeting a German salmon angler in Ireland long ago who had adopted a rigidly logical Teutonic approach to his fishing. Having showed me a rack of twenty-foot rigid poles, he asked what I thought he did when he went fishing. As if it was the most obvious thing in the world, he cried, 'I climb a tree!' When sun shone on the pool he was to be located hanging out of his tree wearing polaroids. From above, the river was like glass. For this Germanic genius it was self-evident that to cast into a river in the hope of catching a fish you did not know was there amounted to a bizarre and undignified expenditure of energy. So he looked down from aloft and spied, from his vantage points along the River Blackwater, whether any salmon were available for the catching.

He then drifted flies, of his own special construction, of course, over the noses of the targeted fish until they lost patience and snapped. Invariably, he assured me, they all eventually break, irritated to a frenzy, like a person with a spider crawling on his face. The idiosyncratic sportsman claimed to have caught numerous fish in this manner. He said snapping-time was always inside three-quarters of an hour.

Thinking on it, catching them on those rigid poles must have made it a mechanical exercise, lacking in the intimacy of galvanic contact. But there was the hunter satisfaction, I suppose, of having behaved in an impeccably rational manner.

I recall a scene one summer on the Saint-Jean River in Quebec where the water is pellucidly clear. I was walking down the river-bank when I came across an angler lying atop a small bush with his hat tilted over his eyes. Striking up a conversation it transpired he was waiting for 'his' fish and the right moment. I pressed him more and he showed me the fish, which I took a while to detect. Stretching far out in front was a rippled pavement of smooth, light-coloured rock. The water looked shallow, maybe three feet deep. Eventually I spotted, nestled into what was no more than a groove, a very large salmon, its back beautifully camouflaged in the ochre tones of the undulating river floor. The angler said he had tried his fish earlier in the day with the sun just rising. The fish had moved and moved again often but never opened its mouth. The next suitable moment would be as the sun disappeared over the canyon side. The angler had six hours to go. He seemed unruffled at the prospect, and sure the fish would succumb. He intended drifting his fly down from some distance above to give the big fish time to see it, and then letting it slide over his nose closer and closer, till … the chapter was written in his mind before it had even taken place.

The interesting time for salmon-watching is late summer when numbers are building for the orgy of spawning. Upstream of the river-bridge to my home is the entrance to a tributary. Salmon gather below the bridge for the shade, perhaps, but also to wait for the right moment to run the tributary and spawn there. The place where they accumulate looks the same as the rest of the river-bed, a trifle deeper maybe, stones studding the sandy bottom. They have stations, places they like to be. These are not, as is often loosely said, 'behind' rocks, rather to the side or below. There they rest, pointing upstream, close to the bottom, occasional bubbles emerging lazily from their mouths, like giveaway wisps of smoke from rainforest tribes.

In the protection of this shady place at a certain point in the autumn the salmon numbers stack up in a diamond formation. To start with, a few just take positions here and there, but as spawning approaches they tighten into a formation. As the days pass and no rain raises water levels, the space they are occupying shrinks and gets cramped with more fish still arriving. It is like a rail terminus with no trains leaving. The water lacks the refreshment of oxygen. I have seen the mass of salmon get edgy and impatient; they start to jostle and swirl at each other. There is a palpable build-up of nervous tension.

One time this was dramatised in a remarkable way. Above the bridge swam a pair of mergansers, paddling on the side of the river. Like a torpedo in an old war movie, a large fish suddenly charged the two sawbills. He launched himself from at least 60 feet and, missile-like, broke the surface enough to create a bow-wave. The mergansers, sensing something at the last moment, rose in a panic of clattering wings and flew fast away.

Well, salmon do not in theory attack birds, but the fact is that mergansers are major predators of salmon eggs, a difficult enemy for the progenitors because the sawbills get their necks and beaks under the water and then shovel through the redds removing the buried caviar. Salmon hide the eggs in their redds and assume they are safe until the little alevins wiggle out in warming springtime sunshine; they cannot remain on duty to stand guard. I have seen a merganser in Canada surfacing from redd-raiding with salmon eggs cascading down its chest. I believe that cock salmon recognised in the merganser pair, with their elongated predator shape and thin heads, a predator enemy. It was a bird-fish interaction I will never see twice.

Prior to rain, the petulant salmon under the bridge are all moving and all disturbed. They squirt forward and drift back, they nudge other salmon, their tails swish and they shift position. Rain falls. I wait for the right conditions to see under the bridge again, despite it being harder with higher water. One time I had counted around 150 salmon in diamond-formation then, following rain, the river-bed where they had been was denuded of every one. The breeding pack had moved on to the final stage: the upper tributaries and the redds.

I was taught by an old fishing ghillie how to read water at this point in the salmon chapter and to detect the presence of a river's spawners from water movement. It is an art. You walk upstream from below, although from above is possible too. The spawners are in certain types of places, at least where I view them they are. They occupy the fast water beside and behind the bigger stones – they like active water with energy. To start with they are not in the fastest riffly current, which is shallow, but in the channels by big rocks. From below you see not the fish but the bulge in the water above where they lie. Their bodies are never long still, so the water has a thicker, darker look. Momentarily they move and a fin-edge shows. Then the fin of the partner fish, close by. If you walk up the bank opposite to the fish you can watch the pair of them. Only if you wade into the water do they swim off. It is not like in the fishing season; these creatures have a special matter on their minds, nothing less than their definitive act. As spawning time approaches they move into the faster riffles.

In Canadian fishing huts and fishing lodges and airports near fishing rivers, one man's quotations often adorn the public spaces. They are the words of Roderick Haig-Brown, a judge in his day and resident on the banks of the Campbell River on Vancouver Island. In his book *Return To The River* he describes the drama on a spawning redd of a female Chinook salmon, a stupendously big fish for the little rivers it breeds in.

No one who has read Haig-Brown's account will feel brave enough to attempt their own description. His spare, detailed and probing simple language turns the enactment of egg-release into a pageant of wildlife drama. He describes the hen's convulsing flanks as she releases eggs, redd-digging with fierce sweeps of her mighty tail, the water current helping the process. Then the arrival of the cock squirting his cloudy milt over the egg pile, the competing immature Chinook rushing in to have his go at contributing to procreation, prior to the whole nest being rapidly covered with pebbles in protection from the throng of potential predators needing just such a feast of fresh protein before the onset of north Canadian winter rigour.

At last he describes her dying, being eaten alive by rot, the fungus which softens and breaks down the flesh. Our heroine mother is left disintegrating on the stones. But, critically in Nature's cycle, her dismembering body flakes feed vital protein to young fish and her distant successors. It is noble writing, and gripping. In stately style he takes longer over some passages of this enactment than the real-life duration.

To watch salmon spawning is an elevating experience available to anyone living in salmon country anywhere. Yet we are glued to wildlife films for their perfecting, high-tech, laboratory touching-up, editing and enhancing. Nothing can give you the smell of the real-life river at spawning, the proximity, and the clarity.

Usually between sundown and midnight, working upstream, the hen turns on her side and scoops a depression in a sandy and gravelly substratum, laying eggs all the while in a steady outpouring. The eggs remain fertile for only one minute, so contenders vie to fertilise them, squirting their cloudy milt. Action is furious. The redds are then covered over with the same stone-shovelling to a depth of up to a foot.

I saw this process one time on a gravel-bar below my house late in November after most fish had spawned. The salmon were same-sized, around 35 pounds. I had recently handled some big salmon and although fish of this size are seldom seen in the River Helmsdale, that was the class of fish I was watching. She lay just in front of him, but instead of a vigorous and exhausting performance these two were in languorous mode. They were so large that no grilse, parr or other contenders were visibly around. Their backs were clear of the water, and the two giants seemed just to nudge each other on the redd. I had two of my children with me and, riding piggy-back, they could see it all from a better height only a few yards across the stream. I almost felt like going away out of politeness.

Enquiring later about the presence of such leviathans, a retired fishery bailiff told me he had long known about these very big salmon. They entered this river after angling had finished, often not till November, and stayed only long enough to spawn. He reckoned they were usually no more than a fortnight in fresh water.

The salmon eggs are clustered in the redds until they hatch, safe from most eventualities except major flooding when rolling rock could smash their soft mounds and disperse the egg collection for consumption by all and sundry. For there are few denizens of salmon headwaters for whom fresh eggs are not a welcome dietary enhancement. Unlucky clutches too near the surface can be frozen solid on gravel-bars exposed to hard frost which has driven down water levels. Redds are safe if there is stability in the river system until they hatch in the spring.

The actors in the conception drama have changed their costumes to participate. Both sexes' noses become extended. If he were a medieval knight trying to unnerve his jousting opponent, the features the cock salmon arraigns himself in might fit the bill. He grows a lower-jaw projection in the form of a solid gristle hook which curves up, sometimes actually piercing the cartilage of his upper mouth, which itself arches, pre-spawning, to accommodate it. The knob has a name, the 'kype', but its purpose is uncertain. Salmon fishery managers have seen cock salmon thrash their heads at male parr trying to get near the females on the redds, but a knob this solid is hardly needed for that. As big cocks charge and chase each other the kype may be a proboscis for belabouring rivals. When the cock reassembles his hormones after spawning and drifts downriver as a kelt, the kype in sympathy shrinks too, till only the familiar small hook is left. Unless this happened he could never resume feeding.

The cock's head attains super-gothic ferocity, being elongated for the spawning by three or four inches, and his skin blackens. At the finale he hardly looks like a fish at all.

When at our local hatchery we had schoolchildren on an afternoon out acquainting themselves with the species for the first time, I remember a fishery bailiff hauling a cock salmon from a deep holding tank and the wide-eyed, disgusting-looking monster squirming from side to side, eliciting a gasp of horror from the young onlookers who jumped backwards. They may have seen some X-rated movies, but this was something else.

Normally, after 50–110 days, the incubation extending to eight months in the colder Arctic, the salmon eggs break forth as tadpole-like creatures, carting as an underbelly appendage the vital egg sac. This bulging picnic is for consumption on the next stage of the pilgrimage, before they can start feeding from the outer world for themselves. As the little jelly-like creature, with its sharp, black, instantly functioning eyes expands, the picnic shrinks, and after six to eight weeks has been completely absorbed. From that time, life support is externally supplied – or existence ends.

Fry, as they are called, eat tiny crustaceans, insect larvae, nymphs and phytoplankton – a variety of miniature organisms that flourish in stream sunlight. They subsist on their hunting skills, which are rapidly developed. In summer heat food multiplies and in winter it shrinks till it disappears, their growth mirroring food availability. The further they range from the safety of shade and cover, the higher the risk of ending up in the stomach of a trout, heron, kingfisher, cormorant, or other assailant. In the fecund backwaters of Scotland's Aberdeenshire River Deveron, where the water is clear and glassy, I have seen thousands of fry massed in corners. The fugitive instincts they need in later life are in evidence early and they move like lightning, even from passing shadows.

The parr stage is marked when they reach a couple of inches. Parr have snub noses, brownish backs, some black spotting, and a few red spots near the lateral line. This line is their nerve system, the strung-out headquarters where their sensory faculties are assembled. Parr have an easy signature in several dark bands running vertically up and down the body, no sign of which survives beyond this stage of their existence. The barring accounts for the term sometimes used to describe them: 'fingerlings'.

Anglers know them as the energetic little fellows that can seize a fly, sometimes almost of their own size, equally in fast riffles or at the tail of the pool in torpid backwaters. We dislike holding them for fear our hands are too hot, so we customarily let them wiggle free from the hook, holding them near the surface to skip off as they hit water.

Just as seagulls are a sign of worms being turned by the plough, so mergansers are a sign of parr shoals. On the famed Restigouche River in New Brunswick, where some of the largest Atlantic salmon abide, flocks of mergansers number hundreds. They fly in menacing sinister squadrons up and down the fish-rich river, making a commotion when they all settle. In the Fifties it was found on the nearby Miramichi River that 86 per cent of the local mergansers ate parr to the tune of over a million each annually! It almost defies belief, but tests elsewhere replicate a gargantuan consumption rate. Mergansers can decimate a salmon population, faster when the water is low. Restigouche kingfishers target parr too and in times past the fishery owners painstakingly shot both mergansers and kingfishers as part of routine salmon protection.

It is perhaps one of the oddest adaptations of Atlantic salmon that some of these miniature parr can be sexually mature. As we have seen, they are capable of fertilising big hen salmon on the redds, nipping in as the cocks pause and ejecting their little sprays of milt over them. Looked at from an evolutionary point of view it completes a portrait of salmon's variable ways of circumventing catastrophe. If all the cock fish in the sea were boiled in the lava outflow of an erupting volcano (to take a fantastic scenario), then the female fish reaching home would not be reproductively marooned. That little barred parr would be waiting, successful fugitive from kingfishers, to secure the future of one more generation of fine salmon.

Parr feed on the full range of titbits that the meagre headwaters of salmon rivers have to offer. Mayflies, stoneflies, other insects and insect larvae, worms and mussels – most things moving and many unmoving contribute to diet. Vulnerable to acidification and very low levels of pH, to chemical discharges from agricultural crops like silage, concentrated effluents, mining tailings, high aluminium and heavy metals, wood dust, oils and the like, parr need clear water and flowing streams. A simple-sounding requirement, but in a land-hungry world clean water is not such a common commodity. As they prepare to 'smoltify', their tails lengthen and the forks in them deepen, their fins grow, the scales soften, and they turn silvery. The great odyssey in the ocean is about to commence.

It is a matter of wonder that such small creatures can be destined to go so far. When birds migrate, they are of a similar size to their progenitors. When flounders and shad and lampreys shift in and out of the salt water on the tides they cover measurable distance on a manageable scale. Other mammal migrants travel in families and herds, adults protecting young. Caribou and elephants and migrating African antelope shepherd their young, fending off predators on their behalf. But these small salmon are unaccompanied minors, with a threat-filled odyssey ahead. On the trip they rub shoulders with whales, they are tossed and turned in the ocean's systems, upwellings and currents and still they adhere to their programmed track. SALSEA identifies the routes and genetic families of some of the journeymen.

When common eels leave the Sargasso as elvers they allow the prevailing winds and currents to push them across the Atlantic towards freshwater lakes. The journey can take years, but the fish are essentially passive. It is the determinism of the young salmon that amazes. Predestined to reach a feeding ground, whether in the North Sea as grilse, or on the Greenland Shelf and north-east Atlantic as multi-sea-winter salmon, they are on a mission, bent on their assignation with copious krill and capelin and other nutritious sweetmeats. The whole challenge is formidable in the extreme.

The Culture

I was in a party of river rafters on the Alaskan panhandle late one summer and we had finished taking apart our gear and were waiting to be picked up. We dawdled around a river-mouth where a multitude of salmon were swarming. Biologists had blocked the small river-mouth with a grid because enough spawners were already jammed in the river and more would overload the small rivers where they bred. Families with open pick-ups were backing onto the edge of the pool and the men were snow-shovelling palpitating salmon directly into the backs of the pick-ups. They filled the rear of their vehicles, pulled tarpaulins over the still-thrashing salmon and drove off. Winter food supply all sorted.

These biblical-scale salmon runs are not all gone. In fact, they continue. It was a year predicted by fishery scientists as likely to be low on spawners, and a multitude arrived.

The world of antediluvian excess, of passenger pigeons in numbers to darken the sky, of fish which break nets and pull trawlers under the waves, of buffalo whose thundering hooves made the American plains shake from far away, these examples of Nature's gargantuan excess still exist in parts of the Pacific salmon domain. It is reckoned that in the southern edge of range, America's Washington State and Oregon, only a tenth of the original runs survive, but north of that runs persist.

What is unknown is the degree to which hatchery efforts by Alaskan fish and game managers are reinforcing migrations. Only genetic testing from the annual runs, against a database of the genetics of salmon used in the hatcheries, would show this, and the record was not taken. There is an element of hybridisation in the run.

I was shown a tributary of the Campbell River on Vancouver Island where pink salmon waiting to spawn were stacked like sardines in a tin. The place was dense with vegetation and only as the fishing guide pushed aside the tree branches did I make out what was in the water. It was like looking into a wine rack where the bottle heads were fish faces. Having spent over a week seeking one lonely steelhead willing to engage with my fly patterns it was a trifle galling to see a stack of fish so dense it pushed water from the river onto the bank.

In July 2010 I was in Vancouver when the sockeye were thronging the bays around the city. Rod fishers were all over, filling larders for winter. There was some edgy banter, too, about whether these super-abundant fish should be returned or not. Conservation talk about perilously damaged fish-runs, even of a different salmon species, had altered public perceptions. The language of conservation and the more acute sense that wildlife values must from now on be looked after has hyped issues, and common sense can get lost. One species gets muddled with another in the public eye and the projection of fishermen as ruthless, greedy hunter-gatherers becomes lodged in the public mind.

Long ago in the history of fish management in western American and Canadian culture it was hard to make the case for the protection of migratory fisheries against the socio-economic advantages of industrial advance, timber-logging, and the power of hydro-energy. Nowadays, in instances of survival adequacy it is sometimes hard to make the case for a controlled take.

The point about the prodigious runs of salmon into western Pacific rivers is more significant, though. The salmon runs dictated human settlement; this can be shown compellingly. No one has applied this information to settlement history in Western Europe. Here the Atlantic salmon, not the Pacific species, was the bonanza of protein delivered by migratory evolution. It is known that the Phoenicians netted tuna in the open sea two thousand years ago. Anyone capable of doing that, and capturing very large fish which were also the fastest swimmers in the sea, could with comparatively little effort have trapped salmon. And they did.

Take the Pacific coast first. In his 2011 book comparing the New World and the Old World, entitled *The Great Divide*, Peter Watson examines the effects of a great climate shift. From around 6000 BC sea levels began to stabilise. Glaciers had been pouring fresh water into the seas, and land had been rising as the weight of ice lifted. This process eventually levelled out. Vast shoals of salmon began to swim up the pristine rivers. A harvest of fish arrived on the doorstep of tribes on river-mouths and it came every year, regular as the turning season.

Peter Watson's evidence comes from the fish bones in river-side human settlement remains. There, human skeletons show signs of arthritis consistent with a diet consisting predominantly of fish. From about 3,000 BC shellfish were added to the menu. Middens grew in size and it appears clans and tribes began to become more permanent and less peripatetic. Cemeteries mark places where tribes wished not only to lay their ancestors' bones, but also places to which they lay claim.

Peter Watson's theory is that the New World, blessed with abundant game and a wagon-train of protein in the form of Pacific salmon arriving before the onset of winter to stock the larders, had no need to evolve and develop agriculture, as had happened in the Old World. Where societies in Asia and Europe lived on cereals and domesticated animals, in the Americas people were graced with abundant wild animals for food. Chief was salmon; north-western cultures used flounders, herring, cod, sturgeon and small oil-rich fish called eulachon too, but most important of all was salmon.

The key to the harvest is the nature of tidal rivers and migrating behaviour of salmon. When the tide fills a river-mouth the fish ride in on it, holding on to the top layer so as not to scrape their stomachs on stones. This way they ascend the river to ascertain whether to continue in the freshwater environment or return to the saltwater and wait for a better moment. But as they return the tidewater level is falling. There is less water to swim in. That is when a river-bed weir structure which had been below water level a few hours earlier suddenly becomes a barrier. There is no escape over the top of it and the unimpeded water flows back through small spaces in the weir. All that is left behind is the fish. They can then be speared or caught in dip-nets, or in a manner of other ways removed from the water. Easy as pie.

There is nothing smart about this: I have seen the same thing happening in Scotland about thirty years ago on the River Ericht, a tributary of the Tay. Stone Age isn't dead! Village boys ran about amongst the rocks as the water levels fell during a dry spell, spearing and catching salmon marooned in pools. Some of them had lamps and flares the better to see the fish as dusk drew in. That scene, long ago called 'burning the water', could have been taking place at any point in the last thousand years. Technically illegal at the time, the occasion pre-dated the era when salmon were accepted as being rare and in need of protection from this primitive-style capture.

Yet the riotous melee had an atmosphere of folk revelry and abandonment to primal energy which somehow stirred ancient memories. Anyone prone to get too sniffy about inappropriate salmon-catching should be reminded that some late-eighteenth-century landowners in New England, unversed in the then-unknown delights of rod-and-line fishing, travelled distances to the Connecticut River to get their fun from salmon-spearing and gaffing salmon leaping at waterfalls.

In the Pacific Northwest the background to salmon capture was quite different. There the salmon was holy and the run was a phenomenon upon which survival hung. Unsurprisingly, the ingenuity, artistry and practical neatness of some of the artefacts developed to capture and process the fish harvest from the sea were astonishing. Salmon were the lifeblood of existence for these people and their fishing culture reflected it. The most famous artwork from the Pacific Northwest is from the Haida Indians, and some of their resplendent work consists of images of fish. Salmon equalled tribe survival and the cultural acknowledgement of this is a feature of the history of the north-west.

Catching salmon was taken to a level of high art in a practical sense. Cedar bark was twined into nets and split cedar boughs were used to make nets and traps. Cedar was deployed too to make lashings for constructing lattices for stopping advancing fish, and wild cherry was tough enough for attaching shafts to nets and fish-spears. Flexible boughs of hemlock and spruce were twisted into fish-traps formed like tunnels in varied designs.

The native people were assiduous in the harvest of their prime resource. The techniques and structures were impressively elaborate. In some of the fish enclosures constructed to hold fish as the tide receded, white clam shells paved the floor, better to show to those peering down what fish were held there. There were lattice mazes with intermittent posts driven into the tidal estuary to snare salmon drifting on the tides; looking for a way out, the salmon swam further in. Different designs were used for varying stream flows and different woods were separated into functions suited to their characteristics; for instance, willow was used for major weirs, being strong and flexible and abundantly available. Stakes held their position, being pointed at the bottom and driven into the stream-bed. On the longer weirs the fishermen built spearing platforms in tripod shapes which enabled them to spot the quarry. Spears were subtly designed with stop-butts to prevent the pointed spear sections being damaged on the bottom.

Plant knowledge had progressed far on this well-endowed coastline. The Indians discovered that the stinging nettle, which grew over head height in those parts, had a property which could be used for salmon harvest. The stalks were cut, dried, peeled, beaten, shredded and then spun into a two-strand twine of exceptional strength. The wood and bone spindles used to do this were in use up to the present time.

In preparation for her brilliant illustrated study, *Indian Fishing*, British Columbian writer Hilary Stewart tried out these techniques herself. Using plants and different woods she constructed weirs and traps and spears and every tool connected to the salmon harvest. She found it took time and skill to replicate the old toolkits – but they worked. In Europe the same knowledge existed and nettles were considered to make stronger twine than flax – in fact the word 'net' derives from nettle. Cedar and willow bark were materials for net construction too. The hoops of nets might be made of bent vine maple.

The north-west Pacific peoples used only materials they had at hand. There were no imported or traded tools or materials. Anthropologists today might term their salmon capture 'organic'. Looking back from where we are now there is something delightfully clean and satisfying about a food provision entirely serviced from the clever utilisation of local plants. Thinking further afield, there are few societies of which this remained true until recent time. The Inuits in the Arctic are an example, and there may be others in Arctic Russia, but on the bigger landmasses, where travel in any direction was physically feasible, there are few. There were the northern Saami and variously named reindeer-herders of the Asian tundra and taiga who relied almost exclusively on reindeer. Generally, though, only societies on the rim of the habitable zone were reliant on a single migratory animal.

Salmon capture was taken to a high art. If the water was moving fast the salmon were swept into a fenced enclosure. The single exit was a grid shelf sloping upwards; escaping fish marooned themselves on the grid, struggling upstream as they attempted to reach flowing water again. Neat.

Snaring fish was a various art. Rocks on the river-bed were designed in hoops or 'wing-dams' with the open end upstream. There could be a series of these ring structures widening out with the river. On the ebb tide salmon fell back in the river-mouth and were stranded. The rock-traps can be seen in outline today, still in place even though modern techniques have rendered them obsolete. The top rocks have been swept away in centuries of spates, but the river-bed structures remain, jawbones from which the teeth have fallen.

They are as evident in western Europe as they are in the Pacific Northwest, but in the former place no one has been looking for them or trying to build a picture of Stone Age salmon capture. If you go to the Grimersta River on Lewis, in Scotland's Outer Hebrides, a prolific salmon system, you can find the same primeval remains of what at one time supplied local Outer Hebrideans with their winter food supply. The most elementary aspects of food harvest have a tendency not to alter much.

Weirs were angled to guide fish towards a centre-pass where the trap would be positioned. I have seen salmon channelled this way in Canada for counting and stock assessment. It works unerringly and the flow of the water keeps the latticework or stake-fence in place. Sometimes densely foliated tree branches are used to fill the bigger gaps. All the system needs is salmon with the urge to go upstream and water pushing the other way. Usually the more delicate lattice structures were taken away after the salmon run and the basic structures, especially when of rock, were left in place. If necessary they were repaired and rebuilt in springtime.

Tricking salmon into net-ends or 'bunts' was a brain-teaser which produced ingenious contraptions. The Indians worked out that salmon could be deflected by the appearance of pendant vertical lines which, had they attempted, the fish could have swum through. But the salmon opted to go in the direction of the tidal current and could be fooled into the upper layer of the water even though the water below was a lot deeper. A loose cats-cradle of connected lines, kept in place by sinker-weights and buoys, was enough to direct the salmon to where spear-wielding fishermen awaited them.

Bunches of rye grass were tied to the floor of the loose cradle of line to create the illusion of a floor or river-bed. This kept the fish in the river's upper level heading for the denser-woven net near the shore through which they could not escape. Guile and knowledge of the quarry were essential in the capture of this turbo-charged fish. A salmon can outswim any creature in the river, and indeed most in the ocean.

In some ways it is peculiar that the Indians never developed the art of rod-angling. In the Azores today medium-sized fishing boats go to sea to take tuna, armed with bunches of fishing poles which are fished manually by fishermen just as day-boat anglers jig for pollack and mackerel. Rod and line is simply the best way of catching tuna. Additionally, rod-caught fish remain clean and attract the highest prices in the market.

The Indians approximated to this with line-fishing by trolling. Trolling from canoes took place in the bays and inlets before the fish range was narrowed by the confinement of rivers. A witness at the time describes what the Nootka Indians did:

> *'For slimness and invisibility the braided leaders were made from women's hair, or in rougher water from the quills of birds or porcupines. A hook was baited with fresh sprat or herring, and the line was attached to the solo canoeist's paddle. The whole rig was sunk with small sinker stones. As the oarsman moved his paddle back and forth a slow jerking movement of the hook attracted the salmon. The paddle was then handled in such a way that the salmon was boated.'*

You may ask, what were the hooks made from in a culture without metal? It is ingenious. 'Bentwood', or wood of hemlock, balsam, fir or spruce branches were used, but taken only from the places there were knots. For knots were denser than ordinary wood and instead of floating, sank. This wood was shaved to the right slimness, then steamed and pressed into a hook-shaped mould. Deer tallow rubbed onto the hook before cooling prevented the hooped construction re-opening. The barbs, lashed on, were fashioned from bone.

The ways in which Pacific-coast salmon were utilised once extracted from their natural element were diverse. Presumably some were used to fuel the energies of hungry fishermen and trappers and eaten fresh. Summer diets consisted of berries and shellfish; salmon was a burst of marine protein. But the bulk of the harvest was preserved for winter by drying and smoking. Nineteenth-century photographs show Indians dip-netting, scoop- and bag-netting and catching salmon in a multifarious manner, with the racks of fish drying in the background. Just as the weirs were often enormous structures involving the use of entire trees, and very long and strongly built, the drying-racks could be structures bigger than houses. Fir boughs protected the fish from direct sun and racks were positioned to catch warm winds for drying. Anything near ground level would attract grizzlies, hence the structures were built aloft.

Weather was all-important. There were good seasons for curing and drying fish, which was ideally done outside. If it had to be done inside, as much of the salmon harvest as could be accommodated was brought in. But for the really large-scale curing, space was needed, and that relied on clement conditions. Complete failure to cure the winter food supply successfully could lead to local starvations. There are a number of peoples, like the Han of the Yukon River, who critically depended on salmon runs for their survival over winter.

The V-shaped drying-racks could handle hundreds of salmon sides. Caches for salmon were built on stilts both to catch the wind and to keep bears off, and they were considerable structures. Some were the size of residential log cabins. There is a photograph of a cache built on several different floors climbing a single tree and connected by ladders. The Indians had wooden tongs for lifting fish. Strainers for removing them from cooking-pots were constructed of seal-ribs. Knives were made of mussel shells, and fish skins were dried on triangular blocks designed to stretch them. The number of varying utensils created to manage the salmon harvest equals the refinement of a modern kitchen equipment range. But all came from at-hand natural products. Tube-like bottles were made from the hollow necks of sea-kelp fronds.

The salmon were not only used for preserved food and skins. On the Fraser River the oil was taken from decomposing salmon bodies which had been left in troughs in the sun to rot, allowing the oil to seep to the bottom. Oil was procured too from the livers of dogfish and cod, and also from the bodies of eulachon (small oily river fish captured in shoals). Salmon roe was hung separately on racks and eaten when decomposed. Alternatively, salmon roe was sunk in boxes below the tide and rotted there before being consumed. Perhaps this is no more strange than raw salmon or gravlax being eaten in Scandinavia today. To many people, gravlax is the best salmon preparation of all.

The importance of the salmon in north-west Pacific culture is reflected in the artistry which was devoted to decoration of the tools deployed in their capture. Salmon was regarded as a sacred food resource with sacramental and life-saving qualities and was accordingly a repeat symbol in the region's famous art. A nineteenth-century French missionary staying in a Huron fishing village described the eloquence of local preachers whose job it was to persuade salmon to come into the nets and be caught. His sermons were theatrical performances attended by the village in a hushed silence. Salmon, remember, possess souls.

Ceremonies preceded the opening of the fishing season. It was believed that salmon would reappear again only if their spirits had been properly appeased. The Indians regarded salmon spirits as closely linked to the human ones which subsisted upon their bodies. Salmon were seen as possessing a conscious spirit and their returning presence to their natal streams viewed as a voluntary act rather than the gene-driven survival ritual identified by biologists today.

If salmon failed to come back, the Indians believed they had broken sacred taboos, or in some way offended the spirit of the fish. Indeed, instead of perceiving the capture of the salmon as the wily manifestation of the skilled hunter's art, the captured salmon was seen as complicit in its own capture. A willing participant in the scheme of things, the fish was taken only with its own consent, and its capture was dependent on certain conditions being fulfilled. In this sense the link between the salmon migration and the peoples who relied on them was similar to the relationship between the Saami of northern Scandinavia and Arctic Russia and reindeer.

The first salmon caught triggered more ceremonies. On the Lower Fraser the Tlingit peoples take the first sockeye to the chief who in turn carries it to his wife. She thanks the salmon chief for sending this emissary. The whole tribe attends the ritual consumption of this first salmon following a rigid set of rules, cleansing themselves with a special concoction of plants beforehand.

The life-giving fish had returned and the rhythmic cycles of Nature are again underlined and confirmed. Instead of chewing the dried salmon cured in a previous year, people could again eat fresh salmon with the tang of the sea.

In addition, the returning silver salmon were seen as capable of dispelling diseases and sickness. Prayers reflected the belief that while the salmon were being eaten in the opening ceremonies their souls surveyed the proceedings from above. Is this why, without knowing it, the rod-angling fraternity hang salmon replicas on the fishing hut or the sporting-lodge wall?

Most tribes had a ritual involving the salmon bones being returned to the river or the sea. One tribe burnt the bones instead, although usually incineration was avoided. The purpose of the rituals was a new commitment to the cycle which would propitiate the salmon spirits and ensure their return in following seasons. There were ceremonies as the salmon was cut and prayers were intoned by senior citizens in the tribe. The fish was honoured. Not before this was done were other fishermen allowed to start fishing from the rest of the salmon run. Which of us Western rod anglers hasn't toasted a first fish? Perhaps more often we have toasted lost fish, the expression on the face of the worsted angler being the most interesting. We observe remnants of old tribal manners without knowing why.

In one ceremony where the salmon is served on cedar planks the fish has to be handled so that the head is always pointing in the direction of the fish-run, or upstream in the river. The

Lkungen tribe in Vancouver Island send their children to await the first salmon to arrive in the fishing boat. The children carry the fish up the beach and conduct a ceremony involving burnt offerings. Only children eat the first salmon, adults having to wait a few days for their share. Salmon bones may not touch the ground and in due course are returned to the sea.

Californian Indians of the Karuk tribe believed that the poles used to make the booth for keeping spears must be taken from the highest mountain or the salmon will see them, and also that they must be renewed every year. The reason is that otherwise old salmon will have told young salmon about them. This tale not only humanises salmon, giving them the faculty of human sight, but removes the distinction between dead or alive salmon. Breaches of tradition entail the failure of fishing effort; these were societies saturated with faith in the spiritual.

James George Frazer, recounting some of these beliefs in his early twentieth-century magnum opus, *The Golden Bough*, points out that in regarding salmon as having spirits equivalent to human ones the salmon-dependent tribes' philosophy chimes with the modern view of the indestructibility of energy. Energy assumes new forms but does not vanish when one energy-vehicle is transmuted into another – as when fish becomes food. This makes sense of tribal beliefs in the immortality of animal souls as well as human ones.

Amongst tribes less reliant on salmon but more able to catch, say, halibut, the reverence and ritual are invested in that fish instead. But for the majority of the coastal cultures on this seaboard, one or more of the five salmon species were the principal food resource. Beliefs about salmon outnumber those of any other fish.

In her study of these subjects, Hilary Stewart records several salmon stories she encountered amongst the coastal tribes. One maintained that the first salmon to arrive were scouts. Correct treatment of the scouts ensured the bulk of the run following. Several tribes believed salmon were really people who lived in undersea communities. Some of the artwork reinforces this with, for example, a fish carving in an oblong piece of wood with a human in its stomach.

The readiness with which catch and release has been adopted in western European fishing circles surprises some people. Fishermen go misty-eyed. Seen as a spiritual enactment, it all makes more sense. Early people tried to ensure a salmon future spiritually, modern people try and ensure it biologically, but the two are in reality blurred.

Twin children in the north-west Pacific were believed to have a special rapport with salmon, and this was a widespread notion. If twins were born in the village, an unusually large salmon would arrive in the river afterwards. A wayward citizen could halt the salmon run by burying a salmon heart in a clam shell or in a burial ground. If salmon eyes were kept overnight in the house without being eaten, all the salmon would disappear. A shell knife had to be used in the ceremonial cutting of salmon or there would be thunder. Only old women past childbirth could work on, or repair, salmon nets. And because people enjoyed eating the sweet inner bark of springtime hemlock, salmon must too, and accordingly balls of it were adorned with feathers and sent downriver to satisfy the fish.

There were other taboos which required adherence if the salmon run was to carry on unimpeded. Freshly split planks could not be floated down the river and new canoes had to season before being floated. Hilary Stewart links this to the actual fact that extracts of fresh cedar are toxic to fish.

Rules abounded regarding the correct procedures for catching salmon. Children were not allowed to play with the sacred fish before they were cleaned. An offending child might even die. Salmon could not be taken up the beach from the canoes in a basket, but rather by hand. Anyone recently connected to birth or death rites should not handle or eat fresh salmon, risking the cessation of the run. The first salmon were not sold commercially in case the salmon hearts were destroyed or fed to the dogs, another potential risk to the run. A spear fisherman catching two fish with one thrust should not exhibit triumph, or the salmon already splayed on the drying racks would climb down and go back to sea.

The catalogue of means which the north-west Pacific cultures used for taking salmon could be continued. The tools and techniques they had for harpooning, spearing, jigging, snaring and ripping salmon are various and ingenious. They used whale baleen for snoods, bones for barbs, split roots for fish hooks. The subject is delightfully fruity.

Perhaps this is an anthropologist's turf rather than mine. Where I think the key significance lies is in Peter Watson's assertion that it was the abundance of the runs of Pacific salmon which has enabled the Pacific coastal peoples to continue lifestyles unadjusted to modern time in a way inconceivable without the extraordinary bounty of the salmon harvest. The various peoples who inhabited the lands around the Columbia River called the river 'the great table', where people could come at different times of year and get their slug of life-reviving sustenance.

Without that returning bonanza of fish which could so variously be prepared and cured and salted down, and preserved for use for over half a year later, the Pacific peoples would have had to trade, to open up avenues for the exchange of goods and generally interact with the rest of the continent in a different way. Their cultures would have changed long ago. The salmon harvest kept an undeveloped but environmentally benign culture in happy coexistence with the salmon runs for thousands of years. Up to a point, and we will revert to this later, it still does so now.

What has never been looked at is the degree to which human settlement was dictated by salmon runs. One might argue and even be able to prove that Vancouver, at the mouth of the Fraser River, was once used by native people as a salmon capture station. It is easy to imagine it; salmon are caught in Vancouver's waterways now. Backed by the Rockies and without coastal roads and caravan routes trekking over open plains to the rear, maybe here, as was the case further north, a society existed for a long time in isolation from other trade centres, hemmed in by the mountains and living primarily on fish, most of which were salmon. Salmon were the cultural lynchpins. But maybe this is not only true in the Americas ...

North European and Scandinavian cities are mostly sited on river-mouths. Mostly they were salmon rivers. Now that it is known that sea voyagers traversed the Atlantic long before Christopher Columbus, sea travel has an ancient pedigree. No one knows how, but 50,000 years ago humans crossed the water from Indonesia to Australia. Boats that could cross the ocean could cruise the coastline up and down. That may be so, but there is another reason why cities were built on river-mouths, and that is because the larder that needing filling was thus ideally located beside the conveyor belt containing the food. The food was migratory fish.

In the twenty-first century salmon cling to survival in a few rivers in northern Spain and in select French rivers down to the Spanish border. But even today the French have a delightful and powerful folk memory of '*le saumon*'.

One time I was sent by a magazine on a grayling fishing trip to a river in the south-west of France. It had rained stupendously, so my fishing guide and I forgot the fishing and enjoyed a repast in a dripping camping ground which was memorable for the wonderful goat's cheese which his own flock had contributed. With little to do I looked at the rule book for local fishermen. At the back was a section on salmon fishing. To my surprise there was a long and detailed chapter delimning precisely how and when salmon could be caught and all the attendant rules. I expressed surprise to my guide that there were indeed any salmon in the river. He said casually that in fact there were not; the chapter on salmon was there to satisfy just such fishermen as myself, whiling away the time and dreaming of fish that might be – dreaming of fish that only existed in different places, where there were not hydro dams up and down the river, and where pollution had been addressed, and where water-flow permitted their existence. Perhaps only in France would you find that chapter about a fish from another place, but it rather enhanced the occasion for me.

Next day we got back to the action on the grayling and I thought several times of the possibility that somewhere on this river, sometime, there could be salmon again too. The concept had become embedded. The salmon as a cultural entity had a significance despite being absent as a living fish.

The Atlantic salmon has been a lifeline of survival for early Man since the Stone Age. As G.E. Sharp, counterpointing survival with angling, said in 1910, 'The caveman's necessity has become the rich man's hobby.' It has been, as for the north-west Pacific Indians, the most reliable source of returning protein of any. It swims into the larder voluntarily and, unlike the fleet-footed reindeer, need only be stopped from going out again. Seals are large lumps of meat easily overtaken and knocked on the head, but they only make landfall once a year for pupping and their meat is unsuitable for variable curing. No wonder some of the Pacific tribes enunciated heartfelt thanks for salmon's bountiful re-appearance.

There is an intrinsic difficulty in firmly tying down what happened long ago in western Europe. It is known that Cro-Magnon man ate salmon from bones in middens on the River Dordogne. And the indigenous inhabitants of Scotland, the Picts, incised salmon on sacred stones, some of which survive to this day. But the food-remains legacy is not all that it might be.

One problem is that fish bones soften and disintegrate faster than animal bones; they are less durable. Where the middens full of clam and mollusc shells present an unarguable picture of shellfish consumption, salmon eating is much harder to ascertain from bone remains. Historians of Stone Age culture say that three-quarters of all animal bones were eaten by creatures, from deer down to voles, needing the calcium. This is prior to natural biological breakdown. We get only a whiff of what was consumed from rubbish deposits, even with animals and their harder bones. Fish bones are often long gone from recorders' view.

Then there is a possible misinterpretation of the meaning of surviving bark and wicker artefacts. These are shown on the Pacific Northwest to have been used for fish capture. Stone Age historians on the east side of the Atlantic often imagine that these surviving creations were used for carrying things. They may, rather, have been used to trap fish. What were suitable materials for doing this on one seaboard may reasonably be assumed to have been suitable for the same purpose on another.

Then most of the evidence of a salmon culture determining settlement in western Europe may lie underneath the coastal cities which have grown where there were once river-mouth fishing villages. Of England's cathedral cities, eighteen of twenty-five are on salmon rivers – either a coincidence, a practical matter relating to easier travel using water, or something to do with an easily obtained food resource. Who knows? My guess is that salmon presence played a part in human settlement locations. Salmon may have determined early settlement. If it is trouble to take the food to the people, take the people to the food.

If you deduce early diet from drawings and rock art depictions, fish appear as well as deer. Perhaps the fact that the hides of deer were vital for clothing made deer more integral to survival, but in London's Victoria and Albert Museum there is a woman's marriage coat described as of the Gilyak tribe from the lower Amur River in eastern Siberia, made of 60 Pacific salmon skins and dated to about 1900. On the upper back are appliqué semi-circular panels simulating fish scales. There are similar garments in other collections.

Not only were salmon skins used in ceremonial occasions, but Icelanders, inhabitants of the Gaspé Peninsular in Quebec, and the Ainu from the Kuril Islands off Japan, all used salmon skin for clothes and shoes. The Ainu used the tougher skins of spawned salmon for making winter boots. My wife, even, is in on the act. She had a business making fashionable items from salmon skins, with a customer base including celebrities. Of course she did! With its delicately inscribed, miniature, cupped ring patterns and very tough texture it is fabulous material.

Today most Atlantic salmon run rivers in only seven countries: Britain, Ireland, Norway, Canada, America, Russia and Sweden. But European rivers at one time mostly possessed salmon populations. Spain, Denmark, Portugal, France and Germany had rivers suited to salmon breeding, as did the countries round the Baltic. The Rhine, Seine, Loire, Douro, Gudena, Oder, Elbe and Weser hosted large populations of the silver visitor.

There is a dearth of statistical information about pre-industrial catches of salmon in Europe, but the few titbits which can be found conjure up a picture of abundance which is reminiscent of the north-west Pacific. A late-eighteenth-century Spanish study claims that 2,000 salmon a day were caught during the season in the province of Asturias. Another writer extrapolating from this considers that 10,000 salmon a day were landed every day in north Spain in the eighteenth century. Adding to this calculation figures for fishing rentals, which were high, Anthony Netboy in *Salmon: The World's Most Harassed Fish*, written in 1980, says that the annual harvest in Spain might therefore have been up to 900,000 fish. Remember, Spain is a salmon country with some of the smallest salmon rivers. Human populations were low then. Salmon were a key ingredient of survival.

France has the shape and physiognomy of a major salmon location. Long winding rivers meander placidly through forests and farmland and course through verdant green valleys. When Caesar colonised Gaul in 56 BC the legions witnessed salmon leaping in the Garonne, and noted a fish-eating people. Salmon and mullet were the delicacies. Taking their cue from the natives, the Romans investigated salmon flavour and took the salted product back home.

The medieval period is perceived only from flashes of comment, but it is known that salmon were traded over long distances. Anthony Netboy says that by the thirteenth century salmon were being exported from Aberdeen, Glasgow, Berwick and Perth to England and the Continent. That is a fact that takes a while to fully appreciate. Salmon, then, was a major trade item from early time, like gold. By the time of the restoration of Charles II in 1660, the value of Scotland's salmon exports was £200,000 – an enormous sum.

Better-detailed is the trade established by Glaswegian merchants sending salted-down salmon to Flanders, Holland and France in the eighteenth century. 'Kippering' was the name given to a method involving decapitating the fish, removing the insides, including any roe, and splitting it down the middle. The cure was dry, with the preserving agents, principally salt, being absorbed into the flesh. Saltpetre, brown sugar, even rum, might be added. The salmon would lie in this concoction for two days, after which it was dried either by heat from a kiln or by sunlight. Sun-drying could take five weeks. Smoking as done in those days involved the same initial process as today, with the fish in the round then being exposed to wood-smoke.

Pickling replaced salting and kippering, mainly because it was less labour-intensive. This entailed boiling in brine (30 minutes for salmon, 20 for smaller grilse), cooling, then topping with brown vinegar. The fish were exported in barrels to a variety of European ports in regions where salmon did not exist naturally. There were idiosyncratic recipes, as you might expect from a food-conscious time: added to the pickle were bunches of rosemary, slices of ginger, mace, lemon-peel, wine and, in the case of salmon emanating from Newcastle, beer.

London was distinct from European markets in demanding salmon that was fresh. Unadulterated salmon was unloaded in London from boats sailing out of Berwick-on-Tweed and Perth. Again, eighteenth-century Londoners were fastidious. Prices of salmon tumbled as the season wore on. Early-season salmon which travelled in cold weather fetched prices nearly two-thirds higher than later in May, by which time salmon were abundant and freshness was fighting higher temperatures. However, transport in 'kitts' (barrels of 30–40 pounds of fish) was quick: fast cutters of 60–70 tons could whack down from Perth on favourable north winds in 50 hours. When Londoners had to hold their noses the fish were pickled and sent abroad.

Although history recounts that the first salmon packed on ice travelled from Perth to London in the 1780s, Galen, the Roman writer, had reported fish being preserved in snow in the second century. Preservation in frozen water was hardly a sophisticated trick anyway; by the time full-scale salmon netting was underway in the eighteenth century there were ice houses at the mouths of many salmon rivers in Scotland. Winter ice was chopped and packed inside these stone-vaulted, partly subterranean buildings, then sealed off. Salmon were loaded in as and when they were caught.

The volume of trade can be established in some of the local details. The big rivers have clear records, at least of official catches. The Tay is Scotland's premier salmon water. By 1807 the average catch of grilse and salmon was 56,000. Including its main tributary, the River Earn, by the 1840s these numbers had increased to between 65,000 and 80,000, and in the year 1842, to 111,000.

England's Tyne, today the top salmon angling river by a clear lead, has an 18-mile estuary which, during the period of industrialisation, became horribly choked and polluted. But when Tyne waters ran clear, as they do again today, the salmon run was prodigious. Nets took 80,000–120,000 fish every year at one time. This was in addition to some 4,000 salmon on rods. Some days the nets managed to sweep up 2,000 fish, an almighty harvest by the standards of any Atlantic salmon rivers anywhere.

Netting and over-netting then took its toll on returning runs in different places at different times. The Tweed, which at the sea-end divides England and Scotland, had a salmon and grilse catch averaging 109,000 fish between 1811 and 1815, which had shrunk to a third of that in the early 1850s. That contraction had itself halved by the end of the century. Pollution, poaching, overfishing and industrialisation began to hammer stocks of a fish which above all needed unadulterated water and a clear passage.

Brittany has a rocky coastline but French historians of the eighteenth century reckon that as many as 4,500 tons of salmon were landed in good years. Using an average weight of ten pounds per fish, this equates to roughly one million salmon. The 1789 revolution ended this happy state of affairs when landed assets, including fishing rights, were distributed amongst the population without safeguards for maintaining the harvest. Fishing was allowed above the navigable reaches of rivers and the waters were ransacked. Prior to that, sense had prevailed: mills were obliged in law to open their gates by night and on Sundays, and if salmon were held up in their passage to the redds in the headwaters, it was never for long.

Up until the French Revolution the monasteries and landowners had owned and managed the salmon runs. Peter Coates, in his amusing 2006 monograph, *Salmon*, describing the pivotal role of monasteries in medieval salmon capture, writes: 'Salmon loomed particularly large in the worldly desires of religious men.' Because wise use of the harvesting rate was properly understood, there are many examples of early conservation. One of Netboy's sentences on the subject of early French conservation stops you in your tracks: 'Until the eleventh century only fishing for salmon and eels was regulated.' Early control of salmon extraction was evidently a feature of European culture a millennium ago. Scotland had salmon conservation law in place protecting fish preparing to breed by the end of August, by 1030. In England as well as Scotland there was what Netboy has called 'a steady flow' of laws to protect salmon as the lifecycle became better understood. Fixed net operations in rivers were outlawed, and weirs had to contain gaps for the passage of running fish. In 1285 England's King Edward II produced more muscular protection, amongst other measures banning taking salmon fry for feeding to pigs.

Clearly, the lifecycle was properly understood a very long time ago. When you consider what violations have been perpetrated on this species in modern times it is a matter for amazement that anyone can pretend humankind gets any wiser! A law passed in Ireland in 1466 illegalised tipping the effluent from the leather-tanning process into the salmon-rich River Liffey. So they understood too.

The Chief Inspector for salmon fisheries in England and Wales reported that in 1885 at one net-station at Kralingen near Rotterdam 69,500 salmon were caught on that part of the Rhine. Nearby nets took another 12,500 salmon, meaning that in this limited area 82,000 salmon were taken. Furthermore, they were fish of impressive size, the average weight at Kralingen being 17 pounds. Germany, the country containing most of the length of the Rhine, had a huge salmon fishery and its biggest rivers took 200,000 fish a year. However, the Rhine reaches the sea down braided channels in north-west Holland, which are now controlled waterways. The run of salmon collided with a major thrust of European land reclamation. Again, the salmon lifecycle bridging ocean and river, using water fresh and salt, had been its undoing.

The Dutch always lacked physical space and have created a sizeable chunk of country wrested from the sea. A third of Holland was once marshes and saltwater. It is a brilliant feat of engineering, but it is deleterious to salmon. To maintain and protect their land-grab the Dutch have constructed enormous dams. On the freshwater side of them fester big lakes of brackish water. Salmon intensely dislike these water conditions. The problem for the Rhine salmon is negotiating the maze of fish-passes and ladders as they search for a passage upstream; and the problem for seaward-running smolts, physically less able to rise to the challenge, and Rhine kelts, is having to do the journey in reverse, and not being able to reach the restorative feeding in the brine. Adding pressure, continental rivers often contain a suite of fish species, like pike, which devour young salmon.

Clearly Europe had a gigantic salmon fishery long ago. What is impossible to conceptualise is an idea of actual numbers. In Bristol Bay in Alaska, maybe the nonpareil location of salmon abundance, some 40 million sockeye jostled for space in 1970, of which 21 million were fished out and 19 million allowed to reach their spawning grounds. The epic run lasted three weeks and Netboy describes watching it from the air, seeing through the clear water the red bodies of millions of fish, 'like armies on the march', mostly hugging the shores. He describes how once they were past the shoreline habitations they moved on into a landscape devoid of buildings or people or anything, an undeveloped pristine world there for the taking.

Although claims have been made for the scale of salmon runs being the same for Atlantics as for their Pacific cousins, I incline to think it is unlikely the runs of Atlantics, which could spawn more than once, were ever close to this scale, locally in hundreds of thousands perhaps but not tens of millions. The Atlantics had much longer running seasons than Pacifics, another aid to species endurance. Also, today's runs of Pacifics include hatchery stock, introduced to beef up commercial fisheries. We cannot be definitive about pre-industrial salmon populations, but Netboy has a figure for the total Atlantic salmon catch in the period 1964–1975 being 13,000 tons, compared to landings for the combined species of Pacifics being thirty times greater. That gives some sense of modern-times scale.

Another aspect of estimating the numbers of Atlantics involves the fact that runs are attenuated, not single-season events. In big UK rivers salmon arrive throughout the year; the flow of silver fish is unending. Few enter rivers in January, but some do. The Tweed has a ten-month angling season. On the Pacific coast, by comparison, concentrated runs are only weeks in duration. To cling to its evolutionary niche the Atlantic species does not need the numerical multitudes that constitute a sockeye run. It has more safety valves.

In the parts of Europe which resemble the north-west Pacific in climate there is the phenomenon of the salmon which run a river and instead of breeding simply hibernate over winter in preparation for spawning an entire season later. In Russia they call them 'osankas'. It is an extreme example of the variability built into the genetics of the Atlantic salmon to widen its chance of successful procreation; another safety valve. I once caught a May steelhead in northern British Columbia which had hibernated in freshwater the same way.

Whereas there are testimonies from various writers as to the abundance of salmon, including Daniel Defoe describing the amount of salmon being taken in northern Scotland as, 'in such plenty as is scarce credible', some other favourite fables need closer analysis. It is often repeated, not least by the historical novelist Walter Scott, that there were so many salmon in seventeenth-century Scotland that laws had to be passed prohibiting them being fed to servants more than three times a week. The reason probably was that the lower orders were fed kelts, spent low-cost salmon that smelt terrible and tasted worse.

No such afflictions faced the inhabitants of northern Russia, as far as we know. Immured in permafrost for most of the winter, human populations were overwhelmed by salmon populations. Knowledge in this part of salmon range is scant and what runs entered Russian rivers long ago is unknowable. What the Russians call 'tourist fishing' started in 1992. The Kola Peninsular is now a byword in contemporary fishing circles. In 2012 on one of its rivers, the Varzuga, 8,500 salmon were landed by rod fishermen in just 8 weeks, a fact presumably translating into almost terminal human exhaustion from sport. The long-distance caster Mark Birkbeck once caught fifty salmon on the Kola's River Ponoi without moving his feet, fishing the nearest lies first, playing the fish as close to him as he could, then stretching out progressively further.

The Kola has become the destination of choice for many American and British salmon anglers. It is a snout of land protruding east of Murmansk and above the White Sea, facing the Arctic and the Barents Sea. There, the big rivers at one time netted salmon. I was fishing on the Litza in 1999 and my ghillie was the head honcho in the netting time. He told me they once caught a salmon weighing one hundred and eighteen pounds. The big charismatic rivers on the Kola – Rhynda, Kharlovka, Litza – are renowned chiefly for the size and condition of their salmon. Weights go up to forty pounds and twenty-pound fish are not uncommon; when they operated bag-nets in the river-mouths fish averaged ten pounds. The water was so clean we made tea dipping the kettle in the river. The Ponoi, which flows out on the east coast into the neck of the White Sea, is different, being wide, gravelly and slow-flowing, a dream river for salmon in multitudes. Here, sheer numbers are the feature and the run is assumed to be about 100,000. Further east there are the north-flowing rivers debouching towards the Arctic Ocean, hefty great waterways, some going through Cossack country, all known to possess varying amounts of salmon.

The most fascinating perhaps is the Pechora, the longest Atlantic salmon river in the world. It is broad and slow and bifurcates barely inhabited country. An ICES paper reports that salmon spawn mostly at the top end by completing enormous migratory journeys. Investigating scientists reported that one in eleven was found to have spawned twice, and two per cent had spawned three times.

The different lifecycle reflects the half-frozen climate. Eggs deposited between September and November take six months to hatch. The young salmon remain in their natal river for three to eight years before venturing into the Arctic waters. Fed by blood-thirsty fairy-tale-sized insects – which in turn drain blood from the tourist fishers – these juvenile fish reach huge dimensions, some parr breathing down the neck of the one-pound class. Instead of surging out in a rush in May, the smolts depart at stately pace, between May and September. When I was there the ghillies reckoned that ten per cent managed to come back. In the buoyant salmon era of the 1960s and the 1970s, Scottish scientists reckoned that survival as far as Scotland's coastal waters could have been as high as thirty per cent; now it is a fraction of that.

Returning Kola adults are far removed in size from the long-gone 12-million-year-old sabre-toothed salmonid, a creature stretching ten feet and weighing around 400 pounds, and a possible ancestor of sockeye and Chinooks. Contemporary minnows are a mere five feet long and can weigh one hundred pounds. The big females make spawning nests up to three metres wide. My ghillie had a nice image for rod anglers rousting out one of these big salmon: like a boy poking a dog with a stick, eventually it snarls and turns.

The Russians claim that the stock is carefully managed, according to established catch limits. There is no reason to suppose that, with the Slavic keenness for statistics, measurements and science, this is not so. Apart from the fact that northern Russia never experienced the salmon-obstructing widespread industrial development that changed western Europe, knowing what happened there is conjectural.

In Scandinavia Neolithic peoples lived on rivers and lake edges. Fishing was a way of life. Norway is one of the great Atlantic salmon countries today and legislation from as long ago as 900 enacted unimpeded passage for migrating salmon. When Norwegian provinces were demarcated in the tenth century the interior was defined as the mark beyond which salmon could not swim inland any further. Salmon were cartographers, determining administrative jurisdictions. In the Middle Ages taxes from the salmon harvest were a main source of Crown revenues. Norway's northerly latitude and the absence of farmland made salmon fishing a mainstay in pre-industrial society to a degree probably unique amongst salmon countries. The first bag-net was set in the 1820s and by 1903, at the peak, there were nine hundred. Salmon were a pillar of the country's sustenance and enriched a seaboard otherwise devoid of development.

From the 1830s rod anglers began to arrive from Britain and produce significant revenue for the owners of salmon fishings. The British believed they had discovered a sporting nirvana, with wild fish surging up pristine rivers in dramatic scenery, serviced by delighted Norwegian country people who had not imagined that their age-old salmon run could ever lead to such lucrative developments.

In 1882 a book called *Three in Norway* was published. It gives the flavour of these early British salmon fishing adventurers amusingly: 'There is only one word to express this existence and that is Freedom – freedom from care, freedom from resistance, and from the struggle for life. What a country! Where civilised man can relapse as much as seems good to him into his natural state, and retrograde a hundred generations into his primeval condition'. Strong sentiments. Another early pioneer, Sir Herbert Maxwell, in describing fishing for salmon on rivers gushing from glaciers wedged in vast mountains, their crests wreathed in cloud, delimns experiences of intoxicating excitement, ravishing scenery brought to high-voltage life with very large fish suddenly feeling the hook, tumbling down frothing rivers in wild demonstrations of exultant power. Norway took note. Visiting anglers were fulsomely accommodated. In due course the salmon net harvest began to move from rivers and fjords out to sea to leave the rod fishermen in peace. By 1977 eighty-five per cent of the catch was taken offshore.

Iceland, like western Britain, is warmed by ocean currents which push from the west. Despite being at 64–66 degrees latitude, the rivers of western Iceland debouche into a sea which carries mineral and fish richness driven by long-range currents far away in the southern hemisphere. Icelandic rivers are short, none over sixty miles long, and at their tops are glaciers and a moon-like landscape marked by extinct or not-so-extinct volcanoes. Not long ago a volcano erupted creating an entirely new island.

Icelandic records have always talked of salmon runs. In the Grimsa valley it was said that the volume of autumnal salmon bodies made passage across the ford on a horse impossible. Nervy horses disliked the slippery sensation of salmon sliding past. In a wise pre-emptive move the Icelandic government banned river and estuary salmon netting after the Second World War. On barren rivers, where volcanic ash had smothered any natural pebbly redds, hatchery reintroduction helped to re-create salmon runs. Rivers which never had salmon were 'ranched' with hatchery-reared smolts being put in rivers to run to sea, grow and come back again.

The Icelanders had a terrain almost devoid of productive soil; they knew about the sea, which was their larder. They understood fish and how to look after them. The pre-eminence of the social value of fish meant that serious poaching, regarded as deviant, never existed.

Icelandic salmon are smaller than those of most countries but in angling value the rod fishery is a key component of Iceland's economic life. Numerically, its rod catch sometimes exceeds that of Scotland.

Bipeds over their time on Earth have dealt death to a few species. The dodo has even given its name to the finality of extinction. Salmon runs have been obliterated too, and what makes this more remarkable, indeed utterly ominous, is that frequently there was no effort to protect a species whose lifestyle was well understood. Often the obliteration of salmon was avoidable, and owed to a lethal carelessness. A high-value fish was being cut off from its breeding grounds at the upper end of rivers inadvertently, as a pig-ignorant omission. The presence of a thousand years of law demonstrates that the salmon was recognised as important, and yet when it came to new-fangled concepts and development of rivers this special meaning was forgotten or over-ridden. Proto-modernist barbarians executed the past. In a tragic book called *Skeena Steelhead*, published in 2011, Robert S. Hooton relates how a comparable blindness has become institutional in the present-day management of British Columbia's steelhead fishery. He was a senior fisheries manager working for the regional government and, tellingly, only able to relate his experiences post-retirement. Mistakes are reiterated and history repeats itself.

If human progress seems linear in, for example, methods of transport, then it too often stands still in conserving valuable biota already there. We take for granted a wildlife cornucopia until it is without a whisper suddenly gone, and then regret the headlong passage towards an illusory future. The Atlantic salmon once occupied rivers across the whole North Atlantic range. It was a universally known fish for all peoples there. In too many places today salmon populations are a ghostly echo from a lost world.

Renewable energy was first known as rain, and rain flowed down rivers, the pathways for the fecund silver fish. Europeans were using water power a thousand years ago and probably earlier. It is said that for every fifty Britons there was a watermill of some sort by 1200 AD.

The early mills did not trap or block whole rivers; they were wheels to the side, as time went by directed through lades or side channels to divert water and turn more wheels in places out of range of damaging floodwaters. They substituted water power for muscle power, turning heavy objects like flour grinders and corn querns. These early watermills would have sucked through some smolts, and to their detriment, but most of the river remained unobstructed and open for small fish descending to the sea.

Later on came the industrial uses, requiring greater quantities of water and more power. As Britain became the mass manufacturer of the world's textiles the pace of water-use accelerated. The era of cotton mills and wool-scouring needed locomotion; pottery works, steel-making, smelting, dyeing, bleaching and coal-mining, and then aluminium manufacture demanded water-cooling. All came in due course. Britain's temperate climate, conveniently, meant ready rain, and so the country suited the use of water as a power source. Energy from moving wheels was procured from water, from the life-blood of the salmon. Again and again, and in a renewed burst today, flowing water was seen as a way of pushing civilisation forwards, of taking a dividend from motion. Early administrators saw that same rain as capable of removing nasty by-products and washing them into the purifying embrace of the ocean.

Before and while rivers containing salmon were being de-naturalised on a major scale there was the advent of mass-scale netting. As human populations increased and more time was spent working in factories learning the arts of increased production, the rivers and estuaries were treated like free larders where food could be secured at will. Early industry produced rivets from an assembly line, tidal waters were to do the same with salmon. England is a good example of how salmon harvesting evolved.

The Domesday Book, compiled in 1086, listed property assets at the time and already there were many recognised fishing stations working coasts and estuaries. Elizabethan eyewitnesses describe salmon being netted in London's Chelsea and Fulham districts, with horses pulling the boats up the beaches. Anthony Netboy has reported the utilisation of England's salmon from early times and he says that on the River Trent in the English Midlands many streams flowed 'so shallow they can barely support a paper boat, yet at one time they all held salmon'. The Trent, like many rivers in the English Midlands, was re-configured by a network of canals for industry and shipping.

From baskets to nets, to traps, tunnels and boxes, fish-catching devices were installed on rivers with salmon. In 1860 it was calculated that the number of impediments to the free passage of salmon going up the Severn estuary totalled over 11,000.

Where water was diverted by weirs into millraces there might be fish-passes to allow salmon to survive, and there might not. There might have been specific days when the sluices were supposed to be left to run open allowing salmon to run, and there might not. Some salmon populations died off, some survived.

As with other forms of natural resource extraction, official attitudes and approaches were neither logical nor consistent. Archaic fishing methods were continued seemingly merely to pay homage to their antiquity.

Consider the ancient practice of 'haaf-netting'. Deriving from the Norse word for 'channel', this most manual of salmon-netting techniques involves two or three men wading into an estuary holding giant net-baskets in front of them to catch salmon drifting back to sea on waning tides. The baskets are held open by suspension from a solid rail. Try doing that without knowledge or skill and your net will remain empty, and you may fall in. Catches are anyway nominal.

The practice exists in only a few places, one being the firth dividing England and Scotland, the Solway. Demanding exertion, coordination between several netters and indifference to the elements, returns from the fish are outweighed by the costs of nets, licences and fishing gear. But in history-conscious Britain haaf-netting has a relict band of faithful practitioners. It would seem vindictive to ban it in law, and no one is pressing the case. In similar vein, a salmon-catching operation using coracles, skin-made cockleshell boats from the Stone Age, still goes on in Wales. What other fish stirs proto-cavemen to persist with such archaic antics?

A sentimental attitude to haaf-netting and coracles co-exists with ruthless attitudes to salmon survival in other spheres. Builders of hydro-power schemes in today's quest for renewable energy are just as happy to skirt or camouflage the issue with resident fish-life as they ever were when advancing industrial development. The environment, holistic management, the crisis affecting so many fish populations, all turn out to mean nothing when there is easy money to be made.

In 2011 a fishery trust in south-west Scotland was deluged in one three-month period with over 80 applications for the installation of weirs and hydro-schemes on rivers containing migrating salmon, shad and sea trout to the extent that the senior biologist became convinced of the intention to swamp his department and make it impossible to put together proper studies of potential damage to fish stocks as the basis for formal objections to the schemes.

Responsible use of water is not in the DNA of most of us yet. There is an atavistic conviction that Nature is bountiful and curative and will solve restorative issues in the long run.

As we have seen, parallel with the proliferation of salmon-catching instruments was fish-protecting law. There is no shortage of legal protection for the fortunate fish which survived the physical and chemical threats. But behind the formal history is a more nebulous matter of attitude.

Rather as the taking of the landlord's rabbit or hare was not seen as wrong in medieval country districts short of meat-protein, so poaching salmon was for long regarded with an easy tolerance. Poachers entered folklore as canny country folk skilled in devious arts. Salmon were, after all, wild. There was an underlying feeling that they could not therefore be private property, and this belief persists vestigially today.

The same freewheeling attitude is evident in today's sea anglers protesting at being required to buy licences to legitimise throwing baits from the shore into the oncoming tide. The shore fishermen object to being regulated in the removal of 'one-for-the-pot' from the wide-open ocean. Why should they not stand on the tide line throwing worm baits for hungry surf-riding dabs, or delicious bass? In the same way, in yesteryear local householders objected to being prevented from feeding the family on a salmon from the stream that ran past their garden or house. We have not yet written law about jigging for mackerel, harvesting wild mushrooms or other naturally occurring foods like nettles, wild mint, samphire on the marshlands, truffles in the forest, or brambles in hedgerows. But we are on the way there.

Salmon poachers of the past were often treated leniently. In particular on the Celtic fringes of Ireland, Wales and Scotland, country magistrates found it not in their hearts to penalise myth-laden local men operating on 'the dark side of the moon'. A man crossing a river at night in Ireland once famously, and successfully, argued that he had happened to be wading across the river – as one does – when a leaping salmon had jumped into his boot and he had been trying to get the darned thing out as a fishery bailiff apprehended him.

There is often talk of 'leistering', or the use of barb-pronged spears on long handles, as if it were a forgotten medieval practice. Dusty leisters hang over the fireplaces of country pubs as archaic relics, though not always on their twenty-foot long handles. The scene I witnessed on the Ericht in the 1970s was one of many rehearsals to and fro demonstrating the efficacy of the pronged trident.

Fast-forward to 2012. Salmon managers on the magisterial Restigouche River in New Brunswick, one of the Atlantic salmon's greatest domains, every year install barriers to hold migrating salmon back from the headwaters in the Upsalquitch, one of four main tributaries. Why? You guessed right; they would be pitch-forked out and taken home to eat by locals if they climbed into the most vulnerable part of the system too early. Nearer spawning, the barriers are lifted and the fish swim up. By then the ground is slippery from autumn downpours deterring vehicles from the water edge, daylight hours are shorter, and the fish are redder, softer and less palatable. Importantly, there are sufficient numbers to ensure that the pitch-fork brigade cannot obliterate the entire breeding.

In July of 2012 I was at a powwow of the Pabineau Indians on the Nepisiguit River in New Brunswick. Walking into the festivities on foot and sporting a battered trilby, I merged adequately as an acceptable visitor from Scotland with a mutual interest in salmon. Indeed, the powwow seemed to be a transatlantic version of Scotland's summer Highland Games, and I knew the form.

More to the point, I met and talked to those of the Indian band's dignitaries concerned with the salmon in their river. Overcoming a mental hex at the fact that all the men I met looked identical to Marlon Brando, himself part-Indian and active participant in 'red-power' protests in the 1970s about reserving salmon for the original inhabitants, I extracted a stimulating picture of the fabulous river passing by.

The once-mighty Nepisiguit, with its salmon weighing up to forty pounds, was experiencing a muscular revival. Open-pit lead mining using lime had destroyed the original bountiful fish-runs which had carried on until the late 1940s. A paper-mill at the mouth had treated the river as a waste pipe, and as a result the water became choked and de-oxygenated and filled with minerals injurious to salmon. During the 1970s and 80s no one fished there and the beautiful river flowed foul and empty.

However, the mining operation undertook to divert noxious tailings into a nearby river naturally devoid of fish. The mill became uncompetitive and closed. Salmon revival had been quick. For three years a midsummer counting operation had been performed by driving stakes into the river-bed, leading fish towards two Vs which were fitted in low water with fish traps. All the fish heading upstream were taken from the traps, handled, scaled (for information on the sea period, the river period and the quality of diet during both) and measured. A hatchery programme was started. Runs in 2009 numbering 300 had transmogrified by 2011 into a vigorously renascent run of over 1600 salmon and grilse.

Rod fishing on the first thirty miles of salmon water had resumed and there was even a local fishing guide. The guide, whose grandfather had been a fishing guide too, told me that in his childhood salmon had been a major part of diet for everyone on the river. Using chicken wire to make tunnel-traps, the family had never lacked the pink protein. Today's angling, though, in the aftermath of scarcity, is tightly controlled, and areas which acted as honey pots, for example beneath falls, are debarred from fishing.

One of the Brando lookalikes, ponytailed, with pairs of moose molars swinging from his moose-hide jacket and a coyote head sewn into the back, confirmed that in times past salmon as food lasted the whole year, the winter's cured fish supply expiring about the time fresh salmon swam up in June. Spring fish heading for the headwaters, however, were not taken, ensuring the early fish would breed a replacement stock.

The Indians said that spearing was still a favoured capture form, although for the time being salmon stocks are rebuilding in their river and none are being taken by the band. Lamping, a universal practice, was a favourite technique, because salmon under darkness are attracted to light. It is a peculiar thought that few if any means of taking fish have passed entirely from use.

In this community, too, adhered the same widely held belief as that on the north-west Pacific coast regarding the importance of returning waste salmon bones to the water. It seems the ritual significance of the fish is consistent between the native people on the west and east of Canada. Pacific salmon and Atlantics exert the same cultural grip.

The traditional use of salmon by Canadian Indians took a dividend from the migrating species but the manipulation of their habitat by modern Europeans damaged the capital.

The price for unreconstructed primitivism should have jolted those reading the Inspector's Report for England and Wales in 1869: only 9,000 square miles of the productive salmon habitat which measured four times that area contained any salmon at all. Three-quarters of their English and Welsh range was by then empty.

The Atlantic salmon in America had fared worse. By around 1900 America had become the world's leading productive output nation. Salmon, though, was not amongst its exports. Indeed, salmon on the east coast had already been all but exterminated. The shrinkage of salmon range is a story of human expansion and triumph over natural systems, marred by irrecoverable loss of fauna.

No Admission

America mutilated its population of Atlantic salmon more comprehensively than any other country. Furthermore, it conducted this pogrom over a short time. It takes a while to absorb the significance of the report in 1819 from a local clergyman that salmon had not been seen in the Connecticut River for twenty years. That winds back to 1799.

The Connecticut, threading from the Canadian border through the gentle, forested, undulating scenery of New England, with 300 miles unobstructed and available to salmon, was America's richest salmon river. Even the Norse a thousand years ago had commented on the number of salmon in New England and their unusual size. But the salmon-swollen Connecticut was fated to a brutally truncated lifespan.

In the 1780s the river's salmon fed half the population that lived bankside. So abundant was the fish that sellers of shad were obliged to include salmon in the package as a 'special offer' extra. Damming was so fast the salmon had no time to think. The first one appeared at Hollyoke, Massachusetts, in 1795. Just three years later another reared up at Montague, terminal for salmon as it blocked access completely. The Connecticut salmon genome was hung out to dry.

The market pronounced it all: by 1798 Connecticut salmon had quadrupled in price. From abundance to scarcity was a quick leap. But this state of affairs was all without reason: the precedent existed on New Hampshire's Salmon Falls River, or Piscataqua. Here in 1717 a one-thousand-ton catch (100,000–200,000 fish) was reported; by 1750 sawmill dams and over-fishing had knocked this back to exiguous numbers. New England's silver-lode – Benjamin Franklin described salmon as 'bits of silver pulled out of the water' – had disappeared in a few decades.

There is a socio-economic aspect to this otherwise bewildering disintegration. During the American revolutionary war the British controlled the seas off eastern America, blockading fish imports. Armies on the march were forced to eat river fish. Salmon from Lake Champlain in Vermont, and from Maine, fed hungry marauding armies. Following defeat, fleeing sympathisers of the British Crown poured into Canada. By 1783, when the treaty was signed, a population of a hundred people at the mouth of the hugely salmon-rich Saint John river had swollen to 14,000. One thing they knew how to do was fish. Rivers were sieved of their occupants by wandering soldiery. Displaced colonists, wise to the meaning of rivers, when picking farmland rights selected those which included fishing rights bordering the granted properties.

Salmon played a specific part in the 1783 treaty. The new American polity demanded rights and access to Newfoundland's fisheries as part of the settlement. It is said that in the early 1800s American fishing vessels filled every bay and inlet in Labrador. In the next war against Britain of 1812, salmon was again a critical issue. The Newfoundlanders under the British Crown wanted the newcomers forced out of the fishing grounds, whereas the Americans wanted salmon-access maintained and reinforced. The matter was so sensitive that the concluding 1814 treaty left it out, in effect leaving American access unchanged. Not for the first time, Atlantic salmon were linked to the maintenance of human settlement.

Salmon were directly involved in America's spirit of energetic expansion and development vigour. Cotton, though grown in the southern states, was spun in New England. Cotton was to be the Atlantic salmon's lethal bedfellow. Richard Arkwright's spinning jenny creation was smuggled across the Atlantic in 1769. The first American mill was built on Rhode Island in 1790, and by 1815 there were 165 New England mills diverting water from salmon rivers. By 1840 this had grown to 1200 mills and power looms, most of which were still located in New England's salmon territory. Mark Twain, capable memorably of articulating the flavour of pioneer America, sarcastically dubbed the prolonged economic boom, 'The Gilded Age'.

The once-fabulous Merrimack River going to sea in Massachusetts was one of the first to die. Major damming started in 1812, then in 1822 a mega-dam blocked access to eighty per cent of salmon range. Other dams arose, terminating migrations. In 1805 a fisherman could take thirty Merrimack salmon a day; by 1830 ten per day was an exceptional catch; in 1886 the yield for the whole river was three fish.

In all salmon histories there is the tragic moment, long past the turning point, when the capture of a salmon makes fishermen blink, because it has become so rare that they cannot identify it. That moment came on the Connecticut in 1872 when the identity of a wandering survivor confused witnesses.

It is easy to overlook the link between technological and human development in America in the period prior to the various states becoming united at the end of the nineteenth century, and the collapsing status of its east-coast salmon. Politics played its part. But by the late eighteenth century there was an explosion of human population and a rapid increase in the number of textile and silk factories, iron and steel foundries for making locomotives and steamboats, lime, potash, charcoal and tar kilns, distilleries, brickworks, glass and pottery factories. Labour was still scarce, forcing the development of power devices.

After the 1812 war with Britain, rivers and lakes were turned into canals to transport the new surge of finished products. In fact the early settlers, pushing into the Appalachian Mountains in Pennsylvania around 1720, had never put down roots anywhere except on riverbanks. Water was the only link between isolated touch points separated by vast distances. Salmon had new neighbours; today's tabloids might say, 'the neighbours from hell'. It was not until around 1840 that railroads took over from waterways as the principal conduit for goods, by which time some 3,300 miles of river had been canalised and improved. Not until the twentieth century was interest rekindled in improving the waterways both as flood control mechanisms and for better conservation of natural resources and cheaper transportation.

Maine was the principal river state on the east. Large, further north and comparatively undeveloped, it nonetheless had one dangerous crop: timber. Maine was a continuous forest.

Before the era of roads, logs were 'driven' in 'log drives' on the only conveyors – water courses. Horse teams dragged timber-laden barges and scows, shallow river-boats ripping through the shallows where salmon eggs were buried in the gravels. The driving was done in the rain season so that the maximum amount of timber could be floated at one time. The biggest log drives were reckoned to float a million tons of timber. The log-drive season, autumn, coincided with salmon breeding.

When free logs were driven in a mass they formed immense water-borne bundles capable of smashing most obstacles in their path. In the early days the logs were merely floated in twisting and turning jumbled masses, latterly they were tied and bundled. The damage they did to banks and to river-beds was awesome. Water courses were re-profiled. Rivers ran over what had been land and former river-beds grew scrub thicket. The timber loads scoured river bottoms, stripping out the weeds and plants which supported young fish, crustacea and aquatic insects. In places the beds deepened, meaning sunlight could not penetrate to aid growth; sand bars, sawdust bars and timber rubble created new islands. In other places river-beds were widened and shallowed, resulting in the water being stripped of oxygen in high summer, and therefore less able to support invertebrate and fish life. Channels were narrowed then burst open again with the next year's drive. No one spared a thought for the damage to the road made of water.

I spoke to an old man in Canada who as a boy was on some of the last log drives. He said that when they unbundled the logs for lorry transport the weight of the log rafts pushed the saturated logs at the bottom of the stack even deeper into the river-bed. They were called 'dead-heads'. Years later, when the timber bonanza was over and these logs suddenly acquired scarcity value, they were levered out by cranes and dried. It took a week to get the water out and they were despatched to the pulp-mill for papermaking. But he said the state of the river below, where the logs could be jammed five deep in a column, was a sticky, foetid mud hole. One time that same spot would have been a boulder-paved, clean river-bed, prickly with stream life, the building blocks for salmon survival. The unloading bays were turned into gloopy, oxygen-deficient backwaters.

The whole system of forest clearance in New England was inimical to rivers and river fisheries. The first colonists had stumbled into a landscape of vast trees. Their first impressions dazed pioneers wondering at a fairytale forest such as had long gone where they hailed from, in tired worked-over western Europe.

Pre-eminent amongst the east-coast trees was the white pine, sometimes soaring three hundred feet into the sky. These huge trees became the timber cabins and clapboard houses which were the definitive settler architecture of early New England. When the grand primeval firs were cut, sun reached the shady forest floor, the soil dried out and water ran off faster. The temperature and humidity difference inside and outside the tall forest was extreme. This change of land use quickened the water rises and falls in rivers, and fish-life had to adapt to a more volatile ecology.

When timberland was first attacked by two-handled cross-cut saws, a huge amount of debris was left on the forest floor. The settlers wanted lumber they could turn into boards for house-building, and rails for corals to keep animals in and their predators out. The forest-floor brash toasted in dry summers and became dangerously flammable. With fire, the soils desiccated further, whilst pouring carbon ash into rivers. There was a cycle of soil impoverishment and soil erosion. This led to siltation in the ultimate receptacles for all homeless, blown-about, dusty material – flowing rivers.

Forest fires had an almost unimaginable capacity for destruction. The Miramichi was known as the territory of the Great Fire which tore through the watershed in 1825. The meteoric rise in water temperature killed salmon eggs, juveniles and also adult spawners. Fish were broiled even in deep fish holes. It was two decades before even a modest recovery in the fish stocks was reported. Anglers, meantime, sought other rivers.

De-forestation happened faster on the American west coast. Timberland owners were taxed on the value of standing timber; when the land was logged, taxes fell, so it made economic sense to get the trees off the land as fast as possible. This encouraged hell-for-leather logging, driven by a tax climate hostile to the retention of standing timber. However, on the east coast the pressures on land were for alternative uses; tax was not an issue.

New England was converted from a rolling timbered landscape stretching for a thousand miles up the Appalachian Chain into homestead country divided into boxes for sheep, horses and cows. The principal difference between the new settlers and American natives was that the new arrivals brought livestock and draft animals whereas the Indian crop-growers had cultivated corn, squash, gourds, peanuts, potatoes, tobacco, beans and pumpkins. The old users had cultivated corners of the land, the new ones transformed the whole landscape.

Stone walls piled stone on stone, forests were hewn down, and America was transfigured. To remove the forest was a mark of progress, a precursor to the creation of farms, Nature under control. Farming was seen as a virtuous activity and the backbone of the new republic. The period 1600 to 1920 saw the advance of cropland and the steady reduction in forest land. It took three acres of cropland to support each person and cropland grew at the same rate as the human population until around

1850. Much of the timber was used as fuel and even as late as 1850 wood provided more than 90 per cent of the nation's energy. By 1920 wood for fuel had dropped to only ten per cent of energy supply. The rest was sawn timber for construction.

The scale of wood-milling was huge and of the 31,000 sawmills registered in 1840, most small-scale two- to five-person operations, the bulk were in New England. Salmon water turned the big wheels. Sawdust and mill residues wound up suffocating rivers, choking stream-beds. Smolts were sucked into waterwheel races and mashed. Throughout this time rivers were used as transportation conduits, not valuable commodities in their own right.

It was around 1970 that America's remnant Atlantic salmon population hit the wall. The cause was not identified. Atlantic salmon were declining across their range but nowhere quite so precipitously. Were they dying in the sea or in the stream waters, or both? No one knew. Calls to arms about saving American wildlife had always centred on birds and mammals – wild turkeys, grizzlies, pronghorns, whitetail deer but never salmon. The mammal populations were successfully rescued by pro-active federal-level policies.

Whilst the headline American debates turned on wolf reintroductions, the numbers of wintering salmon feeding off Greenland fell and fell further, with ICES quoting a figure of one-eighth of previous numbers. Any assessment must consider the possible reasons why.

Official explanations proffer no neat answers tied up with a ribbon. Partly the reason for this is that the practices which contributed to the final decimation of the North American salmon stock are recent, and many of the managers and policy-makers in this zero-sum game are still alive. No one is wildly keen to discuss this matter.

The conservation movement has always veered away from indignation about abuse of a resource if it has been used for sport, an activity it shrinks from. Supporting salmon might be seen as fundraising for anglers, enough to make conservation chiefs dreaming virginal slogans shudder in their sleep. The conservation movement's firepower never directed heavy artillery at abuses to salmon, a shameful omission.

One factor in salmon decimation was forest-spraying. In the 1960s forest industry attitudes to disease and parasites were one-dimensional. Chemical assault would deal with anything that interfered with output production. When the spruce budworm attacked American and Canadian spruce woods the reaction was a programme of spraying forests from the air. DDT, a chemical since known to persist in the environment and which is lethal to all it touches, was sprayed over vast areas of forest land to kill the beetles. Soon people noticed that DDT left in its wake a gory trail of decimated wildlife.

The best-recorded case was on the Miramichi in New Brunswick where government had assembled a time-series of comprehensive fish records starting in 1950. In the early 1950s DDT was sprayed on one million acres of the huge river's northern headwaters in order to save, in particular, the balsam poplars, the mainstay tree of the paper and pulp industries. The corpses of birds and fish began to appear in the sprayed watershed. It was reckoned that only one in six of the young salmon in the streams survived. The hardest hit was taken by second- and third-year parr which needed bigger insects like caddis flies, mayflies and stoneflies. Even a year after spraying, these insects were few and far between.

The Canadians, despite the apparent havoc caused by DDT spraying, resumed the programme whenever budworm populations revived, right into the 1960s. Two million acres of the great Restigouche and Tobique watersheds took a blast too. In a concession to the ghastly side-effects, the insecticide dose was cut from half a pound an acre to a quarter of a pound. A defoliant used in the 1960s called Agent Orange was sprayed along roadways to keep back bushes – that also killed young fish. Lethal sprays were deployed, too, to control insects on blueberry and other berry crops, plants which in the nature of their soil demand grow near rivers. They controlled insects all right, but too many of them.

The USA, despite growing concerns, continued unperturbed, using DDT at the higher rate of one pound an acre until an all-out ban came into force in 1972. In Maine, where budworm was also attacked with the dread insecticide, trout, minnows and sucker fish were found either dead or sightless, floating downstream, too weak to swim of their own volition.

Blindness in salmon has been traced to use of DDT. Sixty years after these spraying programmes there are still occasional blind salmon found in the rivers of eastern Canada – to whom anglers dangling fishing flies are a sad irrelevance. The most ominous aspect of this cavalier chemicals programme was high incidences of cancer in the years following amongst fishing guides in eastern Canada; sitting in the canoe while the fishing is slow, this subject is sometimes brought up, and with bitterness.

The Miramichi River has been thriving – relatively (although the 2012 run slumped unexpectedly) – so what happened? In her well-known 1962 anti-chemicals polemic, *Silent Spring*, Rachel

Carson describes the happenstance events which saved the Miramichi salmon population from being unalterably damaged.

1954 was the year in which Hurricane Edna swept the east coasts of New England and Canada. Torrential rains were followed by a major salmon run, as fish swarmed onto the east-coast rivers from their winter quarters off western Greenland and the Faroe Islands, the stocks deriving from the period before chemical impacts. The salmon also arrived in streams that had been swept clear by rains. Around the saturated landscape, small midges and blackflies were stirring in multitudes. Because the previous generation of juvenile salmon was mostly dead, the subsequent year's salmon eggs from this unusually strong influx, when they hatched out, found abundant food and fewer-than-normal competitors for it. The well-fed young fish grew fast and reached sea age earlier than usual.

Although runs of smolts had been severely curtailed by chemical poisoning, at least one generation of salmon reached saltwater to replenish stocks in that most forgiving river system. With parr reaching smolt stage and going seawards at varying times, Nature played a role in compensating for the chemical assault.

This needs a little extra explanation. Young salmon are fighting for the sustenance in the feeder-streams. They compete, often with each other, as the only fish capable of subsisting in typically harsh climates. When hatchery fry have been planted out in places that migratory fish cannot reach, an interesting fact has been noted. Luxuriating in a pristine habitat devoid of competitors, they thrive. Growing fast and strong, they have even been found in northern Scotland to reach smolt age after one year instead of the more normal two or three. In Arctic rivers they can remain in the stream, building strength for the marine expedition, for as long as seven years.

Put another way, the Atlantic salmon is sometimes compromised in its survival by being anadromous, sea-living and freshwater-breeding, and needing two different habitats at quite different latitudes for its survival. It makes demands on a wide swathe of Nature. Conversely, its complex trajectory to the breeding event means it has evolved to overcome killer-punch catastrophes. One or two seasons of deadly spraying were countered because the sea acted as a safe sanctuary for adults and post-smolts. They contained the promise of species revival. In the river there was just enough physical protection to ensure that entire age-classes were not totally eliminated. It is the elasticity of the reproduction cycle that makes the salmon such a doughty survivor.

Most notoriously, DDT killed off peregrine falcons, icons of the air, and other rare birds by rendering their eggs infertile. Squirrels, frogs and bees all curled up and died. But at a more mundane level, DDT first hit small insects, which died and drifted down rivers. In the freshwater zones occupied by young salmon, insects were the main source of sustenance, so when young salmon snapped up the contaminated flies, they themselves perished.

Another chemical blitz was launched by forest companies to rearrange the species composition of commercial timberland. Sprays were designed to eliminate one tree species and favour another by making space. At one time the processors wanted tall softwoods, so hardwood forest was killed off to promote a mix of fir and pine and spruce. In the context of today's philosophy of hallowed diversity, this is hardly believable. But it happened, and recently. The same occurred, too, in Scotland, a brainwave dreamed up in the 1950s by the State's Forestry Commission. Some other bizarrely primitive practices, like the bone-headed treatment of the steelhead fishery off British Columbia, side-lining it in favour of commercial sockeye catches, continue into the present.

None of this is a well-attested and well-recorded story; by the 1960s alternative chemicals were being experimented with. There remain patchy accounts from backwoods eyewitnesses and river folk, people who do not rush to give testimonies and make headlines. They chorus the same tale, and it is backed by what they saw, but there has been no official postmortem. The tale of woe was better reported for raptors and other avian species protected in law. Salmon at the time were long gone from the Connecticut, relatively numerous in the northern part of their range, and not a principal focus of protection policy in either Canada or America.

There is another aspect: salmon was not regarded highly as a food. Most was eaten canned, and this came from the Pacific west coast. The former chief of the US Forest Service, Jack Ward Thomas, recalls: 'Canned salmon was not considered a treat. When I was a boy salmon from a can was what we ate at the end of the month when the money ran out.' The profile of salmon as a resource was subfusc in the extreme. It only sharpened in the 1970s with the strengthening of environmental awareness, the Endangered Species Act of 1973, and when salmon survival was linked to native Americans whose livelihoods and cultures, voguish areas of interest, centred around its good health.

Development took a heavy toll. In 2006 an ICES report stated that spawning salmon in the USA comprised 0.2 per cent of all those homing to the coast of North America. Canadian rivers had all the others. Today two milestones have been reached at the same time. The Connecticut River programme to restore Atlantic salmon was abandoned in summer 2012 – bad news; second, one of the hydro-electricity dams which for years had prevented salmon running the Penobscot in Maine, was dismantled – good news. Prior to this only three per cent of the Penobscot's historic spawning habitat was accessible to breeding fish. Another dam is soon to be removed, and a fish-way built at a dam further upstream by 2014. Salmon and anadromous fish are, for once, calling the policy tune.

The Penobscot is a mighty river, big and strong. Its runs are estimated to have reached up to 100,000 salmon a year prior to damming, and its watershed covers a third of this sprawling state. Maine has others – the Kennebec, Androscoggin and the Saint Croix – which all once swarmed with salmon. But dams now outnumber the silver fish, a turnaround from when the Kennebec had an annual run estimated at 70,000. America's hopes for a re-birth of its Atlantic salmon population rest with these northern rivers, where wild salmon from the original genetic strain have survived.

Around 150 dams have been dismantled across the USA since 1999. Many had become obsolete because timber today is trucked rather than floated. Where power was extracted from water-driven wheels, there is fuel-burning. Many of these dams were not de-sedimented and dismantled in careful stages on behalf of salmon, but they were removed. With the first major dam to fall on the Penobscot, a milestone was reached. The arguments for opening up the passage of migratory fish on the Penobscot won the day even against the fashionable pressures for renewable carbon-free energy derived from hydro-power. There is a public excitement about salmon, and the ten other fish species which will benefit from a clear passage, as maybe once there was about getting massive power from water-driven wheels. The fish are free to breed. It is a stirring thought; it takes us a step nearer the pre-industrial stage-set. From now, all eyes will be on the results. Fishery biologists warn that the turnaround will take decades, just as extirpation did, but a corner has been turned.

It is perhaps the territory for psychologists – Western man likes to believe there are fish in the river. Recently a newspaper story reported on long-term prisoners in the USA resorting to art to clear, in their imaginations, the high walls that surrounded them. Many of these artworks depict wild country, wild rivers and their fish. When the rafters, canoeists and other river users pass a fisherman standing in the river they shout, 'Any fish biting?' If you shouted back, 'they are all gone', the river-trip would pall under a cold shadow.

The history of the American salmon is instructive because it represents the worst case of obliteration. Here was a virile, thrusting new country which only 250 years after its inception became the world's largest economy. It is in a way understandable that the rush for growth was headlong, that all was swept aside to get there. At that point, at the turn of the last century, President Theodore Roosevelt came along and did more to conserve and protect wild America than any individual in history had ever done to protect citizens' birthrights. He created millions of acres of national parks. Amends were made, on a grand scale. But Roosevelt was a gunpowder man and an active hunter; he championed mammals and land, not fish.

The squabble over salmon ended in tears, at any rate for the USA. In summer 2012 the prodigious effort made by individual states in conjunction with the US Fish and Wildlife Service to restore the silver fish to the Connecticut, started in 1967, was formally abandoned. Success had remained elusive and too much money had been spent. In 2010 alone $2 million was expended stocking six million small fry and 90,000 larger smolts. Returns failed.

Project managers blamed this failure on the disappearance of smolts in the marine. Others had different, less obtuse ideas. Simply, the Connecticut has five dams on the main stem; outgoing smolts in springtime need to negotiate these obstructions and avoid getting minced in the wheels, whilst migrating salmon trying to breed need to be able to swim on past them in summer and autumn to reach the headwaters.

On the Penobscot further north, the downstream mortality of smolts ranges from ten to twenty per cent at each dam. If twenty per cent are killed at each dam, of one hundred smolts only twenty-six are left after five dams have taken their toll. If fifteen per cent are killed, one hundred smolts shrink to fifty-two after five dams. It is a pretty heavy rate of destruction for a fish that is anyway clinging by a thread.

For those smolts that do survive the turbine wheels, or in high water survive being swept over the Connecticut's 30–60-foot vertical spillways, there is then the negotiation of the bypass channels. These fall woefully short of reaching efficiency targets. But smolts that beat the odds and survive these challenges then have an elongated journey time, needing to swim through chains of oxygen-deficient lakes. Hurdle has followed hurdle. And salmon which fail to meet deadlines die.

Dams accumulate populations of predators, including birds like cormorants which have learnt that stunned fish lie at the foot of spillways. It is no accident that dams are at times mobbed by wheeling birds; then you know the smolt run is on.

In the reservoirs themselves surface water heats up and bottom water chills down, both creating difficulties. The passage to sea proves an endurance trial, a far cry from swift journeys through bubbly clean water in natural rivers.

For the Connecticut smolt there is only wild money on survival to the ocean.

The Connecticut's five main dams do have fish-ways for migrating salmon going upstream. They are said to be functional. But for adult salmon the reservoir above the actual dam often swamps headwater feeder streams by backing up into them. Thus spawning areas have shrunk. In place of life-giving gravels, sterile mud banks stretch into the headwaters. Reservoirs rise and fall as power is needed at the outflow. They are managed for human demand. Fish breeding areas are either submerged or exposed, maybe because extra kilowatts are needed on a public holiday, or demand is slack and it isn't a public holiday, rather than because it has rained in the hills. Dams may have been the Connecticut River salmon's nemesis.

They were different sorts of dams to those domestic-scale structures that kick-started America's growth to economic world dominance. These were power dams for electricity. They worked night and day, not only in daytime work hours, and they were built after the mid-1940s. They belonged to the big dam era, heralded by the Hoover Dam which opened in 1946. These were amongst the biggest structures humanity had ever erected. To many, they defined progress, the conquest of Nature. They have left many of the world's big rivers as what was called by the writer Patrick McCully, 'little more than staircases of reservoirs'. And they bury runs of salmon.

Other commentators on the abortive re-introduction point to a biological fact that the stocks used on the Connecticut came from very different ecosystems. The Connecticut runs in the deep south of salmon range. Tragically, the closest donor stocks could only be found much further north, mainly in the Penobscot in Maine, 300 miles distant. Other rivers had expired. Stock compatibility matters.

A different solution existed, though, while the original strains still survived, and that was to freeze fertilised female salmon eggs. Animal cells can be kept for long periods if the preservation process is done correctly. Managers on the Connecticut could have kept the original stock alive by freezing the fertilised eggs in a process using liquid nitrogen called cryo-preservation. The eggs exist in a state of frozen animation at a temperature nearly 200 degrees centigrade below. This costs money, but has successfully been done with fish eggs since around 1957, and is happening today with the resuscitation of Norwegian rivers annihilated by the parasite *Gyrodactylus salaris.* When the river was cleaned up these eggs could have been hatched and used for the reintroduction. Managers may even have had to wait until all the dams were dismantled, but they would have had one ace in the pack. The genetic strain which had evolved over thousands of years, which recognised the water chemistry smells and tastes (charmingly called by some biologists, 'the breadcrumb trail'), and which is vital for relocating the nurseries, would have been there, alive, intact, bent on replication. The key cards backed survival.

This never took place. Hatchery projects using alien strains were the favoured option. Sealing the fate of the project in spring 2012, only 50 spawners reappeared, a token number considered inadequate to build a self-sustaining population.

Dr Fred Whoriskey, writing for the American Fisheries Society, produces a startling statistic. He says that whilst 19 per cent of the potential Atlantic salmon area is in the USA, the returns of spawners to that part of the North American range is now under one per cent. From the domain beneath the fluttering flag of the stars and stripes, the east-coast salmon has almost disappeared. Almost no one in the eastern USA will have ever seen a wild one in their homeland. As Hoagy B. Carmichael, son of the music legend, has said in a book about Quebec's Cascapedia River: 'Were the USA to have implemented a series of conservation policies in the 1820s, many of the salmon rivers along the eastern seaboard might still be teaming with silver-sided fish.' It was not to be.

The history of Canada, as well as the geography, partly explains the discrepancy. Canada is a vast land, much of it wild and untameable, mostly unsuitable for development and the bulk of it terrifyingly cold in winter. Its waters in the main have not been turned to industrial power, Nova Scotia and the Gaspe Peninsular's Saint John River being exceptions; a lot of the back-country has been left alone, except by the logging industry. In the worlds' emptiest big country most citizens are urban and live within ten miles of the American border. The back-country starts, for many Canadians, at the back door. Pollution and over-fishing may have driven huge populations of landlocked salmon out of the tributaries of Lake Ontario (half-Canadian and half-American) by 1800, but today nearly all North American salmon swim up Canadian, not American, waters.

But Canada was not making the emergent world unfold. Its big industries were resource extraction, like forest products, rather than cutting-edge technology. The United States of America was, and is, at the forefront of history, not on the periphery. History explains the attitude to development and to progress which clarifies the spoliation of rivers on this drastic scale two to three hundred years ago. In the period which saw rivers dammed for power, filled with the detritus of logging suffocating the productive life in streams, and latterly providing turbine-driven power for industrial progress in the world's fastest-growing economy, America was on a set course to stand pre-eminent in the world which no sensitivities about stream ecology were going to brook.

Emerging shaky but victorious from the War of Independence in 1776, America needed to build and build fast. Rivers were put to the task of providing power. Salmon up to this time were found as far south as New York on the Hudson up to Arctic Canada's Ungava Bay, and even to Hudson's Bay facing the Arctic. From latitude 40 degrees northwards there were salmon, it is said, in all of the 2,615 watersheds that drained eastwards into the North Atlantic.

What is known of the fish in these runs on so many rivers, and what can it tell us? What sort of salmon were indigenous to American rivers?

Large runs of grilse which feature in Canadian rivers were absent from American ones. A 1965 study reckoned grilse amounted to only two to three per cent of salmon running into the state of Maine. That has a possible significance; the American stock lacked that safety mechanism of a component which returned from the sea only a year later. A quick reproduction turnaround was unavailable to most American salmon populations. America's salmon inheritance was that little bit less flexible than salmon stocks elsewhere.

There is another, perhaps related, peculiarity: eleven per cent of the fish were thought to be repeat spawners, a higher figure than elsewhere. It may be a factor that the seas between western Greenland and the eastern American coast have less shipping and fewer fishing boats in them than churn through the northern North Sea. For salmon passage, they are 'cleaner'.

In the case of the Miramichi in New Brunswick, probably home to the world's largest Atlantic salmon migration, up to a third of the salmon run reproduce more than once. Salmon coming home again three or four times are not uncommon, and scale-reading has even shown some fish making the home-run seven times. So this Canadian river could still replenish itself if several seasons, even several consecutive seasons, were damaged. There is always another run waiting to come in from the sea. In the attack on their migration routes and spawning stocks and outgoing smolt runs, North American salmon have demonstrated phenomenal resilience.

The reports that exist about the utilisation of salmon by the Indians on the Atlantic coast roughly shadow the more detailed knowledge about the salmon culture of the Pacific Northwest. Weirs, spears, hook-and-line capture, scoop-dipping with nets at waterfalls, all these practices were as common on the east with Atlantics as they were on the west with Pacifics. Why not? They are only ways of transferring fish from water to land. The military surveyor Sir James Alexander, who arrived in New Brunswick in 1844, described, in addition to the usual armoury, the use of a spear the Indians called a naygog. It was like a sort of scissor-motion wooden claw, in which slippery fish were grasped. One time he found two men with 37 naygog-captured fresh salmon, the party replete with barrels and salt for laying up the winter food supply.

In the east-coast rivers there were more other fish than salmon. Sturgeon, shad, lampreys, blueback herrings, alewives and eels were co-inhabitants of rivers, moving with salmon from the sea to freshwater to breed. One plus for the abandoned Connecticut programme is that alewives now run the river again.

Offshore in a richly varied fishery were the immense shoals of the algae-eating small fish, menhaden, also know as 'bunkers' or 'pogies'. There was no equivalent massive fish biomass on the west. Lipid-rich pogies were too oily for human consumption but were vital as fodder for other fish. They formed the keystone diet for most east-coast fish. Indians directed European settlers to the oil-rich possibilities of pogies and by the late nineteenth century there was a fleet of three hundred vessels off the Maine coast around June chasing down this easily netted fish. The catches were used as, amongst other things, fertiliser – a fate later meted out to salmon. Principally, though, the densely packed shoals were reduced for fish oil. The multitudes of pogies may have taken pressure off river salmon for a brief period.

The east-coast colonists at a pinch preferred sturgeon to salmon. These huge and sluggish Stone Age bottom feeders were caught with impunity, a single fisherman being able to land a lot, quickly. Sturgeon populations across the world are endangered everywhere; they were sitting ducks, and they vanished. Serious onslaught of salmon by direct capture started about the end of the seventeenth century, when they were salted and casked. But still salmon were not highly regarded, their price was low, their public image unimportant.

The change occurred around the mid-eighteenth century and shortly after American independence it was noted that salmon in Connecticut, along with shad and bass, contributed half the income of the province. Rivers were filling up with nets and the salmon were being sieved out. Connecticut netting was intensive: 3,700 salmon were once landed from a single haul. Today that is equivalent to the total spawning population for a mid-ranking British river. In today's America it would be a visionary dream.

Drift-netting for salmon within rivers accelerated the decline. In Maine, with the mighty Penobscot River, regulations were introduced. In the aftermath of the 1812 war, despite widespread food shortages, nets were prohibited from stretching over a third of the river's width. Drift-netting was eventually banned within 500 yards of a dam or fish-passage.

Salmon restoration in American rivers was attempted at the end of the nineteenth century. The Merrimack, the Penobscot and the Connecticut were stocked from hatcheries. But there was no focused policy. Depradations continued. Rivers were not safe for salmon. The only season's salmon that survived to spawn in numbers was when high flows physically swept the pollution and the maze of nets into the sea.

On the Penosbcot by the early twentieth century a salmon sighting became a newspaper report.

The 1960s Connecticut restoration effort coincided with a changed post-war political world, western Europe split in half by the Cold War, and a new salmon predator, a nation without any living salmon rivers of its own operating in a faraway place near the Arctic Ocean.

This was Denmark, drift-netting salmon off the freezing seas of its semi-autonomous state, Greenland. For the west coast of Greenland was where a massive swirling smorgasbord of krill, sand eels, capelin, squid and amphipods mingled, driven by oceanic circulation patterns which moved warmer water northwards from the Gulf of Mexico. Greenland had discovered this fish bonanza a long while back; records date from the early 1600s. Up to modern times, Greenlanders had not traded the wintering salmon but ate them themselves. But as market demand grew, prices rose. Fishing just offshore in their small boats from mid-August to November, starting in the 1960s, Greenlanders cranked up this lucrative fishery using fixed nets when close to shore and monofilament drift-nets invisible to the salmon further out. The drift-nets were up to two miles long. To the consternation of the natal states of these fish, the harvest climbed in a few years to a 1971 catch of 1800 tons. Although these winter salmon were rather oily and substandard as food, markets for them were rapidly established.

Now the salmon world knew where the fish disappeared to when they went downriver as silvery kelts, adding a key piece in the jigsaw of salmon understanding. A corner of the salmon map had been nailed down. With that knowledge, another chapter of salmon defence opened.

Back in Canada a different story had been unfolding. Unlike in America during the early 1800s, landings of salmon had been climbing. Canada's east coast was a silver-mine of salmon. The Bay of Chaleurs is the outfall for, amongst others, the mighty Restigouche River, a salmon heaven of clear, steady-flowing untarnished salmon water without any impassable waterfalls, 200 miles long with four tributaries of sixty miles in length. Anglers go glassy-eyed saying its name. A historian of the day says that 10,000 barrels of salmon were removed from the river in the season of 1813. With each barrel holding up to 500 pounds of salmon this equated to five million pounds of fresh fish. One netsman in the Bay of Chaleurs, John Adams, was estimated to have removed 150,000 individual salmon using a single net in a later period, the season of 1874. His net was a mere 810 yards long. There were just over a dozen fellow licence holders; possibly the catch in that year was somewhere not far from a million salmon. That conjures up a picture of Atlantic salmon nearly as numerous as mackerel today.

One lesson of history is that salmon can never stand in the way of perceived progress. Nor did they in Canada. Echoing the earlier phase in America, as the century proceeded more sawmills diverted water. By about 1850 in parts of British North America, as it was then called, three out of four workers were employed in lumbering. Huge expanses of eastern Canada were mantled in softwood trees at a time when timber was used for construction of all sorts, by countries of all sorts. Fishing dropped down legislators' agendas. Timber trading was progressive. The only salmon laws passed were to discourage over-fishing; habitat issues were ignored. Poignantly, this is reflected in the cadavers of salmon themselves. After 1830 a barrel of salmon from the Restigouche River required twenty to fill it, where ten had done the job earlier. The great harvests of the late nineteenth century were of smaller fish. In an unwinding of species survival, smaller salmon were then fit to dig only shallow redds, which in turn were more susceptible to being flooded out in spring avalanches and snow melts, and washed to sea with the mill waste.

Legal protection was a charade. Reports calling for protection and laws were eventually passed, but not enforced. Of the eight hundred mill dams in New Brunswick in 1851 not a single one had a functioning fish passage. Illegal netting was universal. Spawning salmon were seized as they were squirting out eggs and milt. Law officers joined in the frenzied depredations themselves; in any case, they often remained unversed in the law they were supposed to enforce. Their territories of jurisdiction were vast. Courts passed joke sentences on offenders. One observer remarked, 'The spirit of wanton extermination is rife', going on to suggest it seemed as if the person who killed the last salmon would be loudly applauded. The myth of endless technological progress must have been intoxicating indeed.

Gradually supplies from the salmon-exporting regions – New Brunswick and Nova Scotia and Newfoundland – dried up. Only faraway Labrador maintained a commercial salmon fishery. Sportsmen complained about the shortages of salmon in Lower Canada. Salmon became scarcer and scarcer. And prices went on rising sharply. Each user, meantime, blamed the rest for salmon depletion.

In a map dated 1900 the Bay of Chaleurs is closely described with the names of all farming smallholders on both the Quebec bank to the north and the New Brunswick bank to the south, whose farmland ran down to the estuary. Farmers had a right to net in the tideway. As they bought each other out and consolidated these rights, netting became a commercial operation on a new scale. The resulting damage forced a netting ban in 1971. A brief netting resuscitation in 1983 concluded in a final government buy-out of these nets in 1993.

The right to net salmon in the saltwater as they inched towards natal rivers hugging the coastline is consistent with the old land-titles further inland along the river edge. Here riparian farmers were permitted to take a few salmon for sustenance. Land-title was designed to provide those hardy folk who opted for residency in the frozen north with as much food from the wild as would ease their struggle to survive. Unlike in the Europe that settlers had left behind, wild game was not the property of large landowners but rather the State's to dispose of as it saw fit. I have spoken to the children of those old-time smallholders in the northern forests who recall being allowed to take salmon, along with a moose, a whitetail deer, maybe even a bear. Fred Whoriskey calls those salmon-taking rights, 'marketing attractions for getting colonists to move to the New World'.

Those few still alive who remember their youth in these back-country farms in the Canadian forest stress that senior family members disallowed profane over-use of the resources. People took what they needed, in the case of salmon usually grilse or later fish. There was no wider market or trading system as there was no transport. The settlers treated the salmon resource by and large much as the indigenous Indians had done, for personal sustenance and with restraint.

Development and progress changed matters. When dams were constructed to supply either water or power, the provision of fish-passes appears to have been erratic. Such passes as were built often fell into disrepair. A salmon-ladder filled with branches or river debris might as well not have existed.

The story of eastern North American Atlantic salmon has one feature that is absent from salmon management and conservation elsewhere: this is the issue of native rights or fishing by Indians. A primary resource, edible, catchable and valuable, salmon finds itself in the headlights of national politics. Its fate is a burning issue: no fish is more political.

When Europeans first settled in North America they signed treatises with the native Americans who were living there. The Treaty of Boston, signed with 16 Indian chiefs in 1726, bequeathed rights to the indigenous people to fish and hunt freely, whilst the new ownership title was accorded to the sovereign power. This allowed property sales to the settlers. The persisting question was, and is, where one right ends and another begins. Settler land came with normal occupational rights too, including the right to game. Whose right was to have precedence?

I recall the first time this became a real issue for me, when I ventured into snow-cloaked northern British Columbia thirty years ago to fish a steelhead river in May. It was called the Nakina, and the fishing camp was accessed by helicopter and perched on the edge of a forested hillside. The situation was a dream of isolationist beauty, the snow-fed sparkling river winding below, steelhead fresh in from the sea, grizzlies roaming the backwoods, a group of exultant buddies oxygenated with heady mountain air and no one else within a fifty-mile range until we encountered Brian the Indian, spinning to his heart's content off a rock in the most scenic pool of all. Brian subsisted on the top of a river-cliff in a mean hut surrounded by the bones of animals he had eaten. We surmised the bones were left there to lure in other animals – meat attracting more meat.

The guides fulminated against the rights being exercised by Brian to do what he wanted, wherever he wanted, whatever we wanted. He could step in front of us on any pool in which we were fishing and start then and there trawling through the delicious fly-water for steelhead. The corpses of any he caught, if he desired, then left to rot on the sunny banks. And Brian did just that, luxuriating in a treaty nearly three hundred years old which pre-dated shortages of steelhead, and which pre-dated the concept of conservation and limited resources under pressure from the unlimited desire to exploit them. Many dark expressions were aired those evenings in the remote fastness of our cabin-camp.

As recently as 1995 a case about hunting and fishing title was brought by the 'Crown' in New Brunswick, a province laying good claim to being the heartland of Atlantic salmon in the New World. Over time there have been innumerable cases testing the matter of who really owns these rights to the salmon. This one ended little differently from its predecessors. The judge said that the Indian couple who had sauntered down to the Little Main Restigouche River and twiddled their spinning tackle through it were acting within the law. The fact that such fishing methods were illegal under provincial law, and that rod anglers were fishing there too, was immaterial; the natives had a prior right to fish and hunt where they chose, however they chose and whenever they chose. No restrictions.

Adherence to this right by native Indians has over time swung between slackening and tightening. They are no longer the drifting population that signed the treaty nearly three centuries ago. The government in Canada looks after its native people, or 'First Nation', and they lack neither for housing, state benefits, schooling nor health care. Immune from paying a variety of taxes, the First Nation Indians do not need income from salmon to help them survive. However, in recent pronouncements on their political priorities for the future, Indian leaders have stated that making more of the salmon resource is a main policy aim.

Partly on this account the market value of salmon fishing rights in eastern Canada are worth less than they are in a place like Scotland, where fishing ownership as a heritable title protected in law goes along with the unencumbered right to manage the species, and exclusive use of the fishing water. In Canada the government is the owner, seeking an acceptable way of managing a high-profile public resource. When the private clubs of affluent business people were sold leases a century ago, administrators saw the value of having muscular expenditure developing the backwoods, building commodious fishing-camps, river craft and making roads, hoisting in all the appurtenances for making a comfortable life in the bush, boosting employment, and at the same time protecting a vulnerable resource.

Because the fishing experience is so seductive on the superb slow-flowing rivers of New Brunswick and Quebec, the families that own or lease the best fishing-camps are some of the most affluent in the USA and Canada itself. The famed Restigouche is one of the world's greatest salmon waters, a 200-mile meandering watercourse running at often perfect fly-fishing velocity. Its biggest fish are very large and the river is astoundingly beautiful.

Focus on the salmon as a resplendent sporting resource was then so intense that kingfishers were hunted down and shot because they ate salmon parr. Mergansers were salmon-eating voluptuaries too: they could consume three times their own weight of parr in a day. The bounty on the next-door Cascapedia in 1934 was 25 cents each for either bird. It must have been a keen enough incentive for wing-shooters, for seven hundred a year were shot on this relatively short river.

Unsurprisingly the concentration of ownership in few hands on such a place as the Restigouche has been contentious. To deflect criticism that it had become the private preserve of rich

Americans, the largest of the assorted salmon fishing clubs ruled that at least half the members must be Canadians. This was not enough to curb the rumbling unrest, especially as a prominent family in club membership was that of the timber company which river guides believed had been responsible for despoiling the river catchment by injudicious clear-cuts.

Lumbering went through an evolution which was critical for salmon. Horse-logging, dragging loaded wagons from the snowy woods, with trees laboriously cut using the old cross-cut hand saws, was one thing; the forest floor afterwards was disturbed but not scarred. Trees were selectively felled, not cleared over an entire landscape. River well-being did not notice horse-logging. Cross-cut saws were usurped by two-stroke engines in the late 1920s, and when the trees in the woods were turned into timber-fibre for papermaking and chainsaws replaced cross-cuts, everything changed. Now any tree would do, which meant every tree would do. Machinery thundered into the dreamy sylvan scene and the extraction technology rapidly got bigger and bigger. Enormous bulldozers shoved timber stacks into the water to kick-start giant log-drives. River-edge flats were levelled to accommodate tottering timber stacks of hundreds of thousands of tons of lumber. If log piles would not budge, dynamite blasted them into juddering motion. The result affected entire landscapes, their streams, rivers, swamps and springs. This brutalist extraction caused traumatic change to the nursery and breeding homes for salmon.

Ground compacted by jumbo machinery lost its capacity to absorb water. Heavy rain hitting compacted soils resulted in surface sediments being swept towards the water edge. This ended up in spawning gravels, choking them. On the Restigouche the spawning beds happen to be composed of very small stones. The mosses beneath the original forest cover had held out ground-cracking frosts, but now as the tree mantle was sliced down temperatures on the unprotected ground dropped, frosts bored downwards, and dirty puddles replaced absorbent moss quilts. Wind speeds through clear-cut former timberland were two and half times swifter than what had wafted through standing timber. Trees had broken up the air-flow. Less cover meant more blown snowdrifts; in springtime this resulted in bigger floods of ice and melting snow pack. 'Ice-runs', as they are called, were earlier in the season, heavier, and did more damage at the wrong time of year for salmon.

Flooding has changed the Restigouche. The tube-like deep pools affording shelter and shade for big salmon widened into shallower ovals. Along with other rivers in logged-out areas the Restigouche both spread sideways and lost depth, and then it overheated. Sometimes today the water temperature reaches 80 degrees in midsummer. Salmon cannot tolerate heated water. Indeed, they can die in it.

When anglers were obliged by rules responding to shrinking runs of fish to practise catch and release, and did so in warm water, the oxygen-deprived corpses of the released salmon were sometimes located afterwards by guides from their smell. The river zone began to stink of rotting salmon. This became worse as the dry periods of low water levels extended and the water crept further down the gravel-bars. Managers blamed global climate change: locals said it was caused by bad land use and irresponsible tree-cutting across the landscape. Catch and release was inappropriate in hot weather. The resource was not understood and it was not being respected. And the resource was heritage.

Local feelings stirred. For a concatenation of reasons, along the great rivers of this salmon-bountiful part of the world, political pressure rose to wrest ownership and management from timber companies and their friends in government. Today, the angling experience for the Restigouche visitor involves a growing awareness that beneath the well-oiled surface of the fishing-camps, and the manicured traditions of hospitality looking after the anglers, lie more extreme emotions and opinions. Big fish draw big attention and country people who see them find them intruding upon their sleep.

Part of the reason for the eyeing-up of salmon may be the make-up of these New Brunswickers. Their roots often are as fugitives. Some descend from the losing confederates of the Deep South in the American Civil War, and others are the French-speaking Acadians forced from their original maritime landholdings by the British seizing control of Canada in the mid-nineteenth century. They are restive folk who have been dispossessed once too often.

The other vexatious issue which recurs as soon as rod angling starts to struggle is the one of native fishing rights. It is easy to see why.

In summer of 2012 I was in a camp on the Restigouche. Fishing was, as they say, 'slow'. The seven rods picked up one or two salmon or grilse in each of the two daily sessions, but as could be told by drifting over the pools in the old-style, 26-foot cedar fishing canoes, many of the lies remained empty. If you had drawn the lot for that pool, for that four-hour fishing session, you were consigned to cast repeatedly over empty water. For an angler it is one thing to fish over individual fish that are sulky and disinclined, it is quite another to fish over beautiful salmon pools devoid of salmon. Anglers want fish, as well as to fish. In your mind as you ply that sumptuous water with a small fly is the comment from an early aficionado, Dean Sage, who said that you could hear a Restigouche salmon jump a quarter of a mile away. But that thundering splash failed to punctuate the silence.

What was happening? The 2011 run had been tremendous; surely it was not a complete one-off? The pools are some of the famous ones in this almost hallucinogenically beautiful river.

The answer takes us to Tide Head in the Bay of Chaleurs estuary where the fish destined for the Restigouche, the Grand Cascapedia, the Matapedia and several other fabled rivers assemble before venturing onwards to the freshwater. In the estuary the native band called the Listuguj freely net for salmon. I had a look over the operation, taking place in late July, later than the netting normally continued.

The Bay at Cross Point is around 400 metres across with a sweep of sea to the east. Floats indicated nets in a variety of places. At one moment I saw four boats checking nets in different places. I was there at the right time, after high tide, when salmon would be snared by the gills behind their pectoral fins as they tried to get closer to their natal streams. There were plastic barrels containing nets on the quay. This particular quay was in disrepair, but further along there was a smarter quay from which the majority of the blunt-sterned boats motored out.

A set of principles had been loosely agreed with government, including the one that any bigger salmon would be put back to improve salmon numbers for the future. However, the fishing-camp manager who was with me doubted that this actually happened. He suspected that the Listuguj Indians made serious money from the sale of salmon, using the contacts they had established whilst working on steel fabrication jobs in the cities to arrange markets with upper-end restaurants. Other people, who mixed with the local band at sport events and camp-fire evenings, said salmon were sold, which is against the law, and they had seen it happening.

The camp manager said that whenever things got difficult and the local police tried to enforce agreements made to conserve the salmon the netters became militant, blocked roads and railways and waited until the authorities backed off – which they invariably did. Not long ago an Ontario policeman had been shot dead trying to enforce agreements about sustainable salmon capture. The fishery manager's complaint was that whereas catching and releasing bigger salmon was scrupulously followed in the fishing camps, the entire policy looked absurd in light of the indiscriminate netting of the Listuguj folk. It all seemed maddeningly unfair.

The logic that netting dents rod catches is underlined by the fact that in the years when nets were suspended, angler catches in rivers like the Restigouche and the Cascapedia have soared.

Canada has a problem which looks insoluble. One aspect is that recognition of the problem is partisan. If you read the *Toronto Globe and Mail* there is no mention of the point of view commonplace wherever the open-season hunting and fishing rights are actually utilised. If policy-makers get the opportunity to see the camp scene at first hand, perspectives can change. It happened in 1979 with a metropolitan government minister who had never thought much about angling and the resource dilemma. Following a three-day visit to the Grand Cascapedia fishing clubs, and having landed a couple of salmon, he was converted. He stated: 'One must recognise that in certain parts of Quebec a property on a salmon river is as valuable as a small industry.'

Canada remains a schizophrenic country, where urban and country people have widely divergent perspectives on the matter of native rights. Resource allocation generally does not touch affluent urbanites. And Canadian public character projects a form of untroubled nonchalance, connected to the knowledge that its nation sits on one of the biggest national territories on Earth, girt with the world's longest coastline and packed with natural resources, a terrain mostly unspoiled and thinly populated. Critically, though, for the time being, federal conservation laws concerning rare species rank below native Indian property concessions.

I referred already to the powwow I attended on New Brunswick's Nepisiguit River in summer 2012 and what I learnt about river restoration by the local Indian band. I learnt too the First Nation viewpoint on salmon rights.

I had approached a campfire where a grey-haired stocky man sitting on a log to the side did not look up as conversation unfolded. He had an air of distinction, which is why I noticed him. Later on, walking around the dance display, we talked.

It transpired that he had been the signatory, as the First Nation representative, to a critical treaty signed for the Cascapedia River in 1982. His tack was this: the Indians had always used salmon. They never abused the resource, allowed free passage to springers and took late-season fish – by spear, net and trap – from places which would not interfere with the principal reproduction. Salmon was the basic traditional life support of the bands. 'If you live on something, you look after it. Life supports life', he averred. He objected to modern conservationists talking about recreating salmon runs; our people never damaged them, he said, and now we are closely involved in their recovery.

He became philosophical: 'We have an indisputable ownership title, but we all live here together. We always knew the Europeans were never going to leave. But you have to let go at some point. In the twenty-first century we are on new ground. Our kids are at university. Still ... the resource needs looking after.' He was a wise and amusing man; I could see speaking the skilled negotiator. I asked him, lastly, whether agreements struck on some rivers to employ local Indians as fishing guides, partnership ventures, were good. He said they worked adequately, reconnecting his people with their sacred fish.

I found out more about him half a year later. Called Bernard Jerome, he had been the chief of the Maria band during the 1982 breakthrough deal on the Cascapedia. He proposed that his people firstly would limit the controversial netting; secondly, half of all the fishing guides would come from Indian reservations; and third that some angling water would be made available for Natives, but within agreed conservation limits. Salmon would not be sold outside the reserve, to eradicate a commercial motive for violating the agreement. Introducing a more progressive note into the debate, Chief Jerome said: 'What I am trying to obtain for my people is work, not welfare.'

The fact that it has been settler Canadian industry which has damaged rivers – in the case of the one he and I had been standing on, it was tailings from a mine – strengthens the First Nations' case. On the other hand, the better economic case for anglers bringing money and employment into fishing-camps where nothing else would do the same, with no such remunerative alternative use for the rivers, with no damage to the fish-runs, in a modern context is hard to combat. At some point Canada will have to mature to the point that this matter is addressed with finality. This is given extra urgency by the perplexingly depleted North American salmon runs of 2012, estimated at only some 140,000 fish, a drop of a third on the average going back five years. It is indigestible that rare fish can be netted for pocket money by one sector of society whilst the other is ferociously conserving the species at a high cost. Seen from aloft, the 'policy' does not earn the name and is at best obscurantist. Somehow everyone has to move on. Perhaps the Cascapedia model will be the forerunner.

The Old World Atlantic salmon has a different history. The major casualty on the eastern side of the Atlantic salmon range has been mainland Europe. Large-scale logging has not been the issue it was in the west, and native Indian bands and their rights do not feature.

However, 'aboriginal' salmon capture issues do exist in northern Scandinavia with the Saami people and their reliance on salmon as food in a climate where food is scarce. The circumstances in many ways resemble those of the First Nation salmon users in Canada. Norwegian and other governments in the Finnmark (this is the name given to northern Scandinavia, including the Kola Peninsular) are attempting to limit and regulate this catch, which has become openly commercial. What is notable is the level of effort, over a long time, by residents to take their share of the silver bounty.

The Alta River in Norway has the largest salmon in any water frequented by rod fishermen and the history of the struggle for its bounties resonates. To do business with these fish, visiting anglers compete with each other to pay top dollar.

The Alta carves a fast and majestic path through the granite shield of the Finnmark. The area derives from the time before the various Scandinavian monarchies and the Russian Czar had partitioned it, and taken as a whole this part of the Atlantic salmon range can be considered the eastern heartland, with the biggest fish, in rivers devoid of much else but salmon.

Alta salmon grow phenomenally fast, some grilse after only one winter in the sea reaching twenty pounds, whereas in conventional rivers they struggle to attain half that weight. Access to the open sea and the protein-laden wintering larder is relatively unobstructed, an area largely controlled by the Russian navy. In olden times it was inhabited only by the Saami, wandering reindeer herders who moved to the lush Arctic pasture in summer and drove their herds southwards for the winter.

The Alta bisects this territory, crashing through ravines cleaving the rock range, smoothing out into great deltas, sweeping on magisterially to the sea. Cliffs rise above the turbulent waters bathed in the glaring bright light peculiar to the Arctic, whilst wolves and moose thread through the scrubby forest. A rich, untrammelled wilderness for hunters and shooters, the river is the focal point for those living along it, and has long been so.

The fight for the fish never ceased. Since the sixteenth century, Russia, Norway, Sweden and Denmark (Finland at this time belonged to Sweden) have contested the territory and the right to tax those catching its fish. Before that, in the long ago, the salmon fishings were in some sense royal, possibly a vestigial right of the chieftains who ruled the Finnmark in the Viking period. The Alta has had the magnetism of a goldmine, with the difference that the resource replenished itself.

The early 'royal privileges' on the river reflected a situation which was unusually fluid because in the Finnmark there had never been conventional land titles. Thus it was that Swedish, Russian and Danish-Norwegian bailiffs found themselves facing each other in this faraway and dream-laden place, vying to collect tax from the itinerant Saami. It is an unusual history and everything about the place is singular to itself. The great fish swam past, glued to gene-determined pathways, oblivious to the squabbles of the skirmishing stakeholders.

Before the late seventeenth century cross-river weirs were constructed to maximise the catches. Salmon were barrelled up, salted down (two times as much salt being needed as weight of salmon), and shipped to Holland. The Dutch entered the scene as the next wannabe stakeholders by providing capital for salmon removal. The first late-seventeenth-century trading post amounted to about 20 houses. It is extraordinary, perhaps, that even then fishing leases were contingent on the construction of cross-river weirs to support the capital value of the fishery. Partaking in the fishery obliged lessees to exploit it to the full. Custom-built Danish ships conveyed catches to market.

We know that salmon freighters could accommodate 720 barrels and that each barrel contained 24 large and 24 small salmon. So a fully laden ship would sail with around 34,500 salmon on board. This cargo was being netted from the Alta, only 28 miles long before impassable falls, and its sister river the longer and wider Tana. It is still an enormous harvest. The Saami who worked this operation took one other Arctic bounty to the markets: eiderdown.

The economic significance of the salmon is contained in the calculation that a harvest of just twenty-four fish was worth twice an individual's personal tax for the year. Riches indeed!

Free trade finally demolished the royal rights to salmon in 1724. For the following century early-season salmon were taken on the river edges in scoop nets. Then they were captured using mid-river weirs leading to bag nets, later in the season with beach seines swept through smooth-bottomed pools, and in very late season speared with fearsome leisters. An eighteenth-century Alta leister was like a weapon of war: strong, wide and with eight fiercely-barbed prongs. Unversed in rod-angling finesse, when the British anglers appeared in the 1830s Alta locals never believed their spindly rods and minimalist tackle could possibly handle the hefty Alta salmon. Spent fish, stripped of market value, were the dubious privilege of the locals who lured salmon up close for spearing by lighting fires.

The history of this much spoken-of river shows how over-exploitation of the salmon resource was always avoided, even if narrowly when at times protection arrived late in the day. Weirs crossing the whole river, self-defeating edifices by definition, were abandoned quickly. In the mid-eighteenth century a greedy local governor received a warning from the Danish Exchequer that being at once the protector of the resource and its exploiter were incompatible roles. Pre-empting river-fishing by moving to the sea to take the salmon earlier on triggered another sharp reprimand to the salmon-addicted governor.

Organised harvesting of the salmon-runs followed until the angling era arrived with the first questing British sportsmen in the 1830s. Northern Norway was to them the ultimate sporting adventure, a bold trip into wild uncharted parts harbouring legendary fish.

There then began the saga of disputes about how to divide the resource according to the method of capture which, up to a point, continues to the present time. Bag nets commenced, multiplied, and were curtailed. Meshes were widened, permitting smaller fish to escape. The local addiction to netting was such that an Act of 1930 states it would be unpractical even to attempt limiting the number of bag-nets. This coincided with a time of financial hardship. Between the wars the slate-working industry languished and smallholder farmers were faring worse than inland farmers further south. Every salmon was a boon.

Angling was a novel concept. The Lapps were described in the nineteenth century precariously paddling pine canoes whilst harling with rods and bent spoons and flies. But the British type of angling was different, a sort of magisterial arabesque performed for hour after hour. The river was in the hands of a single leaseholder from 1863 to the 1930s. This was the Duke of Roxburgh, a Scottish aristocrat who spent his summers tangling with the river's famous leviathans. Some of rod angling's record catches were notched up in this phase. In one of sporting history's most single-minded missions the Duke and his associates heaved vast quantities of pounds of salmon from their watery element into boats and onto banks. It is a sporting saga in itself. Local people then prised open his monopoly in the 1930s and tickets became available to locally based stakeholders. By the 1960s the attractions of angling with rod and line had overwhelmed commercial fishing with stationary gear, and the use of salmon on this great river had become recreational. Meanwhile, sea-fishing for the salmon continued. Contemporary anglers sometimes find long-line hooks in the mouths of salmon they catch.

Today the auctions of fishing tickets attract thousands of anglers and have become major local events; the river has been democratised. Historians of the river concede that it was the enthusiastic visiting rod anglers from Britain and subsequently America that made them comprehend that the ultimate use of a wild salmon was attached to a fishing-line held by a man paying a lot of money. The ascendancy of salmon as sport over salmon as food as a concept might be said to have been established – but only precariously. Today's democratisation of the Alta involves thousands of locals, an expression of the Norwegians' natural instinct to use their salmon resource themselves. By what method the fish are caught is a matter of sublime indifference. Many of the rod anglers believe it is only because they put salmon back and kill none that they are allocated a key part of the run which coincides with the arrival of the big fish. Foreign rod anglers act as a conservation brake.

The extent to which the river's salmon had become a lifeline and ultimate provider for Alta people became vividly clear in 1970 with the announcement that a dam was to be built on the river to generate hydro-electric power. The development plan made no mention of the fish which had made the river a focus of human population for so long, a household word in angling circles, and which epitomised the wilderness bountifulness of the locality. The usually turgid community reaction violently swivelled: foment was immediate.

Perhaps no river has stirred in its defendants such passion. There were protest meetings, sit-ins, hunger strikes, and a protest camp was constructed. It dawned on Norwegian parliamentarians that they were being confronted by civil unrest. The most sensitive political point was that curbing the flow of the river could be seen as discriminating against the Saami people, to whom, in a spiritual sense, Norwegians conceded it somehow belonged. To liberal-minded Norwegians, damaging this inheritance was unacceptable. Torchlight processions in objection took place all over the country. The menace mounted when extra police were drafted in. Finally, ten per cent of the country's whole constabulary were bussed into this normally forgotten northern promontory.

The dam became a defining national issue. Salmon were discussed everywhere. Although the media focused increasingly on the violation of Saami rights as the storyline, no other hydroelectric project in Norway had excited such opposition. The salmon became a symbol for natural systems and the whole natural world. The Alta issue changed the energy debate in Norway and altered its legal and political processes.

A fact worth appreciating is that the dam was to be built above where salmon could naturally reach, deepening an already deep lake; it would not obstruct their passage. The effect on water-flows is what inflamed objectors. Perhaps only those living beside a volatile and great river, with winter ice-jams of monumental size and force, would have put such store in water-flow. But local people here knew what they were confronting. They lived closer to their environment than energy developers and politicians. It was that contrast which gave special force to the protest movement.

The dam was built anyway.

There have been two notable consequences. The extreme pessimism of those who thought the Alta salmon population would take a lethal body-blow have been proved mistaken – on the evidence so far. The fish survives, though its range in the river has shrunk. The river took a while to settle down to the new flows and wash out some of the detritus of the construction process. The section called Sautso, below the dam, once maybe the best Atlantic salmon fishing anywhere, has been permanently damaged for salmon occupation. The remainder seems relatively unaffected in angling catch terms. Water flows and depths, though, have changed with suburbanisation. One example: the lack of ice-cover caused by warmer water streaming from the reservoir has changed the insect-life, made young fish more active earlier, and is believed to have reduced the survival fitness of salmon parr.

Next, the projected financial reward from the development has not been forthcoming; the scheme has under-performed.

However, the colourful and deeply felt public scepticism did produce concessions and most agree they have been useful. To avoid water temperature problems two sluices were constructed, at heavy cost, to mix water from differing layers in the reservoir and moderate temperature differences in the outflow before the water reaches the river. Water temperature is a vital factor for migrating salmon.

The dam was opened in 1987. A look at salmon catches before and after shows a reduction in the number of fish weighing over nine pounds after the dam, and an increase in the number of smaller fish. The biggest total weight of salmon delivered by rods in the 34-year period, starting in 1974, was in 1975. In that halcyon season 2,858 large salmon were landed, a number never approached since.

Seemingly the big fish have missed the top of the river, now subject to water-starvation and a sometimes exposed river-bed, where they might have once spawned. For river-bed stones on the Alta are generally big; it needs a chunky Alta female to sweep the redds clear with her tail. The smaller number of fish big enough to turn these stones may have reduced the gene pool of the real leviathans. Perhaps it is early days in the history of the dammed Alta to know what will ultimately happen.

Norway went seriously to town on further research about Alta salmon. The study prompted by the dam-building – in tagging, scale-reading and so on – has provided insights. If Alta-returning salmon are caught low down the system and put back in higher up the river than their natal zone, they are disorientated. Salmon, then, follow the radar, or smell the water chemistry, to get to the domestic doorstep travelling upstream. It appears that the river itself is not enough; there must be a sequence of chemistry smells which lead fish to their natal zone. They are like children following clues in a paper-trail; one missed link and the trail goes cold.

Also, it was found that some males never migrate. Home-husbands, they achieve maturity in freshwater and mate with females coming in from the sea; their offspring revert to normal. Studies of divergent genetic Alta populations show that salmon may even be programmed to develop resistance to pathogenic organism and parasites common in the stretch of water in which they grew up. Efforts to know and learn more about Alta salmon stop at nothing: helicopters are counting spawning redds, or 'pits' as they call them there, from the air, to check on the river's fecundity.

Perhaps the greatest worry gleaned from the newly invigorated research work is that up to a quarter of all the Alta salmon caught late in the season from 1999–2006 were escapees originating in salmon farms. Salmon farms now occupy the Alta fjord.

The river has not had to contend with the insidious menace of a witches brew of line-bred genetics before. The new findings about the disease resilience of native fish is relevant to arguments about whether wild runs and farm escapes can co-exist.

The long history of the Alta shows that the commitment of the community in a place where the fish signifies so much, has prevailed. The Alta salmon has had to contend with unsustainable over-fishing, with power developers, and with over-avid tax-collectors. There have not been contests with industries offering huge employment, and there has been no threat from large-scale human population increase. The value of the fish has so far won through.

A net fishery persists in the sea conducted by native Saami and utilising an array of weapons to take pre-breeding fish, including bend, seine, lift, bag and drift nets. There are no quotas for the Saami fishermen and no clear records of catch. The only figures around, and they are nebulous, refer to about 80 tons of salmon which, assuming an average sturdy weight of 16 pounds, constitutes some 10,000 fish. Some express this as 80 per cent of the salmon run. It seems a lot. It represents an old-fashioned mixed-stock salmon fishery of the type which has been condemned across the board in other places. But to date anyway, in this realm where salmon is king, the appetite for rod angling appears undented.

Taken as a whole it seems unlikely that solutions for this part of Norway will ever again ignore the big fish. This is a salmon victory location.

It was in western Europe that once-great salmon rivers have become controlled waterways, regulated for water distribution, straightened and revetted, and a far cry from their original meandering watercourses. Rivers which once braided out into complex networks of backwaters and slowly moving streams have been channelised, dredged and re-profiled, and their flows regulated. Straightened, they could be navigated.

Lastly, they have been dammed. Biologists have shown that up to 95 per cent of water-life is missing downstream of large dams. The first dams, as in America, were built for localised power drives. Later came hydro-electricity dams. These were far worse because they worked through the night. A smolt travelling downstream was going to have to meet those revolving turbine-wheels at some point, unless a side-water lade diverted them round the obstruction, which was rare.

On the Upper and Middle Danube the disappearance of all six of the original species of sturgeon showed what blocking an access route can do. Cut the trees, and the birds don't nest. Many of the European dams incorporated no fish-passes, so the extinction of fish species which need to test the boundaries of the big rivers was assured. Nutrients from high up failed to reach the floodplains, where productivity declined. Water, however, became a resource, on tap, stripped of harmful bacteria, available in containers.

France was superb salmon territory. The words, '*le saumon*' are spoken with a sort of throaty dreaminess. The salmon once luxuriated in the ambience of France's forests and valleys and landscape of serene meadows, oak forests and lofty riverside trees. The Loire is 625 miles long, possessing what Anthony Netboy has called 'gemlike tributaries'. Only one of these, the Allier, still has salmon. The Gironde, formed by the confluence of the Dordogne and the Garonne, once had salmon in abundance, as did the Seine. Now in the Pyrenees there are a few surviving populations of salmon, fiercely defended by their users who go tight-lipped when outsiders introduce the subject. Britanny and Normandy also had numerous short and often fast rivers and it is a measure of what has been lost that Britanny alone, just a corner of France, once landed 4,500 tons of salmon, far more than is presently caught on rods by the whole of the United Kingdom. France, where at banquets the regal salmon was trumpeted in, has lost an almighty native.

Most of the blame lies with excessive fishing and gargantuan poaching, followed by careless damming. In 1920, at one of many interminable discussions stretching over the decades, the exchange of kilowatts for delicious food was questioned. Endless stylish exchanges of philosophical niceties ensued. Adorned with miraculous saucy concoctions, spent kelts continued to be jerked out of midwinter rivers, consumed and pronounced good. In the meantime salmon trundled on downhill in a welter of developments culminating in the construction of nuclear power stations. These sucked in coastal water, containing assorted fish, to cool reactors. Salmon fisherman Ernest Schweibert described it all as: 'A text-book case in greed and mismanagement.' Amen.

Perhaps no event is more symbolic of western Europe's vexed relationship with salmon than that affecting the Rhine during the Second World War. This massive 820-mile waterway, a major salmon residency, had one temporary respite from progressive human mismanagement when the great weir at Krembs was destroyed by Allied Forces' bombs. This allowed salmon, briefly, to reach the up-river breeding grounds again. In the aftermath a few generations of salmon flourished. It had taken world war to abrupt man's relentless chastisement of the river-system.

Then the usual culprits – polluted industrial waste, hydro-electric power schemes barring access to breeding grounds, mining detritus, and generally treating the great river as a waste-pipe – battered the valiant salmon resurgence into submission. By the mid-nineteenth century almost no salmon were left.

A restoration programme using stock from Ireland, Spain, Sweden, Denmark, France and Scotland is presently underway. Dams are being ameliorated to allow salmon passage and there are pressures from European Union legislation which has made water clean-up a legal duty. However, a detailed 2011 German government paper about Atlantic salmon restoration in the Rhine comments that the aim of establishing self-sustaining populations 'is still far from being reached.' The fact is that although 540 miles of its length are in Germany and its source is in Switzerland, other stretches of the river are in Austria, Liechtenstein, France, Luxembourg and the Netherlands. The Rhine salmon has many political jurisdictions to please.

Not every country has squandered the resource. Canada has been mentioned; on the eastern side of range are others. This chapter is not an audit of where there are and are not salmon. It concentrates rather on interesting case histories of human treatment. In 1957 Atlantic salmon eggs from nearby Iceland were used to introduce salmon into the Faroes, the only place where reintroduction has been successful. In Greenland there is a single river, the Kapsigdlit, with migrating salmon. Ireland and Iceland are self-defining major salmon nations, by any measure. In Portugal, and Spain, Sweden, Denmark and Finland, Atlantic salmon exist, but they determine little at national level and are not present in large numbers. Some of the rivers in these and other places are beautiful and undamaged and have escaped being beaten on the anvil of development for various reasons and on them, to the inducted, salmon angling may play a huge part in life at a personal level. Some rivers are being manfully restored. But they are not countries in which the national name auto-suggests a leaping silver fish curved over foaming water.

Such a country is Scotland.

Salmon are in Scotland's psyche. The Greeks had a name for someone under the spell of running water; this fascination may affect everyone in proximity to the wet element. No resident Scot is far from a river. They lace the landscape in his country. Walter Scott, the well-travelled Scottish writer who dwelt in the head-waters of the salmon-rich Tweed, said: 'I have translated every land with which I was connected into the speech of rivers.'

Scots are generically under this spell not least because beneath that water in their mind's eye is a silver fish – a leaper, a fish not only occupying freshwater and salt but also on whimsical occasions the air, a sort of giant freshwater flying fish, sparkling like a star. The theme runs through Scotland's poetry, literature and music and the fibres of the culture. It affects every stratum of society from the Royal family which owns fishing in Scotland to the citizens living on Glasgow's River Clyde, who have started to see migrating salmon again in autumn-time, gliding by within the confines of the city. For this small northern nation with a meandering coastline and mountainous interior the salmon is an emblem and a badge.

History reflects salmon's sanctified status. The earliest salmon law dates from 1030 and was, appropriately, protective. Salmon could not be removed from the water between Assumption Day (end of August) and Martinmas Day on 12 November. That prevented them being killed as they bred. Another important cessation of hostilities against salmon in medieval times was between mid-April to St John's Day on 24 June, bang in the spring run. That was truly progressive. The law protected small young fish in the river as well as adults. In one legislative instrument emanating from King Robert III, killing fish whilst they were actually breeding was a crime inviting capital punishment, a human life for a salmon life. Whether this ever occurred is not recorded. Legislation protecting salmon may almost have kept pace with evolving human populations and the pressures on food supply – a legislative achievement.

There were laws to allow free passage for salmon at weekends: estuary nets snaring salmon drifting on tides were regulated, and weirs and river barriers were required to have salmon-passes. Laws were sagacious in their understanding of the biological needs of the fish: acts of 1424 and 1457 banned weirs and cruives (traps on weirs) which impeded either smolts or adult salmon. It was thus understood long ago that the small fish going out was as important as the big one coming in, an early demonstration of wise use sadly sometimes overlooked today in the rush towards renewable energy from hydro-electricity schemes.

Unsurprisingly, salmon in these early medieval times were not taken from the shoreline or in the open sea. Why bother with that trouble when the fish in due course presented itself for attack within the limited confines of the river? Legislation focused on the vulnerable links in the migratory chain.

Although there are plenty of anecdotal and listed reports of laws being flouted it is also clear from the records that up to the time of industrial development Scotland's salmon stock stayed in good heart. The country's happy propensity to provide suitable habitat for salmon with its long clean rivers, and its high latitude, which meant that midsummer water seldom over-heated, made Scotland from the beginning a bigger provider of salmon than England and one of the flagship countries in all salmon domain. The destinies of Scotland and salmon were entwined at the outset, and it may even be the case that they will be in the future.

The Union with England took place in 1707. Prior to that, and indeed for a long time after it, Scottish salmon were sold in England. With wool and hides, salmon was a staple medieval-period export. England had a bigger population, a more advanced economy, and could not supply its people with enough fish. Warfare and border disputes interrupted this trade sometimes as might be expected, but the English market remained the closest and best.

It is amusing to consider that today everything is different and yet the same. Rod-caught salmon may no longer lawfully be sold. Yet the Scottish rivers remain magnets for English anglers. Thus salmon still provides for Scotland tremendous financial benefits in cross-border trade, but for sport rather than the flesh of the quarry. Scottish farm salmon is sold in England, and in large amounts, but that is a very different matter. The dubious benefits of that transaction for the English consumers is a matter treated in a less sanguine chapter later on.

From the mid-nineteenth century, basic protection was spelt out in detail in salmon fishery acts. It was breaking the law to poison salmon or allow poisonous liquids to flow into salmon-water. Fishing with roe was outlawed, except for catching hatchery broodstock. Killing or obstructing or injuring smolts and fry was illegalised. Killing 'unclean' salmon, or salmon ready to spawn, was made illegal too. Obstructing a salmon fishery protection officer was an offence. So was fishing at night. In the main these strictures protecting salmon were the same in England. As to Ireland, there were subtle differences: whereas in Scotland and England to have on your person leisters and spears for catching salmon was an offence, in the Emerald Isle it was all right to possess these instruments if under cover of darkness! To be seen poaching was not on; to do it clandestinely was given a nod and a wink. Ireland's relationship with its salmon has been consistently more slap-happy.

Not only were salmon-friendly laws passed in Scotland but officers with special powers to protect the fish could be appointed. Potential jail sentences were severe. In the fifteenth century, Scottish laws were passed permitting the destruction of illegal salmon-catching nets and other devices. It is perhaps surprising that to this day fishery bailiffs have powers of arrest on rivers and, in some particulars, powers which exceed those of ordinary police officers when dealing with suspected miscreants.

Under the 1868 salmon acts, on suspicion of an offence salmon bailiffs can demand to see personal identity and address details. They have stop-and-search powers over persons, premises and vehicles. They are exempt from trespass laws. Boats, nets and vehicles can be seized by them. These powers extend six miles out into the sea. Furthermore, they can execute this authority by day or night. Salmon in Scotland certainly meant something.

A book published in 1590 describing the firepower being directed against English salmon gives some idea of the sorts of assaults the tentative salmon nosing its way towards its breeding grounds might be expected to encounter. Namely the use of 'fire, handguns, cross bows, oils, ointments, powders and pellets ... to stun and poison fish', without starting on the list of nets and traps which could ensnare them. It is impossible to think of any other creature which elicited this amount of predatory interest. A hefty book on game and fish laws in Scotland contains a text on salmon which fills 150 dense pages. Indeed, almost special linguistic training is needed to work out what is intended!

In this way the treatment by its people of its salmon is perhaps an allegory for a nation's human interaction with the whole environment, along with its denizens.

It is now being better understood in marine fishery circles that property rights may be the key to commercial harvesting guided by enlightened conservation. Japan understood this centuries ago and demarcated property lines in the sea for offshore fishermen. Scottish salmon have fared as well as they have because of their solid foundation in property rights. In Scotland, title to salmon fishing is a heritable property right. A private individual can own the fishing rights for salmon and access to them as well as the means to manage the fish. This differs from England where management by government over-arches private fishing rights. In England and Wales the government can follow any policy it wants and apply them to someone else's property. An example: at the moment, salmon hatcheries are out of favour with government agencies whilst a large body of river-knowledge comprising owners and river-keepers, on rivers with inadequate runs, is demanding them. There is an idealogical impasse.

Which system works best? The market tells all: salmon fishing beats in Scotland are worth a lot more.

In Scotland, management since the 1862 and 1868 Acts has mostly been corporate in nature, performed by district salmon fishery boards. Amended in 1986 the original acts created these boards, elected by assemblies of stakeholders, to raise money and manage the fishery. They were constituted to include salmon netsmen, although in the twenty-first century salmon netting is a dying practice. A board has statutory powers and obligations to protect migratory fish, so is founded in law.

The merits of the 41 boards have become obvious over time. Boards are framed to properly represent the owners who fund management; they have been streamlined to incorporate local angler voices; members serve without charging for their time; and they can react to local issues rapidly. They must respect the salmon laws of the land (like prohibited salmon fishing on Sundays) and adhere to the fishing season set for particular rivers (opening and closing dates can vary between districts and individual rivers), but can take action on local issues. An example might be removing invasive weeds. Alien plants have appeared in the last ten years in Scottish rivers. They can be controlled by targeted action. For example, successful curbing of Japanese knotweed, giant hogweed and other invaders on rivers in south-west Scotland was the result of coordinated action by neighbouring boards.

Fishing methods can be discussed with the hope, though not the absolute power, that suitable restraints, dependent on water height, speed, pool-type, etc., will be exercised on fishing owners and their anglers. Some rivers have slow deep pools unsuitable for fly-angling where spinning tackle can be deployed more sensibly. But spinning is a contentious affair, seen by some as a fishing method more akin to coarse fishing for the non-migratory denizens of lakes and ponds. Boards can try to moderate conflicting voices on such things. Members are there to serve the salmon acts rather than their own economic interests. Private owners still have the power to use any legal method to catch salmon; but in practice boards tend to unify approaches and bring into the open any rumbling discontents. Boards can run events like fishing competitions to generate interest in their salmon fishery, and encourage angling through ticket sales. The finance for boards' operation comes from levies on fishery owners who receive fishing rents from anglers.

In the wide frame, boards can voice the interests of migratory fish to planners. An example is in the initiative being pressed by government to 're-water' certain parts of Scotland which have lost river-flows owing to hydro-electric schemes. This entails trapping water in one river and piping it into another one; some call it, 'playing God with rivers'. Sometimes re-watering even converts east-coast water into west-coast water, redirecting it across Scotland. Often this is to compensate for existing 'de-waterings' from power schemes of an earlier time. Although there are government bodies supposed to consider wider environmental impacts of new schemes, in practice, boards are best placed to argue the specific consequences for migratory fish and for local employment. Employment consequences are a consideration supposedly written into all rural legislation, but boards know best whether workers, and how many, would be affected if fishery interests were somehow violated.

European law affects Scottish freshwaters, for example in the special protection afforded to species like freshwater mussels and lampreys, and salmon themselves on some rivers. Again, boards can present the case for the protection of salmon and salmon workers most comfortably.

Scotland's treatment of its salmon, however, is not a history of undiluted beneficence.

It is not commonly understood to what extent Scottish rivers have already been twisted out of their natural paths to accommodate other purposes, some waters robbed and some boosted. Scotland's engagement with hydro-electric energy is an obscure subject although it affects the country from north to south. In the 1950s a Labour government minister, himself Scottish, determined there should be 'a light in every glen'. Hydro-electricity using large-scale dams was to be the method. The headwaters of many rivers were impounded and often salmon migration paths were blocked. Big rivers like the Tay are dammed in many of their tributaries.

A long time ago I stood on the bridge below my house, which crosses the River Helmsdale, alongside a visiting American. He stared awhile at the water and, turning to me, asked in wonderment, 'Is this a natural river?' With the exception of the headwater dam, built a hundred years ago to control flows and help salmon, I thought, of course it is. Now years later I understand the pointedness of his question: most of Scotland's river flows are compromised and altered, somewhere, somehow.

To compensate salmon, the conscientious 1950s' government long ago conducted some enormous engineering schemes. On the Conon in Ross-shire, in the eastern north Highlands, water was diverted to a west-coast pipeline and four dams were built on one medium-sized river-system. In compensation the board received a massive hatchery capable of accommodating over two million young fish. For many years the power company tried and tested new designs in fish-passes and lifts for ascending fish to ease their passage.

Presently bailiffs catch smolts in April and May high in the system and portage them past the dams 26 miles downriver, returning them to the water fitted with electronic tags. These can be read by sensors at the dams when the fish has completed its huge migratory circle and reappeared for spawning years later. Up to a thousand smolts a year are tagged in this way. The research information thus gleaned represents a major effort to pay back the Conon River for its lost headwaters. And the river has survived. Managers can look at the annual rod catches, averaging some 1,500 fish a year, with satisfaction. Physical improvements continue, with a major tributary presently being re-accessed by salmon for the first time since the 1950s.

Many of Scotland's main rivers have been affected by the 1950s damming programme and although one or two have been effectively de-commissioned for migrating fish, in the majority the fish-runs continue, albeit somewhat injured.

Scotland is a place where most matters are discussed with passionate vigour, and salmon fishing is amongst them – a grizzled old-time fishery manager told me that airing a view on salmon was akin to walking the Gaza Strip! Maybe that has something to do with the fact that in overall terms salmon in Scotland have survived. Consider the statistics: on the keynote rivers, and indeed on some others, catches by rod anglers have been steady for the last thirty years. Apart from in the west Highlands, where the sea-lochs sacrificed to pen-cage salmon farming have pushed wild salmon towards extinction, Scottish rivers generally speaking enjoy steady migrations of the silver fish.

Salmon angling is never far from the news, season opening ceremonies are widely reported, cars with fishing rods attached travel roads as a normal sight, and tackle shops maintain a light-bulb presence in high streets otherwise rendered ghost-like by the advance of out-of-centre supermarkets. The daunting task of estimating the value of Scotland's fishing in 2010 produced a notional figure of £425 million sterling, with an annual value to the Scottish economy of £120 million. No one knows the exact numbers because rentals remain private agreements between individuals and can be cloaked in added-on accommodation charges, ghillieing wages, and so on. Certainly the old culture of salmon netting in Scotland has decreased greatly, leaving more salmon free to ascend rivers, but rod angling in the jewel-like Caledonian hinterland fares well.

Scotland's engagement with salmon has lasted a thousand years. It is akin perhaps to that of any other tribal history.

Across their range, some salmon have been lost and others have been saved, and then had to be re-saved. As the threats to salmon embedded in perpetual development mount, so too have the efforts to protect what is there, and what has been. There is a story of human victory against adversity to be told too.

The Passion

The history of salmon is a history of passions. There have been tremendous acts of damage and there have been tremendous acts of faith. Faith because the fish which is the repository of such commitment travels a huge distance unseen and unmonitored before its re-arrival. Its boomeranging migration extends so far and so wide. Sureness in its return is a faith akin to astrology.

A text written in Latin in 1517 by the Principal of the new Aberdeen University, Hector Boethius, describes the salmon lifecycle with clairvoyant understanding way before his time, only mistaking the amount of time salmon spent at sea. The good monk imagined that they grew to adult size in twenty days at sea, a growth rate even a genetically modified farm salmon would under-achieve! The point, though, is that the biology of the leaping silver-armoured visitor was understood. The rules of wise use should have been laid down. Early salmon protection law shows that its vulnerability was understood too.

The perennial problem for the Atlantic salmon was its demand upon the environment. Salmon need clean waters and waters running free. In their own ranging lifestyle and their joy in leaping (unusual in fish) they epitomise freedom.

Humanity's expansion and development encroaches upon the free and wild. It happens everywhere – whether in the demands on Amazonian Indians to be settled and rooted instead of roaming the rain-forest in a rotation of seasonal camps; in the compression of range for reindeer moving northwards to Artic tundra for summer and southwards to the milder taiga in winter; or in the salmon's need for the refuge of freshwater for breeding and the unruly sea for fattening. It is both physical, as when dams block salmon migrations, and psychic: when Stalin cleared the reindeer herders off the Russian tundra and imprisoned them in camps, their spirits collapsed and they died. As humanity extends its grip over more and more of the Earth's benefactions, the interface with salmon sharpens. One time the life-support system for early Man, the salmon is now being treated as an expendable though glamorous incidental: a luxury which can be foregone.

This critical dilemma has produced in recent time some extraordinary salvation performances. The United Kingdom is a heavily industrialised country with one of the world's highest population densities, yet it still retains a substantial salmon presence.

Britain has been the locus for some impressive initiatives and endeavours. One of the most important was the report by the Scottish judge, Lord Hunter, which was published in 1965 and recommended a ban on catching salmon at sea with nets. Mostly these were mobile drift-nets, catching salmon by the gills with invisible curtains of monofilament suspended from the sea surface and drifting on the currents.

Jack Hunter was a rumbustious figure, full of humour and fun and a keen angler of the river where I live and work, the Helmsdale in Sutherland in the north Scottish Highlands. I recall an evening in the local hotel where his lordship and two fellow judges threw a party. The barman, for reasons unknown, failed to show up so Jack Hunter performed this service. I did not see him noting down much about the bar bill, but maybe he did. Drinks were on tap and on the tab. At any rate, pints were liberally distributed and good fun was had by all. Towards the end he recited some favourite poems, inviting a chorus recitation of the catch lines by the jolly assembly then collected in the bar. Did a singing judge stand swaying on a table? My memory is a little hazy ...

The good judge, though, knew his stuff on fishing. His report had shown an average of 610,000 migratory fish, salmon and sea trout were caught off Scotland in the ten years since 1954. It is a striking number. Critically, he spotted that four out of five were caught by commercial fishermen, the leftovers being for the anglers. He realised that such catches were a cavalier use of the resource and threatened the survival of salmon. What was going on was not only unscientific, it was archaic. His recommended ban on freewheeling netting for salmon at sea was accepted and legislated.

It was shown to be predictive and right. In due course the English drift-nets off Northumberland were also cut down, many of them mothballed and the remainder served with a termination date. The Irish drift-netting for salmon was also outlawed. Jack Hunter, a passionate sporting fisherman, had perceived a new fundamental. If salmon patrolled a huge range, what a glorious fact that was, but it was in natal rivers that capture should concentrate. What was caught could then be recorded properly and, if necessary, regulated, and it would yield far the greatest economic benefit. Catches could be matched to salmon abundance. The Hunter Report was informed and far-sighted.

The folding of the Irish nets is a British as well as an Irish story. An Englishman, Brian Marshall, involved in fishing on Hampshire's River Avon, lodged a petition with the EU claiming that Ireland was flouting the Habitats Directive and catching other people's salmon in the sea without asking them. The Habitats Directive is the EU's main instrument of environmental protection.

The Irish drift fishery, using monofilament nylon, operated around the headland of Donegal and down the western coast. The boats fished inside the 6-mile limit as fishing further out was illegal. Migrating salmon in any case appeared to hug the coast. When the nets were being pulled, extracting amongst other fish what was reckoned to be three-quarters of Ireland's own run of grilse, plundering seals took a few more.

Marshall showed that his own river far away in south-west England was doing everything possible to save its salmon – releasing those caught using barbless hooks, abolishing worming, ruling for fly-only spring fishing, closing seasons early – whilst the Irish were intercepting them at sea, rendering these conservation efforts fruitless. He cited evidence about bad practice by the Irish netters from English scientists as well as those of the Irish government's independent review, the Salmon Review Group. He even gave grid references for affected rivers. He alerted the horrified French to the fact that more of their mythic fish were ending up in Irish nets than in Gallic rivers, as revealed by the number wearing French tags. The fish were no more Irish than swallows are French because they traverse France to reach their wintering grounds in Africa.

French river restorationists were fizzing. Between 2001 and 2003 it was calculated that a few Irishmen off the west coast of Ireland were extracting over half the European Union's total catch of salmon. Yet European rivers were making herculean efforts to get their fish back. The Irish tourism industry and its 30,000 licensed anglers demonstrated that visiting anglers to Ireland had fallen from more than one in ten of all tourists in 1999 to under one in a hundred in 2006. Rod catches of salmon were less than a quarter of their number 40 years earlier. The salmon scene in Ireland had been disembowelled, a ghostly parade of sepia photographs. As was the netting job itself: where once a thousand families earned their living from netting salmon, now only some fifty remained.

Owners had lost interest in their salmon fishings and in parts of Eire there was a virtual free-for-all, a collapse of management. The few faithful visiting anglers who did appear found print marks in the sand from a pre-breakfast angler testing their beats out for them at dawn, and as soon as they left at teatime a shadowy figure would filter from the undergrowth. Before long more flies or worms or spoons were sieving through the water for the last remaining salmon.

I remember fishing the Slaney in the south and finding a group of indistinct figures fade in front of me as I arrived on the pool, then slot into position again behind me as I left in the gathering dusk. Outside the pub that night there was a salmon in the basket of one of the bicycles leaning against a tree. The local lads happily discussed with me the difficulties of catching a particular big salmon which we had all seen rolling on the fly with its mouth obstinately shut. The owner back in the big house, cradling his whiskey, was resigned, dumbly acknowledging control had slipped beyond recovery on his magical salmon waters sliding under the grand trees. There was a sense of abandonment and doomed hopelessness. The few who tried to improve their fishing operations by bettering the habitat, or stocking and sending fit smolts to sea, saw the returning adults being brazenly gill-netted in the bay, within sight of their river-mouths.

Yet to the Emerald Isle the economic value of a netted salmon was 22 Euros compared to 423 Euros if caught on a rod, a droll discrepancy. This was not a policy, it was a surrender to expediency.

The case against netting was overwhelming. It was only because the netsmen had political friends in high places that the anomaly had been allowed to last so long.

Helping to keep the reality of the baseline salmon economics at bay was the fact that the Irish had received a lot of money from Europe. The living was easy. Resource-waste was affordable. European goodwill had become part of the Irish feeling of goodwill about itself. Suddenly that turned sour. Breaching the Habitats Directive was plain unacceptable. On the second attempt Brian Marshall's courageous salient, fortified by Orri Vigfusson, won through. Instead of cheques Ireland received warning letters.

There was never the need for legislation; Ireland's salmon-net protectors could see the writing on the wall, the risk of becoming a fishing pariah in the international European organisation that underpinned the whole shamrock economic revival. In late summer 2006 the nets were unceremoniously illegalised. Not all was lost: to coat the pill another cheque was produced, for 35 million Euros, paid in three instalments to mitigate tax.

Brian Marshall's private petition had worked. Salmon interests, already buoyed by the elevation of salmon to a species worthy of the EU's special protection in certain places, noted this. Under European Union rules a private person can lodge a petition of objection about breaches of EU law. The petition summarily lays out a case. Qualified people in Brussels are obligated to examine its credibility, and they do so scrupulously. Salmon interests noted that the system could work for them.

There is a bizarre, even surreal, postscript to the case. It is hardly believable. In 2011 the net-addicted Irish began a new assay. Ignoring the international resolutions that mixed stock or indiscriminate salmon fishing should be phased out, including Article 66 of the UN Law of the Sea Treaty, Irish government scientists finagled a new case arguing that, using genetics, they could demonstrate salmon could safely be netted once more. In certain places, where so-called 'conservation limits' had been met, stocks of salmon would not be over-exploited by a fresh assault with nylon. The Irish mist, pumped from backstage, thickened again. There was some truly devious blah-blah to justify the case.

People tend, perhaps, to veer back to habits which are embedded, good and bad; change takes a long time. The Irish love politics and the often bewildering meanderings of nebulous argument. In the end, reverting to their monofilament, like befuddled drug-dependants, whilst dispersing as much Irish mist as possible, was just too much of a temptation.

Also, they have a different attitude. There is an ineradicable sense of mischief. Suffering from some historical memory lapse they see snaring salmon willy-nilly somehow as part of an enduring anti-Anglo-Saxon salient, nurturing an old grudge. They habitually use prawns and worms to fiddle salmon out of their lairs, and one Scottish angler was astonished to find an Irishman walking actually underneath his rod, between him and the river as he passed by.

I like the story of a lady I know who was in the pub with an Irishman. A gale blew outside and the pub was dim, dank and grim, entirely to the satisfaction of the Irishman. The door opened with a blast of wind and in stepped a man in a long dripping sou'wester oilskin. 'Hello, O'Farrel, how's tricks?' queried the seated Irishman. O'Farrel, with a huge smile, merely pulled aside the two fronts of his sou'wester and three fresh salmon were somehow vertically hung by their tails to the inside of each. Of Ireland it can be said that there is indeed a passion for the salmon.

The main theme of salmon conservation in Britain in recent time has been getting rid of nets as a means of capturing the gilded fish. Its core concept is that netting salmon at sea or in saltwater on the tides demonstrably steals the native inhabitants from a wide range of rivers. The net intercepts a fish seeking to breed. The net is careless of which fish or where it is going. Self-evidently such a harvesting method is unscientific. It could not be justified. The Irish nets were an extreme case. They took fish from many countries, like Somali pirates attacking a major trade route for important freight where no other route existed. At an extremity was the risk that the last remnants of a river's unique stock could end up mashed in a net far from home. Interceptory netting could potentially obliterate evolution's sensitively constructed network of genetic strains in one rash moment. It would be an accident like the slaughter of the last great auk, not in malice but in ignorance.

An assortment of bodies arose which tried to tackle salmon netting. The North Atlantic Salmon Fund, based in Reykjavik, brainchild of the visionary conservationist Orri Vigfusson, in the early days did much of the heavy lifting. Vigfusson is an unusual conservationist: a fisherman by heritage he is also a natural strategist and a deal-maker. He took ideas further. Instead of trying merely to illegalise a form of fishery, sometimes with ancient origins, his principle was to accept the netter's right and negotiate a commercial deal to ensure it was not exercised. Critics, who were themselves impotent in the political theatre which Vigfusson made his operational territory, whether international or local, objected that such a deal was not final. The right to net remained untouched. True. But Vigfusson came from a commercial fishing family in Iceland and had a more developed sense of justice. He knew too what history is teaching today, with, for example, the restoration of property rights in eastern Germany to families disinherited in the Soviet era of occupation. You should not in principle steal someone's heritage, even with money. He was able successfully to negotiate with netsmen across the salmon world because he recognised the legitimacy of their property rights. He understood their language and he shared their interests.

If netting partners in these agreements arbitrarily jack up their catches and impair runs, as may have happened with Greenland's netsmen in 2011, impacting North American salmon runs in 2012, it is owing to a flaw in the deal rather than the mechanism's principle.

Vigfusson had one extra knack: he was a public relations wizard. There are many examples. Within 10 days of becoming the Russian President for the first time, Vladimir Putin was photographed salmon fishing with a fly-rod. The trick had the Vigfusson signature, and sure enough there he was in the background, the smiling host. Small man, giant achiever, the Icelander was in contact with every key figure, from presidents downwards. He lives and breathes salmon restoration, night and day.

Some of the most vigorous salmon-netting was conducted in the UK, one of the Atlantic salmon's best survival zones. On the north-eastern English coast was one outstandingly contentious netting operation. A fleet of small boats sailed from Berwick, nudging the Scottish Border, and netted salmon and sea trout offshore, starting in early spring. With a crew of two and up to forty feet long, these boats using gill-nets took big catches. Of what, precisely? Some of these fish were destined to run English rivers further south down the coast as far as Yorkshire. Others would have curled north in their migration and followed coast-hugging currents to filter into Scotland's main salmon rivers on the east. Science has showed subsequently that three out of four Northumbrian-caught salmon were north-swimming and destined for Scotland.

The fishery had no quota or cap of any sort. The netsmen had a 92-day season, weather-permitting. Other contestants on the fishing-grounds were seals, and there was a race to get the salmon aboard before these lethally athletic sea mammals chomped bits off.

Who ate the fish? Ten years ago the catch was sent in thirds to Glasgow, the Billingsgate fish market in London, and Birmingham. Then, salmon were worth £5 a pound in mid-season, grilse £3.50. Today the prices are stratospheric, higher in the spring and falling by a half in July when greater numbers of grilse are around; the buyers are French. Many fewer salmon from nets are available as netting has been steadily curtailed, and prices have rocketed with shortages.

On ecology grounds the Northumbrian drift-nets were indefensible. Inertia in stopping them was in part due to the fact that the little burgh of Berwick, a fiercely contested fiefdom in hundreds of years of English-Scottish wars, was socially a rough corner with sensitivities about ingrained unemployment.

Vigfusson's Icelandic organisation, NASF (North Atlantic Salmon Fund), brokered the initial deal. There were 64 boats licensed to participate in this lucrative fishery. I asked Orri Vigfusson how the negotiations had gone. 'It was a natural discussion,' he said, 'we wanted to retire as many licenses as possible, and the netsmen wanted the maximum payments.' Armed with a cheque for £3.3 million sterling, NASF finally persuaded 52 licensees to retire. Their netting right was non-transferable.

The deal's most bizarre aspect was that the newly fledged devolved Scottish government contributed nothing. This was despite salmon fishing being a major plank of visitor tourism on the east coast and that many of the rescued fish owned Scottish birth certificates. It was assumed that either Scotland's rookie government was reluctant to pass money to any English fishermen, or that it shrank from appearing to support rod angling, a pastime associated with leisure, class and privilege. And it was true that many significant salmon fishing rights in Scotland hailed from ancient property rights of local chieftains and big families.

Whatever the reasons and the sensitivities, this large chunk of money had come from British anglers and the English government. The last £1 million was raised from private sources.

Cheques came from far and wide, £10 notes arriving anonymously by mail.

The solution did not float everyone's boat. Salmon conservationists said that the more inactive netsmen departed enriched, leaving energetic ones to ramp up their subtractions from the salmon run. Instruments called T and J nets, similar to bag-nets in being anchored and stretching from the beach, were initially not mentioned in the deal. In the nine years following the buy-out, sixteen remaining netsmen reduced to fourteen. The north-east drift-nets in 2010 declared a catch of 8,000 salmon, a fraction of the old hauls, which sometimes exceeded 45,000 salmon with an additional 30,000 sea trout.

In the same year the River Tweed, which flows to sea at Berwick and whose feeder-streams had supplied the sea-nets with young salmon, recorded the best rod catch in its history, of 23,000 salmon. On the Tyne, just further south, the fish counter had immediately registered the increase in fish able to reach their spawning grounds, vindicating the buy-out: four times as many salmon ran the river by June 2003 as were counted before the nets were reduced in June 2002.

The postscript to the saga was the late 2012 announcement by the British government that the remaining netting operations had to close within a decade. There was a neat twist: after 2022 no further compensation would be paid. Netsmen could figure out for themselves whether to go to the effort of maintaining all the gear, launching the boat and selling the fish, or taking the compensation money and folding up their operations forthwith. From 2012 T and J netsmen have to demonstrate that they do not take mixed stocks, which will presumably be difficult.

The position of the Scottish government meantime had become yet more perverse. The controlling nationalist party had started to encourage the revival of this discredited way of taking salmon. Wild salmon interests blinked in disbelief; what next, had they not noticed the international accords, the science, and the public support for salmon conservation? Indeed, the first move by the Scottish government, to support a salmon-netting firm's application for a European grant to rebuild their commercial enterprise, came just when international delegations were struggling with Greenland to buy off a further five years of harvesting in the wintering grounds. The Greenlanders could have said, why are you paying us not to net and giving money to your own folk to do it more? As it happened, they desisted. But it was looking as though the Scottish nationalists' dislike of rod anglers and the visitor industry was turning into a phobic obsession. The alternative conclusion is that provincial politicians oblivious to the outside world, and domestically keen to appear muscular and contrary, were reverting too easily to base instinct.

The north-east drift-net fishery issue has a parallel further north; that is in coastal salmon-netting by Norway around the Finnmark, Norway's northernmost county. Over 15 years, catches have averaged 200–300 tons – about the same as the river landings of rod-caught salmon from the Finnmark's 43 rivers. International scientists say that between 60 and 70 per cent of the spring salmon caught in this Norwegian operation are from Russian rivers. The Norwegians are doing what the Irish west-coast drift netters did and what the north-east English drift-netters did, pinching fish on-passage travelling home to breed.

The protesting Russians were stymied in circuitous talks for two years. They stressed that the salmon being taken by Norway are destined for the now-famous Kola Peninsular rivers which have become a honey-pot for international fly anglers. These are Russia's only visiting sportsmen in any number. Top Russians fish there too. The Governor of local capital Murmansk said that sea fish for eating are available in many other species. Backing this line, and saying that Norway's own rivers too could benefit, was the Norwegian River Owners Association.

Russia and Norway are intertwined in numerous ways, not least joint interests in cooperating in sensitive treatment of any Arctic developments. Once more, Vigfusson's NASF is embroiled in the negotiations. It is hard to see that this classically archaic sea-netting for salmon by Norway can last for much longer and indeed, at time of writing, the Russian bear is stirring to protect its own. If the Norwegian river owners are right, some rivers on their coast as well are due a recovery.

Recovery stories have a hint of magic. They also have heroes. The salmon resurrection in the River Tyne in north-east England is almost a parable. The chevalier is an obstinate, outspoken, plain-speaking man operating in his own district to re-create a salmon run. The men in black hats are the fishery boffins who find to their horror that a reintroduction programme is working in defiance of in-vogue theory and official lines of advice.

In the long ago the Tyne was a fabled river. The year 1873 saw the Tyne subjected to a panoply of contraptions yielding 129,100 salmon, quite aside from fish squirreled away on the dark side of the moon at sea and in the estuary. Such huge takes cannot continue forever. Yet even in 1922 anglers topped 4,000, a respectable total for a medium-sized river. There followed 40 years of brutalisation in which the mighty Tyne was filled with everything from sewage to farm, mining and industrial wastes. By 1959 the rod catch had transmogrified: it was zero.

I once telephoned some old-timers to get a feel for the history of this chilling collapse. They agreed the river had become a sewer, but one old fellow said that despite the chemical obstacle-course the occasional wild fish still managed to swim in, past the long 18-mile estuary swilling with filth, and reach the tributaries where water was fresh and cool and clean.

Angling, meantime, had died.

It is a quirk of fate that the creation of a new local body, the Northumbrian Water Authority, with the twin functions of supplying water to the region's homes and industries and treating their wastes, should inadvertently have fired up a man for whom the river's recovery became a life-mission. His challenge was to remedy the destruction to salmon wrought on the Tyne by having its tributaries blocked off.

In order steadily to supply water the Kielder Reservoir was created, a giant lake opened by the Queen in 1982. In the process, 10 miles of the North Tyne, containing the gravels where the once-monumental run of fish had hatched as alevins, was submerged, and the Kielder Burn further up-river was put beyond the reach of breeding fish.

Obligated to do something for salmon the authority had two options: to build either a fish-pass circumventing the 172-foot dam, or a salmon hatchery. For the fish-pass to work, over 44-foot-high boxes would have had to be constructed, laddering their way to the dam-crest and over it. As most Tyne salmon only sought their upstream spawning areas in September they would have faced this exhausting and labyrinthine ascent after spending many months and most of their strength in the river.

Many might have been too weak to muster the energy for that final undertaking. A hatchery was decided on.

Enter Peter Gray, not technically qualified but clear-headed. Working as a trainee on the nearby River Coquet, Gray had observed that hatchery salmon were being tipped into waters far colder than their hatchery nurseries. Water-sources were deep-down springs with a temperature of seven degrees. This temperature only moved up a single degree in baking-hot summers. Hatcheries provided water that was consistently warm. Salmon eggs hatched in a mere 56 days. The fish grew exponentially. Sustenance from the yolk-sac lasted three brief weeks. So Coquet hatchery fry were ready for life in the wild by mid-February.

In February, in this bleak moorland just south of the Scottish border, there are no invertebrates, no insects. The uplands are frigid. These headwaters were the release area for the hatchery fish. Coquet fry were being pitched into the equivalent of glacial chasms. Gray realised he had spent his early career in fisheries murdering the species he was meant to be helping.

Gray worked out that returning young fish later might side-step the awkward period in British rivers when late frosts on high-up moors exert a chilling grip, keeping all life dormant. Cooling down water temperature, he extended the yolk-sac period to three months. He looked hard at young salmon feeding behaviour. He saw that in late winter and early spring they mainly subsist off their reserves, spending their energy staking their claims on personal niches in the river. Peter Gray's fish were returned to the river-system not in spring but in autumn. These late arrivals, eleven months old, were super-fit. They were trained to be lean and mean and tough survivors, schooled to combat the perils the river, and later the ocean, would present. Gray's salmon were parr up to four inches long.

He figured out something else, too, a lesson he is now applying in America. Brown trout are fry predators, but when they start thinking about spawning, they stop eating. This happens in autumn when the water temperature falls to about 5 degrees. Peter Gray times his reintroductions to coincide with the attention of predators being diverted by their own reproductive cycle. He used substrate incubators to encourage young fish to emerge from the gravels only when they were ready – that is, when the food supply had heated up. Thereby the fish themselves decided when to start feeding.

Gray hand-fed young fish, straining liquidised livers through tea-strainers as the Victorians had done. Using river-water as a supply, his young fish benefited from the dietary extra of natural small creatures that floated through. They learned to cope with natural turbidity and rainfall flushes. He kept night-lights on to attract midges and flies which fried on the hot fluorescent tubes and fell into the water, training young fish to compete, to gobble natural insects – and cut the feed bill. To increase young fish fitness, every two weeks he cranked up the water-speed in the tanks; sofa-time for these teenagers did not exist.

Gray claims he can guarantee a 95 per cent survival rate for his native immigrants after a year put out in the river. In nature this figure is a fraction, optimally touching ten per cent.

Gray's other prerequisite was a plenitude of young fish: one year the Tyne accommodated up to a million stockies. When other re-stock programmes fail, Gray looks at numbers. He deduces that half-hearted, ill-thought-out programmes, using inadequate quantities of young fish, are in truth designed to fail.

In his programme every release was documented, every fish-batch origin recorded. If there were young fish superfluous to needs he supplied neighbouring rivers where salmon numbers had fallen. He was indefatigable, committed and logical. His working week could top 90 hours.

The Tyne moved from being dead to being pulsatingly alive with salmon. Anglers rejoiced: salmon could be resurrected. Gray was dubbed Father Tyne. Amazingly, but in character, the whole operation had been cheap. There were a lot of pluses lined up here, except we are dealing with the Atlantic salmon, a highly political animal.

Peter Gray's reign as hatchery manager on the Tyne coincided with the ascent of a contrary philosophical approach, even tenet. Parent fish must be from the home river. It was called the theory of genetic integrity. Secondly, habitat management, not fish management, should be the focus. The argument continued that there was no need for the artifice of hatcheries if only the river itself was purified and welcoming for salmon.

Gray believes that if the genetic integrity arguments had attained the unholy grip they have on official policy now, and been forced upon him, the Tyne and the neighbouring rivers he helped to stock would never have recovered so dramatically. As for hatcheries, he showed that intelligent management produces rapid results.

It is not only in fisheries that the habitat versus species argument persists, it is in environmental debate across the board. This view puts mended habitat on a plinth. Give Nature the chance to re-balance. Nurturing the river ecology will nurture the returning fish. Government officials argue this has happened on the Tyne. The official explanation for the Tyne's resuscitation is that cleaning the river and its estuary triggered a revival of the natural run; hatchery work helped to kick-start a recovery that good practice in the watershed would have achieved anyway. Gray's effort, in effect, was a minor sideline.

Peter Gray is a militant for salmon revival. Why move slowly when you can move fast? As purposeful in combating the falsities of his critics as in articulating his vision of hatchery maximisation, he wrote a book about his fight with those he regarded as goggle-visioned scientists from England's Environment Agency.

It is worth taking a step back from this fiery and polarised salmon management argument to consider what is really going on. The anti-hatchery brigade contained respectable scientists and formed a consensus. Where were they coming from? The answer is perhaps in Gray's own discovery. The most sustained and expensive restoration had been tried in eastern America. It failed terribly. Gray has waxed eloquent about the first time he witnessed the reproduction programme in the eastern USA and how horrified he was to find a chronically misguided breeding programme ill-suited to adding a single extra fish to any salmon migration anywhere. So when hatchery-triggered recovery failed in eastern America it was tempting to assume the concept was inherently flawed. That let off the hook 150 years of inept hatchery work. The fact that hatcheries had been used on salmon rivers in Europe for just as long, without salmon disappearing, was an inconvenience.

The background explains why the anti-hatchery lobby is somewhat equivocal when getting to the point. Most fishery scientists concede that there is a place for hatchery assistance with failing runs. They acknowledge that rivers from nearby rivers could play a part in that re-stocking. However, these are caveats to the bedrock principle that hatcheries cripple salmon migrations. The general thrust is that hatcheries release into the sacred wild young fish which have lower disease resistance than wild fish, and compete less well as marine post-smolts than wild fish (research from the Burrishoole fish-station in southern Ireland is adduced on this). The theory extends its critique even into egg-fertilisation: selected pairing-off of eggs with milt by hatchery managers kinks what would be Nature's more random and therefore better solution. Human interference compromises Nature's capacity to repair.

Reading the literature you get an impression of Nature viewed as an ordered and systematic mechanism. It is too neat: those who have watched salmon breeding on the redds view a dynamic, energised scene full of chance occurrences. A simple point: in the wild, pubescent parr squirt milt on female eggs in large numbers, genetically supplanting adult males. Systemised hatchery disciplines cannot reproduce that random effect.

Objective judges can take their view. Is the scientific consensus view right, or has the man with his sleeves rolled up, dabbling night and day with the object of his passion successfully re-vivified a once-great river? Everyone has an opinion, although angler views are unanimous. But this is fact: Peter Gray, rather than subject himself to fashionable government staff self-reappraisals in his old office, is touring Canada and the eastern USA telling eager salmonid nuts how to re-create migratory runs. He is welcomed there as a salmon saviour. Where are his detractors? Sitting, perhaps, in their labs, citing each other's academic work, masticating their theses in the sanctity of private abstractions.

When Gray went to America he was shocked. Here was the country in which hundreds of millions of dollars had been spent

Lower Bergham on the River Tweed, lady angler with ghillie in the boat, early autumn 2011. (© Glyn Satterley)

River Ponoi, Kola Peninsular, Russia, 2012. (© Tarquin Millington-Drake)

Hermione Pilkington, River Helmsdale. She had never caught a salmon before. (© Jonathan Pilkington)

River Sela, Iceland. Lower pools.

Boat-fishing for salmon in Norway. (© Tarquin Millington-Drake)

River Carron at Glencalvie, north Scotland. (© Glyn Satterley)

Fionn Loch. The background mountain is Suilven in Sutherland, north Scotland. (© Glyn Satterley)

Sea pool, North Uist, Outer Hebrides, Scotland. (© Glyn Satterley)

River Helmsdale, north Scotland. Low-profile catchment in open moorland which releases steady water slowly to a winding river. (© Glyn Satterley)

River Helmsdale mid-winter. Beneath the water salmon eggs are slowly developing, young salmon are ticking over, kelts drift to sea, and maybe a fresh salmon has come in. (© Peter Quail)

Female salmon weighing around 14 pounds prior to being released. River Ponoi, 2010. (© Tarquin Millington-Drake)

River Ponoi, Kola Peninsular, Russia. Unusual shot of one fresh salmon and an 'osanka' caught at the same time. The dark fish will have entered freshwater in August/ September, over-wintered without spawning, and summered in the river when the shot was taken. It will spawn soon, over-winter again, and leave the river in the following June about 21 months after arriving. (© Tarquin Millington-Drake)

Salmon ova, some showing yolk-sac. (© Galloway Fisheries Trust, Scotland)

Salmon fry before being planted out, River Helmsdale, north Scotland. (© Peter Quail)

Peter Quail returning home-bred unfed salmon fry in April, River Helmsdale, north Scotland.

Young salmon stages. (© Peter Quail)

A kelt, spawned, returning to sea. When silver they are called 'well-mended'. (© Peter Quail)

River Tweed Opening Day. This is a 20-pound 'baggot' or fish which has never spawned. (© Glyn Satterley)

Stomach contents of a salmon caught at sea. (© The Atlantic Salmon Trust)

Mark Birkbeck casting on the River Findhorn. (© Glyn Satterley)

Otter, salmon capture in an Aberdeenshire river, Scotland. (© Stefan Muller)

The ecstasy of the angler. David Goodman, Restigouche River, New Brunswick side.

Big salmon caught by Nick Edmonstone in August 2012 on the River Teith, Scotland, and held by a younger family member.

Haaf-netting on the Solway, south-west Scotland. He caught a salmon ten minutes later. When the tide turns the netsman faces the other way. (© Andrew Graham-Stewart)

From one tide and a single bag-net, north Scotland. One fifth of this haul was damaged and unsaleable; the proportion could rise to four out of five. Damaged fish were never recorded, dropping into a statistical void. (© Andrew Graham-Stewart)

Hauling a sweep-net at the mouth of the River Thurso, north Scotland, a station now closed. (© Andrew Graham-Stewart)

New Brunswick's Bay of Fundy, from Tunaville to Deer Island, showing the density of cages and why Canadians call it a 'feedlot' system, taken in 2009. (© Tim Foulkes)

Late-season cock salmon, River Ponoi, Russia. (© Tarquin Millington-Drake)

Salmon cages in Loch Eriboll, Sutherland. (© Bruce Sandison)

Stake nets in Lunan Bay, south of Montrose, Scotland, still operating in 2013. (© Andrew Graham-Stewart)

Informal burial-pit on Orkney for diseased farm salmon, shot clandestinely.

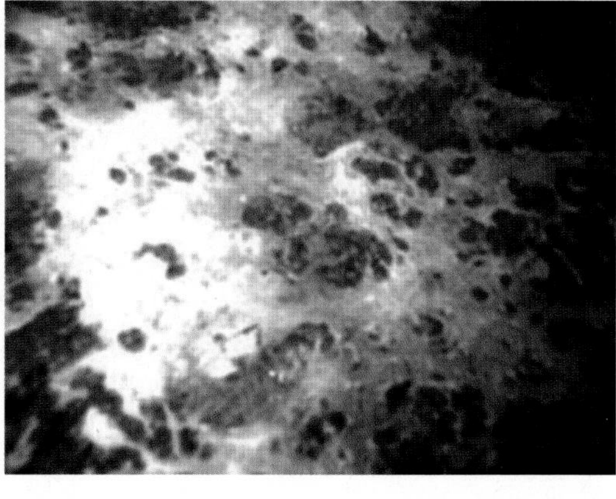

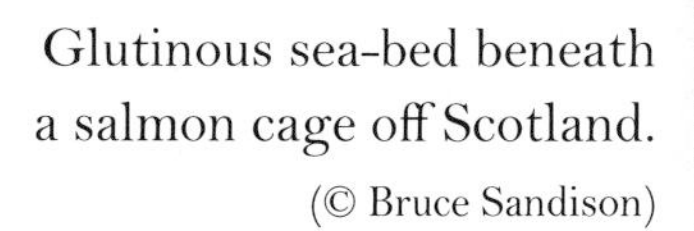

Glutinous sea-bed beneath a salmon cage off Scotland. (© Bruce Sandison)

River Ponoi, Kola Peninsular, Russia. (© Tarquin Millington-Drake)

on salmon restoration – which had failed. He took a deep breath and a long look.

The parr being produced were low grade and flabby, three times as fat as survival demanded. They were cosseted not challenged. The parents were pot-bellied grotesqueries. Broodstock were the length of six-pound grilse but weighed fifteen pounds. Ensconced in the protective cocoon of a luxury hatchery they had never seen real river water, had never been exposed to natural light, had never seen natural food or the creatures to whom they themselves are food. Water-sources were boreholes, usually too warm and with steady temperatures, rather than river-water fluctuating all the time according to the weather. Nearly every hatchery had sluggish water-flows. Water was sterilised, rather than rich in Nature's fluctuating complexities.

The broodstock parents were from hatcheries too: conditioning to the easy life had been inured in them for several generations. They were all genetically related and from the same natal river. Ignoring the amazing adaptability of salmon, managers picked fish from a narrow gene-pool which Nature would have prised open and refreshed by genetic straying.

The fish emerging from this cerebrally determined arena were laboratory weirdos. Nothing was surviving when released. Peter Gray's concept of tough, fit-for-purpose parr on a war-footing for survival was unknown. The pampered pets were being tipped back into cleaned-up rivers fizzing with delighted predators.

It seems extraordinary yet is a fact: America lost more of her native salmon than anywhere else, has spent more money over a longer time to restore them, and has failed more dismally. Americans have spent 150 years persisting with hatchery techniques which in Gray's view were doomed. Gray did not tear up the manual on hatchery practice: it had not even been written.

The Tyne is much-discussed, its saviour is much-disputed, but Peter Gray is talked of and his critics are unknown.

The original Tyne stock was hanging by only a thread. In 1978 Peter Gray lacked enough parent stock from the Tyne to achieve what he wanted in reasonable time. So at the start he supplemented 55,000 Tyne salmon eggs with 350,000 other ova from east and west Scotland. This genetic omelette, he says, laid the foundations of recovery. It would have been interesting had the science then been around to have taken DNA from the parent fish to see what proportion of the native Tyne eggs persisted in the genetic make-up of the established runs later. To the limited extent to which he tested migratory return success using micro-tags, Gray discovered one thing: the only total survival failures derived from eggs he obtained, just once, from a salmon farm.

To lay hands on his hallowed 'Tyne' fish, Gray struck a typically pragmatic deal. Fish in the river were few, but in the Northumbrian drift-nets there were many. Some may have been due to run the Tyne, most were not. Gray's parent 'Tyne' fish were caught by offshore netsmen straight out of the saltwater. Daring as ever, Peter Gray whizzed them ashore in tanks of salt-water, whizzed them onwards 80 miles inland to the hatchery, and there acclimatised them stage by stage to water with progressively less salt in it. To re-build runs of salmon which would command respect, all the fish had to be over 14 pounds.

Hatchery science needs revisiting and clearing of clap-trap and bad practice. It has become a festering backwater of boffinish specialisation remarkable for its repeat failures. Gray at one point asks rhetorically why it is necessary to have a team of genetic specialists in each American hatchery. Cleansing the habitat is an essential component of the solution, but not the only one. There are occasions when stimulating a faster recovery is justifiable and advisable. On the north-eastern English river the Mersey, from which salmon were extirpated by industry long ago, the silver leaper has materialised again. This has happened entirely naturally. Genetic analysis shows that the origins of the salmon are from 37 different rivers. The genetic integrity brigade squirms if queried on this matter. On the subject of how cross-stocking occurred on a wide scale in the past, and was considered routine across hundreds of rivers without evident collapse and tragedy, again they become discomfited.

Genetic straying, then, can replace and substitute for the old stock. In evolutionary terms, that makes sense. A calamity on one river can be rectified by the neighbour, over time. It seems that hatcheries should aim for parent stocks which are similar, approximately. It is not a pure science. To what extent the introduced stocks have to be compatible with the ones they are replacing, and in what special respects, is not yet understood. Somehow Nature's random-ness has to be part of the plan.

Gray's last theme is quasi-political. He believes anglers and local conservationists should run salmon restoration, not distant bureaucrats freighted down with corporate orthodoxies. It is possible to praise America for the lavish funding spent on attempted salmon restoration. An alternative view would be that too many dollars elevated the programme into the realm of the mystical: rough-and-ready approaches might have worked better.

A recitation of the Tyne shows a variety of things. Firstly, a river on the brink was spectacularly recovered. It was recovered using practices at variance with the theories in vogue. The recovery, instead of being welcomed by all, became a battlefield of contending ideologies. Not all was negative: Peter Gray's hatchery theories are now being embraced enthusiastically in North America. If they work, the Atlantic salmon will be fortified over a vital chunk of its natural range.

Last, what does it all tell us about the fish, focus of our thoughts? Perhaps this. If the salmon is treated as a domestic animal it responds badly. To rear salmon for the wild means understanding their biology; Gray even studied their predators and attempted to circumvent them. The salmon is a creature about which the more you know, the more curious you become to fill the other knowledge gaps. The Tyne recovery is a stimulating tale on several levels.

To rekindle a salmon run where there is no natural stock is highly problematic. British salmon managers realised this a while ago, yet up until about 25 years ago anglers had killed most of what they caught. Big salmon were carted home from Scottish fishing trips for the freezer. Slabs of frozen silver in the car-boot were the fisherman's trophies. Some anglers were known to sell their catch and thereby pay the fishing rent. In fact that practice enabled some of the post-war generation to spend their lives on rivers, despite their relative paucity of financial means. There was always a market for salmon when fresh.

Although the more contemporary trend towards catch and release across the board sometimes adopts a holier-than-thou missionary tone, there is nothing new about it. The return of stale fish was made mandatory in law halfway through the nineteenth century. Anglers fishing after midsummer were anyway seeking the few late, fresh fish. It was clear that the salmon nearly always survived being swung about at the end of fishing-line, except occasionally in hot weather and low water when they became de-oxygenated. Why kill a fish that was inedible?

However, the right button was pushed only when the sale of rod-caught salmon was banned in 2003. The ban removed from the moral equation any possibility that anglers were there to make money. Individual rivers attempted to persuade their tenant anglers to put back certain fish at certain times, but the rod-caught fish ban was applied as national law. Hotels and restaurants with salmon in the freezer had to show that they were bought from licensed net stations if asked by the police.

Generally speaking, it is remarkable that the new law bedded down so quietly. It was a sign of the times. Salmon were cherished, and to be protected from brutish commercial exploitation by sportsmen purporting to be angling for the joy of sport alone.

Today, catch and release is mandatory all over the USA, as would be expected after the salmon bruising that country has had, and it is general practice in Canada, with a few smaller fish being allowed for eating by the angler. In Russia fish are released, science and research being high on the list of obligations attending angling. Iceland's release policy is less severe, and obviously on rivers where salmon are 'ranched' or bred in hatcheries for release for sport, virtually everything is killed. Norwegian law faces a dyed-in-the-wool tendency to kill and eat whatever is caught. Nowhere, though, are rod-caught salmon available in a public market.

A century ago American president Theodore Roosevelt realised that the sale of privately killed game was lethal to conservation, and he outlawed it; salmon policy has now caught up.

Migratory fish have acted as canaries in the mine and sometimes governments have acted wisely to protect freshwaters. One example was the concerted action agreed to combat 'acid rain'. This was the deposition which came from rainfall in the 1960s and 70s and was particularly felt in Scandinavia. Swedish lakes recorded plummeting pH levels, or increased acid-readings, and fish populations died off, leaving large lakes sterile. Sweden reported 20,000 damaged lakes, being especially vulnerable because of their shallowness and low counts of calcium and magnesium.

Forest dieback was also recorded elsewhere, in particular in Switzerland and Germany, and traced to the same source.

The trouble came from nitrates and sulphates pumped into the air by coal-burning power stations belching unfiltered fumes. They were mostly located in eastern Europe, and also what was then the USSR, from the use of low-grade, high-sulphur coal. High-altitude pollution drifted westwards and landed on Scandinavia at a parallel latitude. Eighty per cent of Norway's air pollution originated abroad. Germany, umbilically attached to its forests as a national mythic symbol and galvanised by its powerful green lobby, was the first to act to redress this in 1983.

Scrubbers filtering emissions were installed in the power stations whose states had signed up to cleaner air. The result was swift. Air pollution of this type reduced. What at one time had been a free gift from above for farmers wanting nitrates and sulphates on their land as soil enrichers, ceased falling from the sky. Fish populations recovered and tree health responded. Cooperation across state borders had worked to the benefit of all.

The part of British salmon especially affected by acid rain was Galloway in south-west Scotland. The rivers here are different in character from any other salmon waters. They are winding pastoral conveyor-belts of dark water nosing through verdant farm fields riding bumpy hills. Pools are hidden by overhanging trees. Roads are narrow and no planes fly over. White farmhouses dot the landscape, cows contentedly graze in the soft moist air, and there is a feeling of timelessness. I once saw a noticeboard for a new hostelry with the legend 'Just opened' on the top and, underneath, the steadying reminder: 'Now closed down'. Salmon, equally indifferent to time, chug in from the shallow muddy estuary of the multi-channelled west coast Solway as part of a rich, complex and fertile environment.

Galloway salmon had already taken a hit from conifer forest-planting in the hills. Acid deposition, as it was called, amplified the problem, because evergreen needles trapped the drifting particles laden with sulphates and nitrates and soils were rendered more acid by runoff from the needle-littered forest floors. Acidity levels were so high that when it rained hard the water in so-called 'acidic flushes' actually suffocated adult fish with deadly aluminium. Young fish writhed in lethal water acids. Salmon eggs shrivelled in sour pools.

The effect of acidified upper catchments was not dissimilar in salmon terms to erecting barriers at the point the forestry started. From a salmon point of view, any higher up beyond the necklace of needles was a no-man's land, totally sterile. What had been the spawning zones for spring salmon were planted with trees right to the water edge. Streams became black dribbles, inky and sluggish, shunting through dark tunnels threading between the silent conifer blanket, a gothic location mired in stygian gloom.

Upper catchments are where British spring-run salmon breed. Early fish run higher up the rivers. So when Galloway's granite-skinned uplands were planted with trees the early fish were lethally hurt. Their runs faded and faded. Lower down the watershed towards the sea farmland was left intact, and the buffering capacity of richer soils to reduce acid kept the rivers hospitable for migratory fish. All this was starkly evident from electrofishing: high up nothing, lower down healthy levels of salmon fry and parr. But the productive area of rivers was cut in half.

International action to combat power-station emissions was relatively fast. Scrubbers were fitted and the noxious chemicals removed at source. Any changes to British forestry practices to help mitigate the effects for salmon and sea trout, however, moved at another speed. Government fought an extraordinary and unseemly rearguard action to avoid rectifying its disastrous policies.

Fighting every inch of the way to avoid blame, officials scavenged for scapegoats far and wide. Change to climate was unconvincingly cited. To justify dense formations of conifers planted across entire landscapes, the government's Forestry Commission then invented a measurement model which would dictate and vindicate planting policy. It was called the 'critical load' test. This was a figure for water-quality chemistry meant to identify whether soils were too acid or not.

Such a figure should have shown that Galloway's monoculture montane forest-planting was lethal to fish in hills. But the model was devilishly devised with two let-out features. The assessments were predictive: they anticipated improvements over time as forests were established, traumatised soils recovered, and in due course smaller proportions of the hills were planted with conifers in the next generation of trees. The theories gesticulated towards a faraway never-never land, and could thereby make more promises when delivery failed. Fish-lovers had to wait, and then wait some more.

The second escape route was that critical load assessments did not look at biological features. The model was chemistry-based. Fish continued to die off whilst critical load's integrity remained unaffected. All was fine, but the fish were dead. The model was designed to reinforce the status quo. Critical load was a piece of trickery. Galloway salmon recovery was subjected to the worst form of official foot-dragging – what has been termed 'paralysis by analysis'.

The Galloway forests are now well into the second rotation. Uninterrupted landscape-scale conifer forestry has long ago been dropped, showing the defensive nature of the critical load farrago. But widespread recovery for fish is not happening, only the first signs of re-awakening, very slowly, in a few places. To say the government is slow-pedalling over producing new guidelines implies some form of movement: in fact for year after year no motion is discernible.

At one point fishery boards trying to skewer the right culprit for acidification's horrifying levels put their own water quality monitoring equipment in the feeder-streams. This gear recorded pH or acidity. When the first results were published they were disbelieved. Sceptical, the authorities plonked their equipment right alongside. Amazingly, the results were the same.

At that point rejection by the government of the independent fisheries people's claim about acidity toned down. It has been a very hard battle for salmon indeed. At the time of writing the vital figures in revised guidelines about how much of the hills can be replanted with conifers awaits final publication. There is even low-key background diversionary burbling about recovery from acidification, a disturbing falsification. Electro-fishing for migratory salmon and sea trout in the worst-affected rivers still yields no fish at all across wide areas. The streams are often dead. Recovery is no closer, an aspiration. Only a few Galloway waters show the first stirrings of reviving life.

Galloway salmon have been sacrificed to forestry and wood-processing employment arguments. Not for the first time salmon have been an afterthought in a rural policy where forest use is pre-eminent in national planning. What makes the system look somewhere between lightweight and reckless is that final judgements on whether planting should be allowed and with what species is up to the Commission itself. The adjudicator has a major vested interest, and the adjudicator in question has not covered itself in glory over the last 50 years in its awareness and actions to protect salmon. Or water. The fishing writer Bernard Venables contributed this curiously Buddhist remark: 'The first symptom of the health of a society is the quality of the water. When fishermen get uneasy about the quality of the water, it's a symptom that society at large cannot ignore. Life starts and ends with water. If the condition of our water is not right, then the condition of society is not right either.'

With enormous lethargy, however, times are changing. Change is slow enough to ensure that individual and institutional reputations remain untarnished, but the replant in the upper watersheds will be closer to half conifers only. The methods of planting with frothing drains running down hills hurtling sediment onto the sensitive redds have been changed to less intrusive herring-bone ploughing at lower depths, and sometimes to mounding for each tree which reduces impacts of water-distribution in the landscape. Species mix is recognised as important, and an unplanted safety strip acting as a sump, edging up the hills from burns and feeder-streams, is part of the forest plan. The width of this safety-strip is a matter of hot debate, forestry interests straining with unreconstructed ferocity to get as near watercourses as possible; but a buffer zone is at least accepted as beneficial per se. Pine needle tunnels are a thing of the past; when forests are cut new practices leave brash to rot down on the forest floor, retaining more water for river flows.

Admitting to acidification may be a bridge too far, but in the lifetime of a river there is room for new evolution. Galloway's rivers, other things being equal, may one day again have salmon in the top of the watersheds. It will have been a long pilgrimage home.

All along, the struggle to protect salmon has been fought most truthfully by one constituency, the anglers. Fishermen have been salmon's true defenders. Only a shallow cynic would claim that this is to allow more salmon for them to catch: the reason is that salmon have a hold on angler imaginations. To save this species rod anglers have made extraordinary efforts and spent time and money.

What is it about rod angling for salmon that excites that commitment? I myself am a member of the angling brotherhood. I should know. But you ask any group of anglers why they do what they do, and why they spend so much money on this (for much of the time) event-free sport, and they give differing answers. Shelves of tomes have been written on the subject and it has engaged some of the finest literary and judicial minds. At a loss for anything better, I go for the American writer W. D. Wetherell's take on it: 'Fly fishing, after all, is an attempt to make connection with the life of a river.'

One of the teasers lurking in angler minds is that salmon do not eat in freshwater. They are not designed to: when they leave the sea their intestines shrink. There is no reason on earth for them to rise from their comfortable stations to a fly swinging past and try to drown it. The fly resembles nothing they ever ate; it is a fanciful human contrivance. When you fly a kite eagles or seagulls do not materialise to attack it. There is as much connection in logic to salmon and salmon fishing flies as that.

It is easy to see why salmon do not eat in freshwater. With their body-mass they would soon clear rivers of any forms of life. There would be nothing left for their miniature progeny and cousins still growing in the nursery. Salmon's abstention from food in rivers is to succour their own young.

There is one reason I fish that I can grapple with. I cast the fly into the water, dark or sparkling, and I watch it. A train of thought begins. I often think of what the ghillie I know best sometimes says: it looks so good I could take it myself. Then, nothing happens. I repeat the action. Maybe nothing happens for hours as I perform the same seemingly pointless motions. Tedium tiptoes forward. Then another memory enters. Years ago on the River Deveron in north-eastern Scotland a great fly-angler named Andrew Tennant was casting into a slow, almost circular pool with a quickening slick at the tail. On a little cliff above this pool, in dense foliage, is a platform and from it you can see into the pool's shallowing tail. On this day there was a stack of salmon gently finning there, and a gathering of people on the platform. As he lengthened line at each cast the angler's fly got closer. Finally the front fish swished its tail and rose up on the current and inspected the fly. Lethargically, it sank back to its position again. Then another fish stirred from the shoal and it too nonchalantly inspected the fly, then another fish and another. The fish appeared to regard it with distaste. By the time the angler's line was past these fish many had moved to the fly. None, though, had opened their mouths. From above, hidden in the foliage, we could see everything. The point of the exercise was that the angler, as Andrew Tennant well knew, would see nothing at all. The pool from his perspective would seem empty. No ripple, no water-surface bulge, no twitch on the skin of the water. The drama was concealed from its initiator.

So when you go on lashing line across water and nothing is happening, you think of those things. Every angler spends his stillness moments contemplating just that possibility: how many fish saw that fly? It is a psychological angler fact that few fishermen resort to the conclusion that they have been casting over empty water. Salmon anglers have a thinly buried streak of optimism. Call it faith in the fish, if you will.

Let us look at another aspect. What makes a successful salmon angler? I know, I think, some attributes. It is often said you need patience. The truth is the opposite. The best anglers, in my view, are people in a hurry. They are focused. Waiting is not in their nature and they are set on not doing too much of it. Another feature is the ability to concentrate. Hemingway has described how rifle shooters fine their attention down to a tiny, still point before pulling the trigger; anglers perch on this point. Some subconsciously bend over their rods, tense as herons ... until a salmon takes.

It can happen, but it is seldom true that someone fundamentally indifferent to whether he catches salmon or not is a successful angler steadily over a period. Unless his ghillie has the concentration and the angler is merely the instrument of the ghillie's intensity; that can be the salmon's undoing too.

One of the most successful fishermen I know told me that he senses when the salmon is going to come on. This individual on any water routinely catches more of its occupants than others assaying the same. Certainly he casts well and covers the water effectively, but there is also something extra. It sounds a bit spooky to say it is an attitude of mind, but that comes in too. Sir Edward Grey, in his 1899 book, *Fly Fishing*, is one of many who have deliberated over the matter; he remarks on 'some magnetic influence in the angler's confidence'. Then, like all of us, he expatiates too on the huge strokes of luck which attend anglers from time to time, the almost indecent chunks of luck which on occasions favour, dare one say, the least deserving anglers.

I was in a fishing-camp one time in Labrador. To get there we had thudded over the granite rock-scape by helicopter, looking out at miles and miles of featureless stone terrain. It was a great wilderness fishing-camp situated opposite jumbled boulders, mesmerising cauldron-like pools, with a gushing wild river disappearing round a bend to the sea not far away.

In the party was a rare old-timer. He had fished this river many times and he expatiated on its glories the night we arrived. He showed us his flies tied on tempered steel hooks which he had fashioned specially for his fishing week there. His steels were ribbed, not round. These hooks, he promised, with a steely look, would not bend when the big fellas came on.

We began our week, and each evening pairs of anglers from different places in the river-system returned to camp with tales of their successes and losses, or intermissions between dramas. The old fellow, though, had nothing to report. He was locked in one of those sessions which affect us all at some time in our fishing life. The salmon pass us by. For whatever reason, they ignore every artifice we present for their delectation.

On the other side of the assembly was a lady from my own country. She had never fished before – which you would not have deduced, because she knew everything about the business. On the first day she caught a couple of salmon and thereafter, with her wily ghillie, she steadily piled up a creditable fishing-log for the week. As she climbed unassailably into the position of 'top rod' she grew louder, declaiming that she couldn't understand what all the fuss was about, all you had to do was throw in the flies any old how and the silly fish obligingly swallowed them. The old veteran grew more silent. Eventually we lost the benefit of his stories and his wisdom altogether as he withdrew into a closed bubble of trappist misery.

Everyone present wanted him to come in one evening with his 'boots full', as the saying goes, and as the week closed we knew it was not to be. He would 'blank'. We felt terribly for him, and all the worse when the brash lady asked him in front of us all what was wrong. It was a painful time and it is painful to recall it. The salmon on this occasion just snubbed their noses at their committed adversary.

Salmon tales have never-ending human surprises.

A friend of my son's, who had never caught a salmon, was fishing on my home river one day and I was driving back to meet everyone for lunch in the fishing-hut. As we turned the car down the road towards the pool I remarked to my wife that he was about to hook a fish. As I said it, he did. The fishing-week had not produced many salmon, but something about this fellow's approach to the angling made a salmon catch a fact merely awaiting its physical accomplishment. It was unavoidable.

There are physical factors. One is sight. The best ghillie I ever knew has phenomenal eyesight. It is as if he sees under the water. Indeed, in late middle age doctors were confused by his eyes which were somehow burnt-out in an odd way. They attributed the condition to spending a lifetime scrutinising sparkly water. The water-penetrative X-ray eyes were commented on by his client anglers a thousand times. He spots some movement in the water which is a fish looking at the fly. The angler is urged to take a step back and cast again. As he covers the salmon, it takes. The sequence is uncanny. Part of the ghillie's skill is knowing exactly where in this Highland river to expect the fish, but the other is in knowing what the creature is doing under cover of water. There are phrases like 'in tune with' and 'thinks like a fish', but they are clumsy. That is because no phrase really gets a handle on the mysterious connection between some individuals and the fish which feature big in their lives.

Anglers often say that the take, the sudden linkage with a living, strong, vibrant animal in its own element is what marks the card. They live for that kick of resistance, of protest. Why then do we mind so much when the fish gets off? We do. The suddenly slack tackle is like a telephone-line hanging on its cord in the call-box. We feel bereft. The mind floods with a weird sort of cosmic sorrow.

If you intellectualise it, to fish is to change mental focus completely. Once in Argyll in western Scotland on a family holiday, for a month I clambered every day up a steep escarpment behind our house with a trout-rod and fished a silent dark loch nestled between a ring of low rock-faces. I never saw a fish at all.

I got no touch, no signal, I saw no sign of life. Yet to have stopped going never occurred to me. Whether that makes me a fisherman I have no idea; some would say it makes me something rather less impressive!

If I rake about to explain my own fascination there is one other factor. I know this because it is absent when I am fishing for other fish. I visualise the salmon beneath the running water, not only as a presence of the species but as an individual. I see that strong body, that aircraft-shaped sleekness. When I catch a salmon and have it by hand its scales shimmer and reflect the light. There is something about the fish itself that soothes me. I have never had any feeling other than wonderment when I have brought a salmon to the river edge. In greater or lesser degree I unfailingly feel an astonishment that the water has yielded such a creature. Now with the practice of catch and release and the general culture of nurturing the species I have altered in my attitude again. I am worried that the salmon is being hurt, shedding scales on the water-edge stones, or lacking enough oxygen.

One elementary thing, sometimes forgotten, is that many anglers want to catch a fish to eat. Your own catch tastes better, like vegetables grown in the soil by your house. Today's saloon-bar bien-pensants may take lofty attitudes about the brutishness of killing the fish you catch: the desire to eat your fish is as natural and uncomplicated and understandable as any explanation of what it is to fish. It completes a circle, bringing the human back to his roots as a hunter. Resource management should be pragmatic or it excites opposition also tending to the extreme. If the salmon population is adequate and stable there should be no queasiness about anglers maintaining that link and eating the occasional fish they catch. It can be vastly satisfying. If they were prohibited from killing fish on all occasions no one would know what that celebrated flavour was anymore. That in turn could foment its own sort of trouble.

This flavour explains part of the salmon's mighty grip on us. And in the angler the salmon has won a great defender. It is generally true that angler pressure and passion are the forces which have bent politicians to act to protect salmon. Private money financed the net buy-outs and leases, private money paid for court cases for salmon survival, often it has been private money that has financed hatcheries and rearing programmes and keeping rivers in good health to accommodate their most glamorous occupant. Some dinners staged by NASF, designed to muster donations from carefully selected affluent people, have yielded hundreds of thousands of pounds, all in a matter of a few hours. This money has mostly come from people with a fishing rod in the cupboard.

When American and British salmon anglers first went to the Kola Peninsular in northern Russia, east of Murmansk, some thirty years ago, the experience had a pioneering quality. My first flight over the Russian tundra was in a helicopter previously on service in Afghanistan and ventilated with bullet holes. The anglers slumped on the floor on their luggage; seating there was none. One Russian accompanied us. He stood up the whole flight, and despite the racket of whirring rotors over our heads maintained an intoxicated perambulation of the chopper floor, meantime declaiming in Russian and throwing his arms wide and gesticulating outside as if to some distant deity. What he was getting at was clear: this is my motherland. Regard its beauty.

Without warning we descended into the featureless expanse of scrub and rocky ridges onto a concrete pad in the middle of nowhere. There were no houses or roads and there had been no sign of human presence for nearly an hour's flying time. But the spirited Russian disembarked and strode off into the scrubby wastes. It was an inexplicable performance, in some sense of poetic clarity. There was this feature of salmon fishing in Russia, something certainly alien and perhaps touching on the mystical, that grabbed one's attention.

The rivers are magnificent. Some are wide and slow and others are torrents crashing from ledges and out-of-sight ravines. It is completely wild country. Some of the boulders in the rivers are gigantic and while fishing the pools coiling below, you perch precariously behind the buffer of your boulder, lengthening line. To drown yourself whilst fishing salmon on the northern Russian rivers is no hard trick. During winter it is incredibly cold and there is the phenomenon of some salmon spending a winter under the ice in freshwater and spawning the next autumn; in the protracted interval they have not fed. All salmon growth stages are slower in the Arctic. The lakes on the granite shield from which the rivers take their source-waters are alive with huge fluttering insects. I caught my largest-ever brown trout in one of these still headwater lakes where trout were slurping down buzzing creatures the size of small birds. These also nourish the young salmon. The rivers then start an often tumultuous journey to the sea.

For a long time the Kola salmon have been netted in stations along the coast. On the north these face the Barents Sea and on the south Kola the White Sea. When Americans discovered these great fly rivers and realised that they contained some of the world's highest-octane Atlantic salmon, it dawned on them that they had stumbled on a new salmon destination for fishermen, and they knew it might be the best salmon fishing destination of all. It was a discovery when all novel salmon fishing zones had been assumed to have ended, like a re-run of the early twentieth-century British finding Norway. The world seemed to have the Atlantic salmon-fishing domain complete and mapped and here was a new world, an attainable destination which until then had been a military zone with all outsiders forbidden entry.

In constructing fishing-camps international entrepreneurs were faced by logistical nightmares. Everything had to be helicoptered in. There were no roads and no railway. The season for practical operation was just a few months. Camp-building required joiners and plumbers, electricians and fitters on-site, working through the long mosquito-laden hours of daylight in Arctic summers. In the early days camps were only one remove from living outside. My first cabin there was designed with wooden poles at knee level, then canvas above. One friend of mine arrived on a river to find no camp at all. When I saw him a week later, in Murmansk airport, he was almost unrecognisable, a wild, fugitive, matted-hair figure swollen with insect bites and jabbering unintelligibly about huge fish. That some of the fanciest fishing-camps have been built in the Russian tundra is a testament to great creativity, persistence and commitment by a rare bunch of individuals. The great fish in the river were their stimulus and the source of their vibrancy, and the faith that they would return was implicit.

It has done something more than add packed pages to the diaries and record books of anglers. It has forged a communication link with the Russians. It has established itself in the culture of that part of this enormous and mystifying, even bewitching country. The Russian fishing guides – many of whom, when I was there, were off-duty scientists earning better money in tips from visiting anglers than they ever could in their cash-strapped state laboratories – were knowledgeable, enthusiastic and skilled. It was a pleasure being with them. Somehow in that remote appendage to the world's biggest landmass we developed a good mutual understanding.

As a primary fact it made the Russians understand that their familiar salmon had a greater relevance outside Russia than they could ever have suspected. Here was a common fish that was revered by affluent and important visitors. The fish they had taken for granted was hallowed in other parts of the world. Although at one point in recent time it looked as though the salmon resource would become, as had happened so often before in different places, a political football, this seems less likely now. The salmon on the Kola is a way of accumulating foreign currency and attracting visitors from all over. The salmon suddenly is more than food on a rather bare plate. Science-minded anyway, the Russians now have muscular conservation and research policies for their Atlantic salmon. And they have taken up fly-angling like British Edwardians.

The Russians were lucky; their grand salmon had just not been noticed, but for another northern-hemisphere location the luck came in a different form – volcanic magma.

If it seems at first glance puzzling why hot rocks under the Earth's mantle could be to the advantage of salmon, well, maybe it is. But what occurred in northern Iceland about 25 years ago has borne amazing fruit. And when you drill down on the reason behind Iceland's success in pumping life into otherwise un-fecund rivers choked with volcanic sand, one of the main reasons why installing salmon runs is physically possible is that in the hatcheries needed to grow the salmon, the right water temperatures are maintained by mixing hot and cold.

Iceland is a cold place and a salmon hatchery, at this latitude, normally, would have to tackle water solidifying instantly to ice. But in this uneasily volcanic landmass, where not long ago an eruption from the Earth's core belching lava into the surrounding ocean produced an entirely new outlying island, heat is never far away. Go down and there it is, thermal heat hissing from underneath. Therefore the problem of surface chill at the hatchery on Iceland's far north Ranga River, located at around latitude 66, is solved by drawing warmer water from underground, and mixing it with the cold water already there.

For one unique feature of Iceland is both very cold water and very hot water. I have waded into the hot springs near Reykjavik to restore lost bodily functions with outside air temperatures very much the wrong side of comfortable. Icelandic homes are heated by geo-thermal energy, and so are their far north hatcheries. There is no need to have hatcheries in the south, dodging the climate; they can be on-site.

Around 25 years ago innovative Icelanders tried putting salmon parr into ponds and lakes close to Icelandic rivers in the north. They fed them there. These hatchery fish, modified over evolutionary time for rapid weight-gain in a place where summers are short, grew at almost unbelievable rates. Then the ponds were opened so that the water and the fish debouched into the rivers. The rivers may have been bedded with volcanic sand which, from a fish point of view, is a sterile bottom, but not many insects are needed to sustain smoltified young salmon seeking the sea. Also, the rivers were not long. The fishing length of the Ranga, both the east and west branches, is only 19 miles. With a decent current smolts will swim that in a few days.

On the Ranga system salmon come back either as grilse after one year in the sea or as two-sea winter salmon. They enter rivers from late June and continue through August. East and West Ranga differ in that the east branch is coloured a little green, being glacial in origin; the west branch has clear water bubbling from underground. Temperatures are low: 4 degrees rising to 12 degrees in sunny summer weather.

What do these salmon do when they arrive in a river where they cannot breed? They meet anglers. International travellers that they are – although the exact places they winter and put on weight are unknown – the Ranga salmon rendezvous with other international travellers. For the Icelandic salmon fishery is a visitor business. The majority of the 10,000 annual anglers come from the UK, after that from Spain and France, and also from the USA. Austrian, Swiss and German anglers complete the throng.

They are there for the huge catches. Some years, despite the short season, the west Ranga alone has a catch figure of 15,000 fish. Usually, though, between 5,000 and 7,000 are caught in each branch. The fish are generally four to six pounds in weight, although in some seasons a third of them go to ten or eleven pounds.

The Ranga is a creation of fishery managers for sporting use. The icy water would otherwise run empty, barring its char and occasional brown trout. Broodstock for the hatchery is taken from different rivers all over this volcanic land. The salmon rivers are relatively uniform in nature; selecting stock from one particular river or type of river has been unnecessary. Usually up to 300 female salmon are netted, crossed with cock fish also netted, and the return rate into rivers following the sea journey is between two-and-a-half and one per cent.

Obviously this ingenious practice, using rivers that are near-sterile (just a few salmon do find places to spawn), represents a great stimulus in a region of Iceland that otherwise would endure protracted inactivity. There are over thirty guides on the Ranga and each fishing party functions from a smart and serviced fishing lodge. The cost of rearing and feeding smolts bars Ranga owners from making much money from their ingenuity, but they have the satisfaction of having created a significant tourist attraction in a landscape of sterile volcanic lava.

There is one regard, perhaps, in which the Ranga system differs from that of some other Icelandic rivers. There is no need to re-profile pools. Fishing in Iceland, I was at first mystified by the presence of bulldozers parked close to the rivers. Guides told me they were for reshaping rivers after winter ice damage. The rock-braced Ranga maintains its pools more reliably.

Icelandic salmon fishing is unlike any other. The usually clear water means anglers have to stand well back in case they are seen, and present flies with skill and accuracy. You peep into the pool bent low like a hunter. Icelandics are beautiful fighting fish and very strong for their size. Up on the Ranga there is one other angler-stimulant. The volcano in the back country last blew ten years ago. Another blow is said to be on the way. You could be playing the salmon of your dreams as lava waves rolled down, hissing, from the hills behind. It adds that little bit of frisson.

Modern salmon angling is a sport that does not jeopardise the species it targets. Indeed, across Atlantic salmon range angling protects and encourages that fish. The commitment anglers have shown towards salmon has no obvious parallel in any other species. The protection of whales has raised huge sums of money, sure, but those who feel deeply for whales never encounter the object of their passion as salmon anglers do, on the end of a taut and quivering line, finally handling it. It is a more abstract relationship, even than whale-watching in the early days when small inflatables were allowed close enough to the great mammals to see individual features clearly.

If the salmon lifestyle spanning fresh and saltwater has posed sometimes insuperable problems for its survival, the same lifestyle has aroused in its human protectors enormous ingenuity and commitment. There exists an un-straightforward relationship which is complex and strange. An elderly guide I knew in eastern Canada, bred in the river's backwoods, used a phrase that has stuck with me because I am unable to understand it; yet it holds a numinous meaning. He used to say, testing the fly-knot, 'Let's see if that'll keep them honest'. It was only when he repeated it several times that I paid attention. If you analyse that concept you end up with the salmon as a form of river-spirit, maybe unpredictable and unfathomable, but somehow accessible to human reason. The chrome fish transcends conventional human interactive norms. For that and other reasons salmon restoration is a significant history in itself.

The Pressure

The same factor has made salmon runs flinch from the start – call it the pressure of human development.

Maybe in some parts of the Earth the pressure of development is actually slackening, despite growing numbers of humans. There are sorts of land and land areas which the present time has no particular use for. An example might be the hill country in Spain, from which the livestock farmers have departed and where now only the old or the alternative lifestyle folk play out their lives. There are places in Europe from which human population is in retreat, for a variety of reasons. Where I live in Scotland many of the glens are empty where once there were shepherds. Some deer stalking occurs; little else.

But seven-tenths of the Earth is covered not by land but by water. Probably the pressure on the watery element is greater universally. There may be areas that were once fished which are now left alone, but that is because the fish are no longer there. The oceans in general are at the cutting edge of development. The deeps will soon be mined for ore, energy and minerals; the surface already accommodates increasing traffic.

The zones salmon occupy in the northern hemisphere are not less used, they are harder used. Some of this development presents threats. Whilst in the modern time nothing equates in lethality to a barrage barring access to breeding, as widescale damming once did in Europe and America, or to relentless river-mouth netting removing the breeders, there are uses of water which may be equally inimical to salmon in the longer term.

European leaders are pledged to reduce fossil fuel emissions. For Britain this instruction translates into power companies being obligated to source more energy from what are called 'renewables', or sources of energy that do not die when burnt but are plugged in to earthly respirations which repeat themselves.

The most proven renewable is hydro-power, or water-turning turbines. It is thousands of years old, without byproducts or wastes, and has had a role in shrinking salmon range from long ago. Water theft is as injurious to salmon as taking range from the deer, or trees from the nesting birds.

Hydro-power has trapped and throttled many once-great salmon rivers. Indeed, the undammed rivers we have discussed are the minority. Salmon are found now in wild places because power is not needed at the extremity. Salmon's territory has terribly contracted: the silver fish used to be everywhere.

When member nations of the EU signed the conventions on climate change, salmon were potentially affected. In 2008 Europe gurgled downwards into a major economic recession when the banks collapsed. Fighting bad balance sheets, governments inflicted cuts on public services. Many government departments were shredded. At a time they were most needed, as it turned out, they were under-manned.

In Britain an explosion of hydro-electricity proposals was launched at the flimsy government bodies meant to assess their suitability. Time will tell how many unsuitable hydro-electric schemes crept through under the radar and received planning consent.

In Scotland there was a political dimension. A relatively new political party, the Scottish National Party, unexpectedly took power in a devolved government. It had control over most departments, the exceptions being defence and management of the United Kingdom's economy. The devolved nationalist government pinned its colours to the mast of renewable energy as a defining policy. Departments that handled the permissions for hydro schemes were dismembered just at the time the flow of applications intensified.

The bodies mandated to consider hydro-power applications up until then had been the fisheries committees. They were composed, amongst others, of senior scientists and biologists, and they took the job seriously. Sites were visited and individually assessed. This rigour showed up in measured and considered approvals, and a tough standard for getting the green development light.

The old committees of professionals were abolished by gung-ho rookie nationalists. Independents were replaced by teams of civil servants working for a government department. These teams had government objectives to meet and were the instruments of government policy. Then the rump of the department was pared further.

The ground was now laid for renewable targets to be met at any cost, including to the most reliable renewable resource of all, the salmon. Many of those in fisheries considered it had been a cynical political exercise.

The fear of fishery managers is that schemes are glided through planning stages with the environmental downside never being articulated. Aggressive schemes crept through weak defences. There was no such thing as a balance-sheet approach, acknowledging any possible losses for the water-flow being halted. Plans were presented by developers blithely claiming that salmon would be unaffected. Government had instructed planning committees that they expected schemes with commercial potential to be given a fair wind; the biggest schemes were 'called-in', which meant government made the decision itself, unconstrained by local persuasions or local planning opinion. Some geographic areas, like south-west Scotland, were firebombed with multiple applications, zapping the ability of fishery interests to mount considered responses. Amazingly, some applications were accompanied by legal threats if there was any obstruction.

The biggest potential energy output was identified as coming from offshore wind energy. Schemes promised outputs of megawatts not kilowatts. Claiming that Scotland was a world-leader in renewables, the nationalist party leader, Alex Salmond, spicing the electorate up for a vote for total independence from the UK, laid his reputation and political future on the line: all Scotland's electricity would come from renewable energy by the year 2020.

Boggled energy analysts said this was impossible. The Scottish government's response was to encourage the power companies to consider schemes of unprecedented magnitude. There are several enormous ones around British coasts but one especially threatening to salmon is the scheme proposed for the Outer Moray Firth.

This is a wedge of seawater that cuts in from the North Sea towards the north Scottish capital of Inverness. Through the firth run the outgoing kelts of seventeen salmon rivers, the smolts in springtime looking for open ocean and the north, and the homing salmon returning from off the coasts of Greenland and the Faroes to breed. Some of the rivers, like the world-famous Spey, are recognised Special Areas of Protection under European law, specifically on account of their salmon runs.

Migratory paths are unknown in any detail but in broad terms homing fish enter the firth at the north-east end and travel round it clockwise, filtering into rivers to their east as they head northwards again. Some of this knowledge has been gleaned from the historic era of salmon-netting, which once took place all around the shores of the firth.

The proposed wind-energy factory will plant around 750 giant wind turbines, some 550 feet high to the blade tip, on sandbanks positioned roughly in the middle of the shallow firth. Seismic effects will penetrate 600 feet into the substrate during construction.

Sounds may affect salmon migration and they may not. The limited area of knowledge that exists suggests negative effects. It has been shown that fish flee unusual sound waves, that they may dive deeper to escape them, and that they can be distracted and their ability to hunt prey and feed may be adversely affected. An international symposium held in Montreal in 2012, heralding some breakthroughs on the effects of underwater noise on biodiversity, said that there were no widely accepted research models on the subject and that such information was urgently needed.

The venture in the Outer Moray Firth, therefore, is exploratory and carries the risks of unintended consequences. There are understandable unknowns. One would not have expected the knowns to be unknown also.

Almost unbelievably, the environmental firm for the project was unaware at the time of the publicity launch that salmon existed in the Moray Firth and were the existing users – along with seals, dolphins and others – of the domain which was to be developed. So much for the iconic fish which has helped decide the trajectory of human development for so long.

At the initial meetings the consultants said that they thought salmon were found only in rivers! It beggars belief. The same firm, based in Suffolk in eastern England, is handling the environmental side of several other big UK schemes. Representatives of river boards and fisheries scientists present at these early meetings suspected the gaping holes in the consultants' knowledge constituted an alluring qualification for developers in the environment-wrenching schemes which they are advancing.

In the Outer Moray Firth the migratory habits of salmon were a trick the consultants had to hurriedly learn to cover their ignorance of the existing wildlife.

One of the main worries for fisheries' interests was the sandbanks themselves. They are honeycombed with the habitat of protected populations of sand eels. These are the thin, silvery oil-rich fish which are a base building-block of the surrounding fish foodchain. Everything waxes fat on them, and their populations are huge. At one time trawled in catches of over a million tons by vessels from Denmark, which unloaded the haul at domestic power stations where the fish-oil was burnt to heat homes, sand eels have since been recognised for their niche importance in the food web. Now a fish subject to Europe's catch quota system, with regulated landings, sand eel populations are scientifically assessed. Studies show that they are getting scarcer; warming in the North Sea is probably pushing them northwards, like the plankton on which they feed, and like wintering salmon themselves.

Main diners at the sand-eel banquet are salmon smolts going to sea. The smolts find post-larval sand eels near the sea surface coinciding with the time they hit saltwater. Marine biologists say that sand eels with up to 17 per cent pure oil in their oleaginous bodies provide the perfect fuel and conditioning food for smolts facing a daunting journey.

The turbine cities are to be planted bang on the banks containing breeding sand eels. The water is shallower there and the physical difficulties of planting wind towers are thus reduced. Consider a marine turbine. The blades whack round hundreds of feet above the base, causing tremor down the column. When the tremor hits impassable substrate it radiates outwards. The water-surface permanently shivers. The shallow Moray Firth will become a noise-filled place. Linking each turbine to its neighbour are thick bunches of electricity cables transporting the power. These create literally power-full electro-magnetic fields. The developer companies know this but are unwilling to bury cables if they do not have to.

Knowledge about noise effects on fish has escalated sharply as a significant marine management issue. A host of international bodies, including the United Nations, has expressed concern about the increase of noise underwater and what effects it is having. Because touch, taste, vision and smell all have limitations in the marine environment, sound has been recognised as the preferred sensory medium for fish and marine mammals. Noise can result in loss of biodiversity in sensitive marine habitats. That is fact. And wind farms sound, at surface level, like busy airports. Below surface level is another matter.

Underwater is the ideal location for the powerful projection of sound. Because of its high molecular density, water is an excellent medium for sound transmission, as sound travels through water five times as fast as through air. Low-frequency sound can travel hundreds of miles underwater without notable loss of energy. So, how does this affect fish? Research has not been done in the wild, but noise has changed metabolisms and caused higher stress levels for fish in tanks. Where the effects specifically of marine wind turbines have been considered, recommendations have been published about careful planning of arrays of turbines, avoiding critical habitats, and avoiding transit routes used by fish. The family to which salmon belong, teleost fish, is recognised as specially dependent for survival and reproduction on good acoustic reception.

What research exists on noise effects in the wild has been done, unsurprisingly, on cetaceans. Their behaviour is more easily observed. Whales' use of sound is highly specialised and they have extraordinary echolocation abilities. Using sound waves they are capable of communicating across an ocean. Less is known about fish, and nothing specifically on the use of sound by wild salmon, but there is one obvious difference: if whales are discomfited by an array of sounds, they can move away. Salmon cannot, or not without penalty. If salmon are massed at the river-mouth, waiting to ascend, fleeing from discordant sound is likely to interfere with a delicately calibrated breeding timetable. Unlike marine fish which do not use rivers, salmon have to be where they are, when they are there.

At project-launch meetings developers exhibited no comprehension of any of these matters. Their environmental advisers seemed bewildered even by the language expressing the issues.

They battened instead onto the dodgy proposition that salmon may not migrate in the areas in question. Maybe they swam all around, except where the turbines were planned, they posited brightly. Surely the salmon fishery boards would know the answers to that matter, they queried. They waited to be told where the fish were.

The reality is that no one knows exactly where the salmon swim, either as departing kelts or as arriving spawners, or as hungry little smolts. No one knows much about where any salmon traverse the sea, except in general directional terms. Electronic tagging is a means of following fish but it is high-tech, harder below seawater, very expensive, and a technique in its infancy. The Outer Moray Firth is only some twenty-five miles wide at the middle section and the turbines have to be at least one kilometre apart. The power plant is therefore to occupy a big chunk of the middle of the firth. Rotating juddering columns would reach to the skies and a cobweb of pulsating electro-magnetic cables would lace the sea floor. That is not a description of habitat which salmon will find easy. It may not be a place they can tolerate being in.

In the absence of proper understanding of the whereabouts of important local fish, developers promised to monitor any effects once the scheme was constructed. Any damage was not to be prevented but it was to be recorded, or so the promise went. Where there is already a wind-farm in a salmon estuary, on the Solway in south-west Scotland, developers' promises to record effects on migrating salmon have been criticised as utterly inadequate. For there is no way, effectively, of recording anything. It is a paper promise. The Solway has a mud bottom, not sand, so sand eels do not enter the equation, and there are sixty small turbines not over seven hundred giant ones.

When it came to the stage of writing the Outer Moray Firth project plan and formulating an environmental report, a prolix statement was produced so full of holes as to be laughable. The number of named rivers debouching into the Moray Firth was half the true total, minimising the importance of salmon, local rod fisheries, and traditional users of the firth. The authors appeared to be unaware of any data about noise effects on fish being debated internationally at the time. They claim that because salmon and sea trout are in rivers or hugging the coast – in an assumption for which they quote no sources – that the development is immaterial to their survival. No comprehension of the feeding habits of either fish, which are centred on the fish-rich banks needed by the developers, is demonstrated. It is not an environmental statement of rigour, it is knowledge-light guesswork. The authors quote effects of sediment movement, a serious matter for fish with gills, from a study done in freshwater, not in the sea. Their few remarks on the behaviour of salmon and sea trout are factually wrong. With the sole exception of a commitment to bury cables carrying electricity, to be done only in some places and where 'feasible', no mitigations for the protected species already in residence, or any other species, are proposed at all.

This is despite the sure knowledge that various of the potentially affected species orient into rivers using geomagnetic cues. This has been proved in research on Pacific salmon in America. The plea from fishery biologists that seismic disturbance was timed to avoid smolts going out to sea, or a small window of the period in which salmon come in, was simply ignored. If ever a developers' report deserved the epithet 'whitewash', this one was it.

Many marine species which use the fertile firth are ensnared in this marine wind factory. Protected species include common eels, trans-Atlantic migratory creatures considered highly at risk. The answer is the same to all anxious enquiries from stakeholders: results on the fauna and flora and fish and mammal life will be watched. No information is proffered on how this watching will be done. The concept of precautionary principles, or step-wise proceeding, or a development map designed to lower potential impacts on the major fish types, is not mentioned. In the absence of sound information about runs and timings and fish behaviour, final plans came up with the same reasoning: we will proceed with our original schedule and see what happens. Paraphrasing: we will hope for the best. More likely, we will clamber onto the munificently subsidised renewable energy bandwagon while political need ensures that it lasts. For other countries have tried offshore wind energy and have withdrawn owing to failed technology, high cost, and new smarter power sources rendering the Brobdingnagian technology obsolete.

So how will anyone know if runs of salmon fail? Fish counters on river systems are few. The developers have shunned interest in these instruments where they do exist – for obvious reasons. They have never asked for the available baseline data. Attuned to the deceits and specious exculpatory arguments of the salmon farmers, anyone can guess their devious persiflage in anticipation. The runs may not be so bad anyway, anglers always complain; climate change is pushing the fish somewhere else; salmon follow cycles and river owners ebullient from the recent good times will have to get used to thinner pickings; we are providing clean green energy and should not be the Aunt Sallies for disreputable sportsmens' imagined troubles. There will be claims that the salmon are being caught on remote unmonitored pathways in their migrations, outside 200-mile national maritime limits, by unnamed states, far from the virtuous clean energy engines occupying the doorsteps of their homes.

Actually, there will be no need for argument or even speech. The project will cost billions of pounds. Will energy companies dismantle projects of this scale because fewer salmonids allegedly came home? To spell it out is to see the pointlessness of the syrupy promises to monitor developments.

The other technologies pushing at the door of Scotland's renewables enthusiasm are tidal- and wave-power inventions. One involves anchoring structures of rotating blades, similar to wind turbines, on the seabed of the Pentland Firth, thought to be a main migration route for Scotland's homing north-coast salmon. This firth, shallow with a sandy bottom, has one of the most powerful tidal races in the world. Again, no one has a notion about what effects the scheme will have on salmon. Because both formulae involve structures which move in the water column, it has been suggested that fish could collide with them and be damaged that way. Once more, impacts on salmon are guesswork. Maybe that is the wrong word: no work has been done on the matter at all.

The country so closely identified with salmon seems ready to override its needs without a backward glance. Why?

Politics raises its ugly head. The First Minister in Scotland's devolved parliament may be called Salmond but he is uninterested in the eponymous fish. Bizarrely, his deputy's surname is Sturgeon, even less propitious; we know what happened to them. Salmond's focus is publicly endorsing himself through the full independence of Scotland in a referendum vote in 2014. A main underpinning for the claim that an independent Scotland could function is energy sufficiency. Enter renewables. His Nationalist Party has deleted nuclear power as an option and, groping for eye-catching announcements, has lodged the claim that it will lead Scotland into the sunlit uplands to become a world leader in renewable energy.

Scotland is not Iceland. In Iceland the government recognised the importance of the sport of fishing for salmon as a main policy plank, and Iceland possessed a bubbling ocean of fiery underground heat suitable for energy. Scotland is vexed by a longer and more twisted history, and has defunct, not active, volcanoes. Its metaphorical volcanoes instead sputter from its tangled feudal and cross-border history. This has forged an idiomatic culture with a strong sense of nationhood.

Despite having a landmass dominated by wild country and being renowned for its unspoiled physical beauty, Scotland's culture is of an ex-industrial society. Its role in sub-sea exploration, and energy and gas exploration, in which it is a contemporary leader, has replaced metal-bashing as the defining national activity and is the economy's twenty-first-century pivot. The rural side of life is peripheral. To protect wild salmon would be to protect the playthings of the old landowner families which retain some of the better-known salmon fishing rights from the time when they ran national affairs. It would be a nod in deference to the past.

Salmon angling is casually portrayed as a toff's game rather than an occupation for the common man. To knock salmon is therefore doubly satisfactory, the fish of the privileged takes a hit and those who pursue it do too.

The reality is that salmon in Scotland have been argued about and legislated for over the centuries because they are of interest to everyone, especially in the places they exist. No creature has attracted greater legislative attention. In truth, salmon have the glamour to wake up anyone, fisherman or not, in their home rivers. That is why modern management systems generally attempt to get local anglers and communities entrained in the protection and also the enjoyment of salmon. Residents near decent salmon fishing can buy seasonal angling permits for nominal amounts. The fish swimming past the garden at the mouth of the river has to earn safe passage from those whose houses it passes, and fishing managers recognise this.

Salmon protection is popular across a wide field, but to politicians fixed on Scotland's Central Belt, where most people live and vote, the salmon is still a creature with a whiff of Victorian exclusivity. Indeed, it is a fish which entranced Queen Victoria, and the idea that progress in the form of renewable energy should be hindered because of salmon and sea trout angling in the nationalists' perspective is simply absurd.

Furthermore, to pro-actively encourage and support salmon carries no political gain. No dramatic signature action is required. No one anywhere ever went to the hustings on the promise to keep rivers clean. Leaving things as they are was never a rallying cry for politicians; change and forcing change is what differentiates them from the throng. No government minister or department in Scotland is mandated to look after salmon. Under the EU's Habitats Directive the salmon is bracketed with many other natural biota, most of which have no mythic or economic significance at all. Indeed, it is their baggage-free neutrality which makes them appealing to a swathe of modern society. So the lamprey, a rare, inedible, parasitic sucker fish which hardly anyone has ever seen, is vested with parallel legal status to the venerable salmon.

At the point at which EU law meshes with national law there is a tension between legislation to protect the environment in the wide sense and a concomitant commitment to maintain and enhance employment in the rural areas. At the simple level of legal definition, salmon is a species needing protection alongside rare shrimps, and unheard-of sphagnums and bivalves. Its role in the rural economy earns it no special favours from government administration, which partly explains why the proponents of the Outer Moray Firth wind-energy scheme were caught napping when the presence of salmon was brought to their attention. Edwardian natural history generalists, like the monumental polymath Sir Herbert Maxwell from Galloway, are out of vogue. Today, every specialist is focused on their own subject only, and even in environmentalism generalists are a rare breed. That eases the passage of human development which impacts across the environment with a wide sweep.

The salmon is harmed by default rather than design. Historians have often expressed amazement that despite the great fish's interface with progress and development so few people rose to defend the star-spangled stalwart of their cultural and dietary past. Dams were built without a backward glance; nets swept up the lifeblood of the species unremarked; now salmon factory farms spewing lethal bloodsuckers have been dumped in their migratory pathways. Most persistently, salmon survival has been damaged by attempts to supply energy for developing society. It is about to happen again. The energy the salmon is able to supply in the form of food, the older contribution to human life, has been long ago overtaken. For the salmon the message is: fit the mood, or else!

Extinction Vortex

Families can quarrel, as we know. Alongside the wild salmon thwacking with his tail to power through the sea to reach home, another lookalike salmon materialises, with oddly similar replicas drifting around in the vicinity too. The other fish are different from the wild fish, but also alike. Clearly salmonids, they are bigger, their extremities are blunter, and closer study shows that their noses are rubbed, and the fins are worn-down stubs rather than filigree wavery appendages. The tail is round not square. Lacking the same homing impulse they behave differently too, appearing undirected, even indolent.

The storm has subsided now but hours ago these drifting salmon were the circling prisoners in a Hotel California of special devising. All of them had been swimming clockwise round and round a cylindrical webbed enclosure, but now, for the first time, they are experiencing the sensation of being able to move sideways, even up and down. Where until today they had been in the company of tens of thousands of their own kind, confined by tough polyurethane netting, suddenly they have space. The outside world is no longer viewed through quadrangles of super-strong twine but offers clear space, a free environment.

There is another extraordinary difference. The seawater seems filled with substances. Their previous home had been a sterilised hospital; the inmates met no one except replicas of themselves, thousands of them, a ghostly enclosure of mirrors. Here in the open sea other fish dart about, the water column contains shrimps and eggs and fishy beings, and the temperature changes at different depths. Unobstructed light dapples the surface.

Critically, there is no snowstorm of pellets raining steadily down. Pellets had equalled growth. They had allowed a small fish to reach seven or eight pounds, or more, in only eight months, a growth rate almost equating to blowing up a tyre. In this weird and limitless wonderland the absence of the rainfall of pellets was one problem which might prove tough to rectify. For now the escaped salmon will have to find food for themselves.

The Atlantic salmon is a wondrous fish, we know that, but it has one further capacity which may yet prove its undoing: it is susceptible to being domesticated. It can be farmed as intensively as any creature on Earth and still grow and maintain body health. Unlike cod, which grow too slowly, or turbot, which are tricky to domesticate, or many other saltwater fish for their own special reasons, Atlantic salmon are flexible and manageable. In common with cows and sheep and pigs and horses, salmon are amenable to human management.

Fish have been farmed in China for thousands of years but they are freshwater vegetation-eating species, like carp. The Atlantic salmon is a carnivore, like brown trout, sea bass, bream and tuna. Perhaps because they epitomised wildness no one had considered they might be farmed like rainbow trout. But their susceptibility to replication and steady predictable growth proved almost surreal. As farm fish, in pen-cages suspended in seawater instead of feed-lots or outhouses, they became as manageable as chickens.

Some fans of the wild salmon have found this sufficiently disturbing to alter nomenclature. They have defined farm salmon as a separate species. Even fishery scientists refer to one species having two separate biologies. But they are the same.

The genome of the Atlantic salmon is unusually complex, consisting of 28 pairs of chromosomes in North American salmon and 29 pairs in European strains. It is more complex than that of any mammal and twice the size of the human one. The salmon that swam from the net-pen when the storm broke its eight-point moorings and overturned the structure is a cousin of the wild one. A Norwegian cousin for sure, with some programmed differences which are highly important to the compatibility of the two fish, but nonetheless a close relation, a regional variant from the same family.

The Scottish wildcat from the Highlands is now probably extinct. Just at the moment when no one can find one any more, conservation bodies have launched a posthumous rescue appeal. After the event is the normal timing for rescues of this type. But the reason for the wildcat's final vanishing is miscegenation. Crossing with wandering domesticated cats has bred out the survival qualities of the original wildcat. The famously wild and impossible-to-tame wildcat has entered the lists of legend. Hybridising did for it, and that is the threat posed by farmed salmon to the truly wild type. More later.

Salmon farming started in Scotland in the late 1960s. Trout farming had been long in existence and it occurred to pushy pioneers to try the same thing with salmon. Net-pens were hammered together out of wooden planks, the hatchery skills which had conducted programmes of enhancement for salmon fishing rivers for over a hundred years were put to use cultivating fry from eggs, and salmon were transposed as smolts into aqueous cages to see if they grew when fed buckets of fishy mush. Which they did.

Furthermore, they performed the right tricks in a location which had been a headache for politicians for a very long time. Salmon grew in the sea in parts of Scotland where everything else had gone or was going. Human existence in the west Highlands was in retreat; livestock farming no longer flourished and was subsidy-dependant to a frightening degree. The wool price had collapsed and instead of providing a third of a sheep farmer's income its value had fallen to a tenth; latterly the cost of shearing sheep became more than the wool was worth.

The manse had an unholy grip on the lifestyles of the bowed population, fierce ministers drilling into their mute congregations the imminence of the doomsday finale. Emigration was the normal exit for the young, and drinking was the accepted panacea for the rest. Farming hung on, shakily, but the hills were overgrazed and over-used. No one would claim it was a triumphant point in the country's evolution.

Politicians and those mandated to stimulate development latched onto a new industry which seemed to tick all the boxes. Here were the sea-lochs from which many of the migratory swarms of fish, such as herrings, which occupied the inshore fishing fleets in the days of sail, had departed. Here was a youth population looking for work. The sea lochs had no other users, barring occasional leisure boats and the local creel-men and potters. Buildings lay abandoned along the shoreline and the perpetually wet weather seemed more acceptable if you were on the sea anyway.

Most cogently, the north-west coast had something else. It was in a sense the wellspring of Scotland's identity. Here the notorious internecine clan battles had been bloodiest and most treacherous. Scotland's culture leans on the west, the motherland of Gaelic poetry. Even east-coast poets veered towards the setting sun for inspiration. There was the nation-defining sadness of depopulation kick-started two centuries earlier by the Clearances, when west coasters more than their east-coast cousins boarded ships bound for America, Newfoundland and Canada and found there, as well as unencumbered land, the same salmon they had filched from home rivers in Gaeldom.

The west was the perennial sore point for administrators. Poor soils limited agriculture; from the wonderful flora and bird-life little economic dividend could be extracted. The once-valuable kelp industries had been displaced by modern alginate production. West-coast humour defined resignation laced with witty barbs. The west coast cried out for a passage into the future.

That is the background to the warm welcome given to salmon farming in the early years. It was perceived as a way by which the enterprising crofter could lift himself into the modern era and defeat the condemnation of history. It would supply a food export from a coastline synonymous with unspoiled wildness. It was an alpha-plus proposition and few people remonstrated with the concept.

Development agencies like Scotland's Highlands and Islands Development Board poured funds into this new receptacle, and when there were teething troubles, like fish escaping and sea-farms being wrecked in storms, money tracked money and then more was found. Politicians fell over each other to ride the wave of discovery and conquest. It all seemed so commendable and obvious.

To ensure that there was no undue hindrance and because no one could see what might happen, serious regulation was never seriously considered. The sea had always operated as a commons, especially on the west coast where the nearest neighbours were an ocean away. When a government department was selected to handle the new industry the government chose the fisheries department in charge of trawling and seine-netting wild fish. They had a novel form of agriculture on their hands, but they chose a department used to dealing with wild capture to administer it. Agriculture had been regulated and strictly vetted for two hundred years, and epidemics and disease outbreaks resulting from intensive production had been wrestled under control. Essentially cage-farming was livestock farming, but in saltwater. In the haze of heady enthusiasm it was seen as something new and different.

Whilst the fisheries department that was given charge of the new industry had some distinguished scientists on its staff, the disease risks to wild fish of the same species and also to sea trout were not considered, and the scale and dangers of the parasite problems inside cages were underestimated. When the penny dropped, warnings from the alarmed fishery department scientists were brushed aside. By that time the government had the bit between its teeth, the new industry had been acclaimed, and it had been pump-primed. Political forces had taken over, and they were not to relinquish their grip. The new industry's side-impacts were an unwelcome complication. This malfunction of governance lay behind the ghastly tragedy which was to unfold.

There was a freeholder or landlord in the form of the Crown Estate Commission (CEC). Misleadingly titled, this is a property-owning body, descending in authority from the landholding rights held by medieval monarchy, which remits its profits to the UK Treasury. The CEC owns the sea bed from the shoreline out to six miles. It opened the book as a new landlord offering leases on sites for which there had been no comparable market previously. The commissioners could now look forward to leasing parts of the sea bed to eager and often subsidised tenants. Suddenly their capital asset had achieved novel dimensions.

There were no precedents and again there was no foresight. No one really thought about any of the ramifications. What transpired was a landlord issuing licences for the use of a national asset but without any responsibility for the state of the site before or after its new utilisation. The landlord took the money but had not been stuck with any duties. In a further bizarre twist the CEC was the body officiating over and regulating the lease process. It was the adjudicator in an industry in which it was the end-beneficiary – and it had a monopoly. A stranger scenario would be hard to imagine.

The freshly fledged salmon farm industry was looking for sea lochs. They had the saltwater needed for growing-on smolted salmon, the tides refreshed the waters, and they were close to roads and communications. Even though the latter were poor, they were to become upgraded as the EU tackled infrastructure in remote rural locations, and within thirty years west-coast roads were smart. Some of the only traffic was fish-farm related. The west coast provided the clean image of a pure and beautiful environment with which to bless a sunrise industry.

The food already had a cachet. It was one formerly reserved for the affluent; salmon was a luxury enjoyed by the elite. Salmon farming was to make the fish not only affordable but, finally, the cheapest protein on the slab. It was like manna from heaven, available to all. The marketing people had achingly beautiful sea-lochs drenched in westering sunsets with a leaping silver fish as the eye-catcher. It brought the sparkling sea into ordinary kitchens. Its flesh had the pink promise of coldwater succulence, its shape the torpedo slimness of an acrobat. Salmon farmers were eventually to sponsor photographic competitions of pictures from the fabled west coast. Scenery would be used for all its marketing worth.

What photographers were not invited to snap was the bit that would have betrayed what was really going on, the sea bed. The footprint there, in the real workplace, was ugly.

At the beginning, growth in Scotland's new food-output industry was steady but not fast. For the decade up to 1980 industry growth was incremental not dramatic – Scottish annual production had attained about 800 tons. Accidents and storms and escapes, and trouble from seals which appreciated the delicatessen opening on their doorstep, provided the pioneer salmon farmers with plenty of worries. Nothing was that easy, and the first salmon farmers were innovative, resilient and resourceful. The industry attracted those prepared to take risks and to work hard.

It was a muscular exercise; 25-kilo feed bags might be handled nine times before reaching the fish. Dirty nets were hauled ashore and manually brushed. At harvests of two or three tons, boxes were filled and loaded onto lorries by hand. Work squads consisted of five or six men. Later on, with bigger volumes, twenty tons were hand-netted from the pens in a single day. Lines of men with clubs despatched the fish, some weighing as much as seventeen pounds. Clubs were branded with the inscribed logos of their owners; one manager said the killing-line resembled a scene from a martial arts club. Long shifts lasted fourteen hours. An old fish-farm worker reminiscing said it was surprising they were not all hunchbacks given the amount of physical exertion their work demanded.

Presumably because of the marine connection, several original business pioneers came from the shipping industry. These men at least knew the location where this new form of food production would set up shop. In the early days they built pens for salmon out of wooden rails and suspended their nets in the sea below. Four-metre-square pens contained around 4,000 salmon which were sold to market at weights of between five and eight pounds.

Progress was erratic. By the mid-1980s cages had grown to twelve metres across and hung down about four metres. A collection of cages was linked together by roped walkways. The sea loch looked different but not dramatically so. The protein engine-room, after all, was below the water. A cage might contain 10,000 salmon. At the beginning the fish would be smaller than the ten-pound product favoured by processors today. When the salmon were ready for processing, suction pumps removed them from the corners of the pens into which they were herded and they were rolled down chutes towards killing and freezing lines. The industry had attained that degree of automation by around 1986.

The success of the early ventures depended heavily on the sea-loch site. For example, in western Ross-shire, Loch Kishorn enjoyed full refreshment of all its tide-driven water after only three days. Salmon were always in clean ocean water because any detritus was sucked out to sea and disappeared. The sea-lochs which had slower tidal exchanges quickly ran into water-quality and other problems. The sea acted as the refreshment agency the way that rivers had in the eighteenth and nineteenth centuries when industry needed a receptacle for production wastes. Tidal flushing was everything. As salmon farming developed, only the less good sites with weaker tidal flows were available. The best had gone and been tied up in long leases by canny fish farmers. If a site across the loch became available they would buy that too, to keep others out rather than use it themselves, or indeed to use it over time, relocating the farm when the localised effects of massed fish production began to impact the health of the next crop of salmon.

What happened to the water that was sucked out by the tides, and what happened to the chemicals, surplus food, urine and faeces in it, was never asked. The sea was a toilet lacking filtration or plumbing.

Early salmon farming developed its own peculiar business practice reflecting the particular circumstances of production. Producers of salmon smolts in the freshwater lochs sold their fish to the bigger farmers in the early grow-out areas in the west Highland sea lochs and the Shetland Islands. Market readiness came about two and a half years later, at eight pounds.

The payments system explains why the salmon farming industry gravitated towards compression. In the early 1980s before the arrival of vaccines, up to thirty per cent of the smolts could perish after being moved to saltwater. The sea farmers took the view that payment should be on the proportion of survivors after three months of translocation. Smolts that died moving from freshwater to salt were the liability of their original growers. Business deals varied, but a further percentage of the smolt stock might only be paid when the fish were finally harvested some thirty months later.

Norwegian banks, luxuriating in oil revenues, and minded to spearhead the salmon farming venture, took a kindlier view than their Scottish counterparts of these tenuous and unusual arrangements. Early smolt growers made money inconsistently and were ultimately vulnerable because their fish had to leave freshwater at the time of smolting, around April. Like for soft-fruit or dairy farmers, smolt growers had a weak position in the market. Smolt growers could not hold out for better money; their stock had to be moved when biological changes dictated. Sea farmers dictated terms to their suppliers in the freshwater lochs and rivers.

This systemic weakness reflected the strangeness of the industry. The smolt producers who grew young salmon in freshwater lochs from the egg stage tended to be small-time operators. Typically, they lived close by the lochs. They had to be ready to jump up in the night and attend to water supplies freezing up or getting clogged by spates, oxygen filtration fading, power cuts, or a host of hitches threatening the survival of the fish. Grow-out farmers at sea, watching the weather forecast, usually also lived close by. Salmon farming in the early days was a hands-on business taken up by locals or pioneers who came in to utilise vacant seawater.

The big fish in this pond were the feed companies. They had the whip hand because the feed price, at around forty per cent of production cost, was so high. Therefore when small independent fish farmers, enlarging to keep pace with the upbeat industry, were unable to meet the feed bills, they were bought up by the feed suppliers. These were almost invariably Norwegian companies. Not being members of the EU, the Norwegians overcame the difficulty of exporting marketable salmon to a foreign trading block by using their subsidiaries in Denmark.

There were new problems farming in the sea which had never been considerations for farmers on land. Terrestrial agriculture had a two-dimensional environment to deal with; salmon farmers had a three-dimensional one. They were perched on an undulating skin of water. There was experimentation about how to grow salmon faster. Early managers developed an eye for stewardship and watching the condition of individual fish. It pertains still on the good salmon farms, watchfulness from the sharp-eyed stockmen and the managers.

There was an enemy, however, which surged from the abyss. It became the biggest hurdle to unending progress extrapolating from the success of early salmon farming. It has now apparently spread from salmon farms, according to the Royal Society, to infest wild salmon all over the north-east Atlantic. This is the parasitic, blood-sucking sea louse. Familiar to anglers as the mini, crab-like attachments on salmon 'just in from the sea', in freshwater they drop off.

Suddenly this roving marine parasite seeking a host found them in tens of thousands – even millions – all in a confined area and all zinging with zesty growth and condition. These Olympian athletes of the salmon industry were confined in their cages like blood sacrifices laid out by gore-fixated Amerindian tribes. Captive salmon never ventured into freshwater, which breaks the cycle when sea lice attach to wild fish. The picnic carried on and on. Sea lice proliferated at ghastly speed.

The sea louse, as fate will have it, is a key animal in the future of the Atlantic salmon. In the North Atlantic there are several sea louse species, two of which affect farmed and wild salmon. The smaller one, Latin name *Caligus elongatus*, is found on eighty species of fish and is the lesser of the two horrors. The other, *Lepeophtheirus salmonis*, as its name implies, is a salmon specialist; indeed, it can only complete its lifecycle on salmonids, either sea-trout or salmon. Its larvae are capable, with the help of wind and sea currents, of moving 28 miles in a fortnight, and it is present year-round on salmon farms. Its range stretches as far as the tropics. The lifecycle is common to both species.

Sea lice are crustaceans and therefore moult like lobsters. The outer shell, which is shed by moulting, is made of chitin, and it is this shell which salmon farmers assail with chemicals to rid themselves of lice. At the last stage of moulting the bulbous female louse attracts a paired-off male which waits to pounce when the chitin shell is binned. The problem is that the four moulting stages are carried out whilst attached to and feeding off either a host salmon or sea trout.

Start with the egg. Eggs hang out from the rear of the female louse in pairs of strings. After being released from the egg shed by the female from two egg-strings, each capable of containing several hundred eggs, the larvae can exist in the sea's plankton for a limited time. Fast-growing, the wee bug reaches adulthood at differing speeds depending on the water temperature. If the sea is 10°C it takes 38 days, longer if the water is colder.

The hungry larvae have a week to locate a host. If successful their specially designed antennae drive into the epidermis of the fish and hook into the blood and slime supply. The larva's front end may lodge beneath the fish scales.

Almost immediately it moults again. During the next four moults the free-riding parasite feeds on the salmon's skin around the attachment point. The rate of moulting again is temperature-dependant, ten weeks in typical North Atlantic spring temperatures and just four weeks at 15 degrees. A louse off Scotland can replicate itself in thousands every six weeks. A female louse can produce between six and eleven broods over her lifetime.

In exchange for a relatively short life, Nature has given the louse excellent adaptability. It has the ability to crawl around on the host and colonise new feeding zones using its rasping mouth parts. The scientific description from the research director of the Atlantic Salmon Trust, Dr Ken Whelan, is horror-film material: 'Impacts on the host's skin include epithelium loss, bleeding, increased mucus discharge, altered mucus biochemistry, tissue necrosis and consequent loss of physical and microbial protective function.' The host suffers blood anaemia, impaired breathing and a damaged immune system.

In her breeding life a female louse can produce over 4,000 eggs, each of whose larvae seek new feeding grounds. Some sea-going salmon and sea trout smolts have been found with a carapace of larvae, their own skins invisible. Ken Whelan, while working off the west coast of Ireland, found that it was at the less visually apparent larval stage of the louse cycle, when they are just tiny dots, that most damage can be done. He proved that the dramatic collapse of western Ireland's treasured sea-trout populations was linked to *L. salmonis* infestations in 2010. The fact that 95 per cent of the lice originated on western Irish salmon farms had been established as long ago as 1991.

The salmon louse and the salmon share a preference which ensures collision: they both like the upper surface of seawater.

That sophisticated animal the sea louse is attracted too by vibrations which lead it towards a potential host. Researchers into lice have found that *L. salmonis* is attracted by other fish species, but it fails to latch on. It is assumed that there is some chemical recognition specific to Atlantic salmon which dictates the instruction to attach. Lice are like sharks, they select the weaker fish in a batch. The smaller the host the deadlier the result of louse attack. This is why finger-long smolts are especially susceptible. Weak smolts are easy meat and rapidly sucked lifeless as essential body fluids transfer from the fish to the parasite.

In all these effects damage inflicted by the second type of louse, *Caligus*, is less lethal than that from *Lepeophtheirus salmonis.*

Lice are comparable to fleas on a dog but can be as lethal as ticks on a sheep. When the parasite digs deeper in, fish can haemorrhage. Voracious feeding may result in the fish's muscle showing through. When there are deeper lesions the lice feed vampirically on flowing blood. Lice eat salmon alive and some of the photographs of skinless salmon heads and jostling lice boring into what is left are stuff to unsettle a hardened film censor. Owing to the louse lifecycle, a salmon can play host to several generations of lice simultaneously. With a million salmon swirling round and round salmon cages occupying a limited cubic area, a single farm in the period between lice treatments may be the locus for hundreds of millions of the blood-sucking parasites at one time.

Eating off the mucous coating on salmon is like picking the wings from a dragonfly. The slime is the protective layer interposed between the fish and the environment. A salmon lacking slime is vulnerable to bacterial infection. Although the link is unproven, it has been shown that lice carry bacteria in their gut. Skin damage changes blood chemistry, and the salmon has subsequent difficulty maintaining salt and water balances. Rubbing by farm salmon on the edges of pens is not only avoidance from the pressure of dense numbers, it is the fish response to a skin-irritant. Salmon attempt to dislodge the invader as a person scratches a tick bite. A salmon farm company director told me he thought that jumping was triggered similarly.

The way salmon farmers have tried to control the blizzard of rapidly replicating parasites is the chemical history of salmon farming. In 2012, the last year I visited salmon farms, the virulence of sea-louse swarms was necessitating up to five treatments a year. Louse treatments were ramping up. The furious battle with parasites is little known to the public.

The number and quantity of chemicals used by salmon farmers is mind-boggling. The business has spawned its own chemical arsenal. In 2011 in the Scottish industry 35 medicines were licensed to keep salmon clean, and 25 anti-fouling substances were available to unclog nets and cages. Drug manufacturers facing the challenge of resistance to treatment in sea lice from single concoctions were pushed to recommending suites of chemical compounds as possible solutions. This proliferation of chemicals coincides with the efforts by the European Union to ban or reduce those available to crop growers on farmland.

Diseases are attacked with antibiotics if they are bacterial, and with disinfectants like chlorine and hypochlorite. In Norway in the late eighties more antibiotics were deployed to combat disease on salmon farms than the combined total being used by humans and farm animals. Had that been known, consumers might have blanched. They would certainly have been shocked to hear that the bacteria which developed resistance to these antibiotics, and most recently were incorporated in their feed pellets, are now thought to have developed their resistance in the sediment-sludge beneath salmon pens. Resistant bacteria were not found in areas without salmon farms. Antibiotics used on salmon farms can spread to nearby shellfish, potentially affecting wider food safety.

A member of the Scottish Parliament on a fish-farm visit asked innocently why the cages were not closer together in order to localise the spread of contamination, to which the fish-farm worker, momentarily off-message, replied, 'In case we cook the loch'!

Anti-foulants are pressure-sprayed on nets to clear debris and growing organisms. Metals leaching from cage structures and used in physical treatments on fish include the heavy metals cadmium, lead, copper and zinc. But if the treatments were being used to clear, say, molluscs from nets, what were they doing to the molluscs not on nets? Given our contemporary concern for contamination of the terrestrial environment, the failure to measure seawater health is extraordinary. The water is the element in which the wild fish grow, including the crustaceans that we eat. No one knows what effects this continuous chemical deposition is having on the inner coastline or indeed the currents which drag dirty water out of the sea lochs and away into the circulating ocean. Present assessment of the risks of oil-drilling in the Arctic has focused on potential leaks of fossil fuels, natural substances which break down in seawater, into the wider ocean after accidents. Why should regular and persistent dosing of the same environment with compound chemicals, which are persistent and break down slowly, as used constantly by salmon farming, be regarded as of no concern? The industry claims that fewer chemicals are being used to treat individual fish, skating round the fact that the industry has expanded and the total load being released into seawater soars with mounting production.

There were warning signals enough. One of the worst salmon-farm diseases is infectious salmon anaemia or ISA. It first occurred in Norway on a salmon farm in the late 1970s. Once present in a cage most fish are doomed. It is capable of existence in both seawater and freshwater, and is untreatable with drugs. The only way to even begin to get a handle on ISA is to thin down salmon densities, fallow infected sites and move salmon farms further apart, all of which involve collapsing output. It remains a killer threat for salmon farms after decades of combat. Late in December 2012 an ISA outbreak on a south-coast Newfoundland fish farm obliged the government to order the destruction of 350,000 infected salmon. This followed another major outbreak there only six months earlier. ISA comes round like a bad penny.

Norwegian research has showed that sea lice are likely vectors or transfer agents in ISA outbreaks. The worst-affected farms were often close to processing plants. Blood water from the processing factories was fizzing with the virusues which affect the blood of living salmon. Salmon which die in the cages themselves before they can be removed, in some cases up to twenty per cent of the stock, if not properly disposed of, also became a pathway for repeat infection. In Scotland in 2012 the reported deaths of cage salmon was 8.5 million, sixty per cent higher than the figure two years earlier; insiders say true losses are unknown because of the scale of non-reporting. Red-faced industry spokesmen solemnly referred to 'naturally occurring amoeba from the wild' as the cause of the trouble.

Disposal protocols for these 'morts' (as dead fish are known) are unclear or non-existent. The authorities, in the form of SEPA and local councils, when asked about the destination of 8.5 million carcases in 2012, passed the buck. Others were responsible. One council which did not duck the question said the morts were converted into fishmeal, ratcheting up the stakes with a host of further unedifying questions. When you consider the physical volume of hundreds of thousands of putrefying fish, the absence of any protocols is inexplicable. On the Scottish islands small farmers were paid to bulldoze them in an ad hoc fashion under the sand. Enjoying the revenue, they have been reluctant whistleblowers. A picture forms of a coastal ecology wracked by infection epidemics, lacking a functional carcase-disposal policy or a functional waste-disposal policy, repeatedly re-infected in a disease cycle beyond the grasp of weak regulators. Again, the sea is being used as a toilet, lacking filtration or plumbing.

The nutrient loads imposed on sea lochs by salmon farms have overwhelmed natural cycles, according to World Wildlife Fund (WWF) researchers. They have linked higher incidences of toxic algal blooms, and their geographical spread, with the pumped-up nutrient load. The phosphorus from Scottish salmon farms was estimated in the year 2000 to equate to discharges from nine million humans, and the equivalent nitrogen sewage load from three million people. Government records and measures none of these factors, yet Scottish salmon farming on a short length of coastline stands accused of distorting nutrient cycles more than in any other European sea-body in recent time. The biologist Allan Sefton has called Scotland's wilderness west coast, 'the most polluted aquatic environment in the UK'.

The rush of nutrient enrichment affects the growth of phytoplankton or plant production in the sea and can render shellfish poisonous. Toxic algal blooms resulted in a series of recent scallop-eating bans. It is estimated that knock-on effects may hurt sea mammals and birds through their consumption of plankton-eating fish, and also damage the larvae of cod.

Pollution protocols are so flimsy as not to deserve the name.

The way that salmon farming is dealt with by government is eerily similar in different countries. The obtuseness of officials is highlighted in the situation in New Brunswick where salmon farming was allowed to dream up its own rules of operation. When finally change was forced and coercion introduced, the language was of disease 'management' rather than eradication. Bizarrely, not all salmon on a diseased farm needed to be killed. Even with this ineffectively targeted culling, 9.6 million farm salmon in New Brunswick in a single continuous disease cycle were destroyed.

Surreally we are suddenly back in the eighteenth century, before disease transfer was understood. Businesses managed to stay afloat owing to government rescue aid, a cool CAN$50 million by the end of 1999. Money was forked out to the farms where malpractice had caused cyclical epidemics, thereby perpetuating the dirty business. Whilst the vote-nervous provincial government of New Brunswick favoured continuing aid for disease-struck salmon farmers, federal government finally pulled the plug on more cheque-writing to the industry with a last $10-million flourish in 2006.

Parasites have attracted the greatest chemical response and for these pesticides were the counter-blast.

An array of pesticides has been used and, as treatments fail, abused. Lice mutilated young salmon and disfigured some adults so much they were un-saleable. Despite the fact that no environmental review had been performed about its wider effects, and despite the fact that it persisted in seawater for days rather than hours, hydrogen peroxide was the chosen weapon against lice. It was used after they had started to move. Teflubenzeron was the weapon in the arsenal used to kill them at the moulting stage. Dichlorvos, an organophosphorous compound, was another stock-in-trade louse treatment. A recent innovation is insertion of lice-controls in feed. Emamectin benzoate, capable of impacting lice at all stages of growth, is injected into the feeds.

Cypermethrin, a pesticide related to pyrethrin, was used both legally and illegally in different places. When the authorities bore down on its distribution, salmon growers located an agricultural chemical with a different name but containing cypermethrin. The Conservation Council of New Brunswick found an anonymous memo circulating the fish-farming world known as the 'cookbook'. It described how to procure and illegally use an agrochemical containing the vital cypermethin.

This chemical is highly toxic to fish, aquatic insects and crustaceans. In one notorious event 60,000 lobsters worth CAN$700,000 died downstream of a salmon farm with traces of the dread substance in them. There was an out-of-court settlement with a group of salmon farmers who had all accused each other of the offence. What volume of marine life has died as a result of cypermethrin being broadcast into the marine environment in the various places where there is salmon farming will never been known. No one is looking for an answer.

From the beginning the treatments showed their limitations. Hydrogen peroxide could not be used without risk to the fish in higher water temperatures. Water colder than 9°C was not authorised for teflubenzeron. In-feed treatments involved fish ingesting differing doses depending on their appetite at that time. As treatments were ramped up, cross-resistance occurred between unlike chemicals. Salmon farms became the underwater theatre for chemical experimentation. The industry coined a new term, implying a form of gentle persuasion rather than poisoning – 'therapeutants'.

In the meantime the manufacturers themselves truthfully labelled many of the chemicals used as highly toxic to fish. Ignorance was no excuse. Commercial and competition pressure dictated measures taken to combat lice in a battle that in the end was always likely to be won by the parasite not the host.

Every treatment had its own 'withdrawal' period – that means the time following treatment during which the fish cannot be marketed or consumed. These varied from country to country and province to province. Incredibly, in a consumer-conscious food industry, withdrawal periods were sometimes left to the judgement of salmon growers themselves. A popular chemical called ivermectin usually had a withdrawal of 180 days, an indication of its toxicity. Some pharmacists warned in vain against its use on salmon. Ivermectin is excreted by fish unaltered, accumulates in wild lobster tissue, can kill crustaceans, and persists in bottom sediments for a month. It is so powerful that at higher concentrations in one incident it killed 80 per cent of the adult salmon it was meant to cure.

Fish farmers were desperate. Slice, which contained emamectin benzoate, was another product in the medicine chest. A neurotoxin which affected brain function and development, Slice was only classified in Canada for use as an emergency drug. But it was warranted for use more frequently as disease ramped up.

By 2003 forty-seven million salmon had been treated and earlier cautions about its suitability had been set aside. Its persistence in marine sediment was passed by in favour of protection of this pampered new food industry. Lobsters were behaving irregularly and moulting their shells prematurely. No matter. Inconvenient rules about residue levels were simply ratcheted upwards to allow more liberal use. These levels were much higher than allowed in other food production, like the American beef industry.

Chemicals battled each other for the brevity of withdrawal times; the shorter the period the faster fish could be moved to market. Chemicals were licensed in shorter and shorter times, sometimes in a matter of months, although proper registration took up to five years because of intense lobbying from salmon farmers. The industry had produced a genie which could not be put back in any bottle. In the early days lice on fish on the processing line was no big deal, but as their wider effects began to be understood, and the industry had to work harder to maintain its wild and natural image, fish with lice attached to them disappeared from the production lines.

Considering the strength and number of the chemicals in widespread use it is amazing looking back that the impact on the receiving environment was never explored. It is particularly astonishing given the forensic examination of chemicals being used on land farms. Pyrethroid sheep dips had replaced organophosphorous dips. Farmers were being pressed to reduce nitrogen use and deployment of all herbicides and pesticides. With schemes to restore naturalness to farmland and farming, epitomised by public distaste for genetically modified food, use of the land was becoming more sophisticated and more cautious. Broad-brush approaches were being binned.

At sea everything was different. Salmon farms were left with the guidance: watch out for what works. Where did these chemicals go? What were their dispersal pathways? Wider effects were not considered. There is no understanding in any country of the fate or destination of aquaculture chemicals in the marine environment. We know in agriculture what happens to nitrogen applied to soil. We know in detail. Aquaculture has been allowed to use the sea as an unlicensed dump.

Warnings about these matters were routinely articulated, including by senior scientists, and routinely ignored. One former head of department in Scottish fisheries commented that the scientists who made progress in government were the ones who were, 'amenable to discipline'. Planners cannot be blamed for permitting the industry expansion; they relied on professional guidance. And the clear-thinking scientists had been muzzled.

If one disregarded matter was the effect on the wider environment, another was the effect of extreme chemicals, specifically on shellfish, with the same characteristics as sea lice. After all, crustaceans are a major shellfish family which includes lobsters, Norway lobsters and crabs. Lobsters and their like also moulted and grew new skins, and they were some of the highest-value creatures in the in-shore marine theatre. If the chemicals targeted the chitinous shells of crustacean sea lice, what were they doing to the shells of lobsters a little way down the sea loch? That question was never broached by the regulators.

There was a good reason for this: no regulator with responsibility for that matter existed. For example, in Scotland the Scottish Environmental Protection Agency (SEPA) had no specific remit to cover it. SEPA conducted surveys of sea lochs up to a point, performing some limited testing of seawaters at special locations. But looking for any downstream effects of powerful chemicals used on salmon farms was not their bag.

What salmon farming needed from the outset was, as one of the pioneer salmon farmers expressed it, 'a bobby on the beat'. That is to say, an independent watchdog empowered to oversee the entire industry function. The post has never been advertised.

In so far as they had a serious role in this matter, SEPA looked at the benthos of sea lochs, or the bottom layer. This was the area where in parts of Scotland valuable reefs with all their attendant life-forms were to be found. But government searches were occasional, localised and usually not under the salmon pens themselves. The salmon farm industry was treated with kid gloves. As for the department of fisheries, why, they were involved with formulating quotas for North Sea cod and haddock and the like. Assessment of the shellfish sector consisted of updating catch records; whether lobsters had shells on them was beyond any official ken.

This misalignment persisted even as the Scottish shellfish sector rose in value and finally became of more economic importance than all the trawling and seining and long-lining put together. But that is not the same thing as saying that the salmon farm industry, an epicentre of chemical exfoliation, had no effect on white fish and pelagic species like mackerel and herring. It is to say that no one was looking at it.

Metal contamination from fish farms was disregarded also. Copper is used to inhibit algal growth on pen-cages and on service boats. Copper is lethal to fish, as any hatchery manager knows. Zinc, iron and manganese are components of fish feeds. Other metals leach from metal pen structures. Around salmon farms residues of metals often far exceed guidelines. Elevated metal levels have been matched to the exact start of salmon farming industries.

Salmon farm companies became nervous of growing consumer concern about chemical use. Lateral thinking produced a good idea: clean the dirty fish with lice predators. Enter a small marine fish, happy in the same waters as salmon, equipped with a mouth like the sliding mechanism of a telescope and designed to suck periwinkles and other food from their anchors – the wrasse. Fish farms began using wrasse in pen cages to clean their lice-badged salmon. The wrasse were provided with imitation kelp fronds in which to take cover.

It worked, but there were shortcomings. Populations of wild wrasse from which the cleaning squads could be sourced went up and down; the population was vulnerable to heavy seine-netting. Fish farmers began breeding their own wrasse, but that proved problematical. Wrasse needed special feeds, sex differentiation was a puzzle, and wrasse stress levels, fish farmers claimed, needed investigation. So the aquaculturists reacted, as usual, by asking the Scottish government for financial help now to address the problems of wrasse-farming, and, as usual, they got it, over £2 million. Consider: a financially pressed government doled out aid to highly-profitable foreign multinationals in order to investigate the stress in cleaner fish, themselves introduced to attack out-of-control parasites on other fish now immune to chemical assault. Strange, but this is salmon farming.

Critically, there were more salmon in cages than the wrasse could handle. As lice found the salmon supply an irresistibly immediate host so wrasse found the lice a pleasing repast. But lice overwhelmed the wrasse. It was one thing for wrasse to clean manageable young salmon; adults were a proposition too far. Then, wrasse had a nasty habit: they liked salmon eyeballs and could suck them out. Blind salmon usually died. Using one species to counteract another can have unforeseen side-effects. This one was tricky indeed.

Wrasse utilisation was a neat idea and a useful public relations story, but sea lice proliferated too fast for the lice-eaters. Wrasse became part of the lice response, but a limited one. The chemical solution was the big gun for the big picture.

We will look back from the future and ask, what was going on? Eastern Canada is where the most particular research has been carried out on the effects of salmon farming. The Conservation Council of New Brunswick had this to say in 2008, concluding a chapter on chemicals and metals used on salmon farms: 'Claims that there is no environmental impact are either misinformed or dishonest. Yet governments allow this industry to operate as if it is having no impact on the receiving waters and the plants and animals that live on them. This is unjustifiable and irresponsible.' No one can say we were not told.

The lessons simply never sunk in. Instead, they were ducked. When government officials from salmon farm countries have been quizzed about chemicals they bat away the queries with vague language. These things disperse, they are absorbed, they are nothing to worry about.

Wrong. They are. That was the lesson learned – supposedly – when it was established that smuts of soot locked in Greenland's ice-fields hailed from the industrial heartlands of China, northern Europe and north-eastern America. It can take a mere ten days to push air particles round the world. Water is little different. We all know the stories of messages in bottles crossing the oceans. The North Pacific Gyre, a gyre of seawater which moves in an arc from Alaska, past California to coastal China, and then back to Alaska, contains discarded plastic from all over the Pacific. It has formed a floating carpet some say as big as Texas. Sailors travel through it for days on end. The sea circulates like atmospheric systems. Those officials saying pollutants will just go away are deceiving people, or they are primitives. The 'global village' was a term born in the 1960s; first it was meant culturally, but then it took on an environmental meaning too. Today's international protocols to abate climate change are based on the understanding that effects in one place affect another, half a world away. By now we are all supposed to know these elementary realities.

There is a further problem with fish farm chemicals. Application rates and methodologies recommended for chemicals were not always followed. Worse, they were ignored. Many people connected to the salmon farming business confirm that doses to combat diseases and parasites were frequently exceeded, sometimes by huge amounts, as desperate site managers tried to combat the effects of over-crowding in a valuable crop. It is not a murmur of chemical abuse, it is a drum-beat. Again, this matter was brought to the attention of government by senior civil servants; again it was ignored.

I had a long talk to a diver employed on west Highland salmon farms to remove dead fish, the starkly termed 'morts'. His testimony was nothing short of horrifying.

He described how sea-louse chemicals are administered. A tarpaulin is meant to be slid underneath the pen to be treated and up the sides in order to contain the chemical. The chemicals are mixed and poured in and the fish are left in a mild solution, normally for around half an hour. It is time-consuming and hard work. There is an easier way and the diver had seen it being used, not once but repeatedly.

Fish farmers in a sea loch with little tidal exchange wait for a slack tide. That means no water is moving into the loch or out. The fish have been starved to make them hungry. Then chemicals are poured into open water along with the feed. The starving fish feed in a frenzy. The chemical, meanwhile, languishes motion-free in a flat tide and all the cages on a farm can be treated at once. No tarpaulin to get in place or remove; instead of two or three days the whole operation takes two to three hours. Then the tide arrives. The chemicals and the spare feed are swept along the loch-shore, round the loch-edge, and in due course out of the loch. Any embarrassing evidence is now at sea, link-free.

But consider what has actually happened. The entire loch has been used as a bath. There are chemicals everywhere. The fish farmer can use heavier doses as he is saving money on administering them. Any shellfish still extant in this enlarged treatment zone is likely on the chemical down-drift to be wiped out. The diver recalled one incident where what he called a 'massive pulse of concentrated chemicals' killed every lobster in a retaining-pond down the loch-side from the fish farm. The lobsterman's complaints to the salmon farmers were dismissed: he had been hit by algal bloom. How he had been stricken with algal bloom which had not affected the salmon farm sited closer to the sea was unexplained.

This was only the first chapter in the disturbing testimony which followed. The Uist diver, let us call him Don, tells the story of when chemicals were used in huge overdoses prior to his diving in to remove morts. On morts, the numbers get interesting.

On this occasion there were 4,000–5,000 dead salmon in one pen. He attributed the deaths to overcrowding and bad practices. Sometimes he had been called to sites where pens had sunk from the mass of deceased fish starting to rot in them; he calls these scenes like diving into 'thousand island dressing'. Dead farm salmon are notorious for their awful smell.

At any rate, this time he found his diving gear and put it on. But the suit had been disinfected in undiluted iodine. He became seriously ill whilst working below and was sick underwater. Neat chemical was all over his body. He only just managed to drag himself out. The dose had been two thousand times in excess of what was needed. Don says that dilution mistakes with chemicals were normal. The fish farm workers, he says, laughed it off.

Don describes the substitution of cheaper illegal chemicals in place of legal ones, a malpractice reported in many salmon farm situations. He saw it often. Bottles with broken seals were re-filled with the rougher substitutes. He called the risk of the fish farm being found out, 'zero'. No one ever looked.

Don himself is a sheep farmer as well as diver. He compared the two sets of regulations, the sheep farmer being subjected to routine testing and checking with unannounced visits from officials. He described the two food-production industries as being in 'different worlds'.

In his view, from familiarity with salmon farm operations and the people working on them, site managers are pressurised by their company owners. They are asked to grow fish faster, to larger sizes, on less feed. No parasites. Nothing must get in the way of production targets. Contrary to industry claims that salmon aquaculture has improved its practices beyond comparison with the long ago, Don says that the best site managers, old-fashioned husbandry professionals conscientiously checking their charges for signs of trouble, have largely gone. What he calls 'drones' have replaced them, people who know little of the fish-culture process but who obey orders.

He introduces a new evidence-twist. He described how the condition of nets on a salmon farm was often a good indicator as to the true sea-loch ecology and what practices are being followed. There are various marine creatures which would naturally colonise nets and clog them up; the assortment changes seasonally. Spat from mussels, sea squirts, queenies, hydroids (a relative of sea anemones), kelp and various drifting marine animals latched onto nets, shifted by tides and currents, in the early fish-farming days. They needed to be brushed or hosed off or dislodged with chemicals. That takes time and costs money. A pen-cage lies idle. And the licence to operate stipulates the number of cages allowed on the site.

However, if the sea loch has had its marine organisms eradicated by repeated chemical pulses, hey presto, clean nets. Nets through which salmon can get the vital refreshment of freely flushing clean water and oxygen. Whether there are any sea squirts around is not going to be of much interest, not to anyone. Contrary to the story projected by the salmon farming industry, Don describes a scene today where nets are cleaner, lochs emptier. He paints a picture of the local creel men trying and hopelessly failing to pin environmental degradation and shellfish deaths on huge corporations which employ smooth-talking media-savvy publicists 'selling snake-oil'.

Don moved on to the socio-economic aspect of his case history. It is a key part of the understanding of all salmon farming, wherever it occurs. The places he worked were on Scotland's western islands. They are closed communities, short on jobs. Salmon farming was often the main employer. The salmon farms fortified ageing settlements with at least a smattering of working-age families. Efforts to tear back the veil on bad practices were seen as poor form by other locals. At the extremity, they feared for their jobs. He describes the fish-farm atmosphere frequently as a conspiracy of silence. Speaking out resulted in physical remonstration.

I tried several divers with stories to tell but most of them backed off from being quoted. Not so Donald Macleod, a lobsterman from Lewis. He works a twenty-foot boat and fishes solo. He described how his catches had fallen by up to two-thirds since fish farms had begun to populate the sea loch. He described how he and other shell fishermen in Loch Sealg discovered their lobster and prawn catches falling off sharply. They found dead and dying prawns and lobsters in the creels; the small local crabs had all vanished. But when they asked about the deployment of chemicals they tended to be rebuffed and fobbed off by the fish farmers with condescending explanations. The theoretical regulatory body SEPA privately conceded that intensive sea-louse treatments had been going on, sometimes with unpermitted chemicals.

Donald Macleod noted that severe outbreaks of sea lice were followed by barren periods in the sea lochs. Good fishing zones had been zapped. The further out to sea and far from shore he went, the more prolific the shellfish. His previous fishing ground was sterile. In place of prawns and shellfish there were invasions of carrion-consuming and poison-bearing starfish. Long-time creel-man Donald MacLeod sometimes wondered, with discomfort, if the shellfish he sold for a living were themselves safe to eat.

On a land farm there is a record book. This applies to a stock farm or an arable farm. What chemicals have been used is recorded; what dosages over what area or on how many animals. Even the purchase date and expiry date of the chemicals used are logged. Machinery is tested. A farm sprayer on a crop-growing farm is checked annually in an examination taking several hours. Each spray-jet is examined for efficiency by a specialist person in case the chemical load on the land is more or less than allowed. The person applying the spray himself must be certificated and trained. Chemical application is a highly sensitive matter, made more so by legal actions about spray-drift hurting the health of those nearby.

The overall chemical burden being applied to European land by its farmers is falling sharply. This is partly because soil testing has resulted in areas being subjected to dosage restrictions, as in nitrate vulnerable zones, or forbidden altogether. Every year fewer chemicals are allowed on European Union farmland in a general movement towards a less-dependant and more natural mode of food production. Application of chemicals using global satellite positioning is now greatly refined. Computerised sensors on spraying machinery dictate precisely how much chemical is needed on any part of the land. Larger farmers in particular have taken up GPS-controlled applications both as a more efficient use of expensive chemicals and to avoid land being over or under dosed. Wise-use application with less waste. The honed sophistication of chemicals use has come a long way on farmland.

Salmon culture is in glaring contrast. Chemicals are used in ever-greater quantities and ever-greater numbers to combat epidemics and sea lice which, especially since 2009, have acquired immunity. Checking is minimal, training is optional (except in

Norway), and the industry has a large degree of self-regulation. Sea-lice data collection in Scotland, from the time the parasite acquired immunity, has actually been cut. Official documents now show that the Scottish government was bullied into this 2010 reversal by strong-arm industry lobbying. The industry, not for the first time, dictated to the regulators.

There is no meaningful threat of loss of the operating licence for fish farmers. Licences, like compound chemicals, endure. Compare this to stock farming on land, where individual farmers are not infrequently banned from having farm animals and whose farms can be closed instantly as bio-security risks. Cattle farmers with foot and mouth on one animal are de-barred from moving any stock at all. Compare it, too, to sea fishermen, operating in the same arena as salmon farmers. In 2012 there were several high-profile cases about the severe treatment being meted out by courts to fishermen who had flouted some ingredient of Europe's complex Common Fisheries Policy. Found with a few fish in the hold without quota, and the fisherman faced jail or a fine or both. Would anyone care to compute the damage done to the seas by that handful of the wrong dead fish calibrated against the insidious lasting harm wrought by repeatedly dosing open sea with strong chemicals on an industrial scale?

Physical over-crowding, to an extent which would never be allowed for land animals, takes place below the waves, out of sight. Some salmon farms now contain one-and-a-half million fish. Individual pens can hold 200,000 salmon. These holding-pens are not large, just one hundred feet in diameter and maybe the same in depth. As senior British fisheries scientist Dr Richard Shelton said long ago: 'The industry is much too large relative to the receiving habitat.'

A small cubic area of water is being occupied by multitudes of fish worth enormous sums of money. A single sea loch could today contain more cultured salmon that the estimated number of individuals of the whole species in the wild. The weirdness of it is encapsulated in the latest industry-devised formula to assess acceptable stocking rates: fish farmers talk about what percentage of a water body is salmon and what percentage remains water. If ninety-eight per cent of the containment is water not fish, that, apparently, is all right. Land animals at least have the unlimited air above.

Birds in aviaries occupy a cubic area. The mathematics on this would be complex as birds are winged, but if zoos held birds in aviaries in comparable densities to which salmon are held in pen-cages there would be a hullabaloo.

In 2012 there was a public outcry in eastern England when a farm partnership proposed a large modernistic pig unit to hold eight thousand sows. Planners prevaricated, and the strength of public objection eventually led them to turn down the planning application. The situation with salmon farmers, in a primitive output-focused industry run by large international companies, which has fought tigerishly against attempts at control, where waste management is left to the sea, is unrecognisably different. Don the diver concludes: 'The situation is getting worse. The business is owned by Norwegians. It is not their environment. They don't give a rat's arse what happens in Scotland.'

Norway is the home of salmon farming and the industry leader. The country has an almost unending coastline, 3,000 miles of it. Much of it is protected from storm surges and waves owing to a jagged profile incised with numerous long and deep fjords. Facing the Atlantic the water is warmed by the North Atlantic Drift and is therefore favourable for salmon-growing.

The Norwegians knew how to grow salmon in the fjords before anyone else had attempted it on a commercial scale. In 1969 smolts were put in suspended nets in the sea and harvested two years afterwards. It is said that salmon farming in Norway received the approval and support from government that has been the industry mainstay because this small nationalistic Scandinavian social democracy, with its acute sense of liberal humanism, was eager not to be seen as solely a fossil fuel extractor, subsisting on pumped fuel from the biggest natural oilfields outside the USA and Arabia. Norwegians like to present conspicuously green credentials to the world.

Politicians acclaimed the industry as a flagship accomplishment. World leading again came naturally. With only four and a half million inhabitants, and beyond the reach of migration from the EU (of which it is not a member), Norway is a very rich country indeed. Fossil fuel wealth has been used by the government to back salmon farming whenever there has been serious trouble – an inconvenient paradox given their green credentials. The power of salmon farming in Norwegian politics is said to be formidable; and the north and west where the industry operates is over-represented politically.

Norwegian national affairs are not transparent from the outside, but it is said that Norwegian banks have stepped in behind the only big national food export industry whenever needed.

When there was a trade dispute in 2008 about whether or not live salmon ova from Norway could be imported into British salmon farms the Norwegians cited free trade in pressing their case for access. This was despite the fact that in Norway precautionary disinfection of the eggs was performed by the same companies selling them. Hardly satisfactory. At that time no live fish material from anywhere was allowed to be imported into the UK. Independent fish farmers in the Scottish industry pleaded for a quarantine arrangement, in a closed re-circulation hatchery, to double-check against importing new diseases or, more pertinently, so far unknown diseases. They said that fish disease shifted with shifting fish, as it had with gyrodactylus salaris in Norway and with infectious salmon anaemia all over. The Norwegians counter-argued about the performance characteristics of their home-grown eggs. The UK industry, in any case mostly Norwegian-owned, lost. The Scottish government shrank from even minor impediments inconveniencing these bold international Nordic investors.

Norway has used its deep cold fjords as natural salmon farm zones along the coastline from Stavanger in the south upwards to Troms County in the north. Less well flushed than shallower sea lochs in Scotland they are also far further from markets. To reach France, a main buyer, takes four days by road instead of one day from Scotland. But the number of fjords is huge; Scandinavia's western coastline is jaggedly indented end to end. Some fjords are jam-packed with several hundred net-pens. Information about Norwegian salmon farms is not easily accessed (the Norwegians know the value of language as cover) but the government figure for the population of salmon in pens in 2010 was 290 million.

Where these farms are most concentrated, wild salmon have almost totally expired. Around 120 rivers have lost all or most of their original salmon stocks. Norway's salmon rivers number 550, so a fifth are maimed or deceased. Biologists believe that the disappearance of the remaining wild strains could follow in time. In some rivers 80 per cent of salmon caught by sport anglers started their lives not in rivers but in hatcheries for aquaculture.

Not only have wild fish been overwhelmed by sea lice but their home rivers have been ravaged by a more immediately lethal parasite, this time a freshwater one called *Gyrodactylus salaris*. Gyro presented a nightmare on a new scale: affected salmon simply died. The parasite spread outwards from a government smolt hatchery in the mid 1970s. It sent not only Norway but the whole eastern side of the Atlantic salmon world into a spin of apprehension. This tiny creature could have spelled the beginning of the end.

So severe was the effect that in order to purify rivers for potential re-occupation by salmonids the government conducted a scorched-earth policy where the virus had struck, literally killing all life-forms and possible Gyro vectors within an affected water catchment. Successful treatments must eradicate every single fish to cleanse the system. Rivers were meticulously mapped so that no hidden pocket of poison remained undetected. Spraying teams scarily clad in chemical-warfare white zoot-suits and resembling post-atomic decontamination personnel marched in lines across catchments treating every water body, big and small. Aluminium sulphate and the chemical rotenone were used. It was a dramatic response to a dramatically lethal parasite.

After 40 years battling with Gyro, and facing up to the need for multiple treatments for a chance of elimination, there are a few signs of recovery. Norway claims twenty rivers have been restored, including the multi-river system of Rana in the north, and fourteen more are in the five-year quarantine prior to being declared Gyro-free. Others remain infected. Great salmon rivers like the Laerdal still hang in the balance. The government claims it is gaining ground, an asseveration contradicted by some of those actually on the ground. Lost rivers are a highly contentious issue domestically and hard facts are difficult to come by.

What makes the story yet more compelling is the way biology favours the salmon when under this dire attack. Most of the rivers treated had a reserve of older fish still in the sea. They are the re-population gene pool. The elasticity of the salmon lifecycle may make the critical difference between a river surviving, and Norway losing one of its tantalising wildlife treasures. If the government considered a population was likely to get infected, or potentially endangered, eggs were frozen for re-awakening when the habitat was clean enough to succour them. It is somehow a very salmon story.

Other countries potentially in the Gyro zone took precautions to keep it out. In Iceland all fishing gear, on which the killer parasite can attach for up to half a year, is sterilised before being allowed through Customs. This is done by freezing or by chemical cleansing. In Scotland some rivers insist on anglers signing declaration forms certifying that they have not visited any Gyro zones within the last half year. Free disinfection is frequently offered. Gyro has the capacity to wipe out salmon stocks entirely within any water catchment that it penetrates, and might be the most lethal threat ever to face wild salmon. The aftermath of salmon culturing has yet to be worked through fully.

There is a reason – of sorts – for lax rules about salmon escaping from the Norwegian fjords. Escapement of fish from Norwegian salmon farms means something different biologically in the country where salmon genetics originates. It is the big-framed Norwegian fish that salmon farmers everywhere wanted in order to maximise growth from expensive feeds. In order to attain commercial sizes fish farmers did not want early-maturing grilse which were too small for smoking and ordinary processing. Using big multi-sea winter salmon from rivers like the Namsen, this possibility was reduced. The same heftier fish had better sea-lice resistance, a further bonus.

Salmon farm bloodlines all go back to Norway. The best strains come from just a few sources; salmon aquaculture's gene pool is very narrow. If farm salmon escape from fish farms in Norway, which happens routinely, the escaped fish may not be genetically similar, but they are attuned to the same climate as the wild ones.

Broodstock genetics is not of only academic interest; it is of the essence. In spring 2012 Scottish salmon fishery boards, which manage rivers, out of the blue received a novel request. Salmon farmers, who until that point had been cold-shouldering the champions of wild fish because of criticisms over the proliferation of sea lice and farm escapees flooding natural rivers, asked wild-salmon river owners to become their customers. Salmon farmers needed new genetics. They wanted broodstock eggs from the so-far uncontaminated rivers of eastern Scotland. And they were prepared to pay. River owners thought for a few moments. That was all the time needed. If their precious genetics were sold, crossed with Norwegian bloodlines, and the new hybrid salmon then escaped, their own gene pools at home risked being back-crossed by new alien hybrids. The witches' brew of escapee/wild genetics would get even harder, if it came to it, ever to unravel.

If the gene bank was ultimately the most valuable possession of salmon fishery board members, as was being slowly recognised, this was a non-starter. Which is how the boards were advised by their umbrella organisation, the Association of Salmon Fishery Boards.

To the Norwegian state, the salmon is a different animal. It is not the fish of ancient lore, the quiddity of the creature culture. The Norwegian state has accepted that a consequence of salmon farming is the loss of many of its once-great salmon rivers and the replacement of original stock with fish-farm escapees. Some areas have been kept clear of salmon farms in the hope that original strains will survive. Others are officially 'national salmon rivers', but still have farms in their vestibules. In the rest, policies imply the species is expendable. Given the affluence of this closed-off north European country, it is perhaps an odd posture. Perhaps.

It is not the first time Norway has led the world on the sea. It was once the world's principal whaling nation. Having exhausted whale stocks in the northern hemisphere Norwegian whalers moved to Antarctica and harpooned the giant mammals in the freezing oceans there too. Several species of that great creature were driven to the verge of extinction, but the Norwegian whaling effort only relented when operations became uneconomic owing to the paucity of the surviving quarry. Indeed, harvesting the filter-feeding or baleen whales peaked as recently as the 1950s. Only in 1986 did Norway finally abandon most of its commercial whaling, persisting only with more numerous minke whales. In salmon farming the independent, hard-headed, nationalistic attitude is recognisably the same, and salmon farming was well underway by the time Norway's commercial whaling had shrunk. Norwegians held the lead.

When will intensive fjord salmon farming come to an end, as whaling had to? That question may depend on a creature as long as your fingernail, the frighteningly versatile sea louse. For sea lice discovered in the Norwegian fjords a louse mecca; they swarm over salmon in concentrations numbering millions. Salmon may carry hundreds of lice where any number over ten is considered to increase the risk of death; smolts are routinely found with over fifteen times the quantity of lice considered to be fatal.

Louse counts began to mount steeply in 2009 and since then government spot checks have been introduced in what is recognised as an emergency. Salmon farmers in Norway are obliged to conduct and report on louse counts regularly. Standards are set for permissible numbers of louse per fish. If a farm is heavily infested treatments must be completed within 14 days. At the time of writing it is unclear whether farmers or parasitism will win this battle. Epidemiologists would back the louse.

Norway is also known for the porosity of its pen systems. The tight regulatory grip applied to its successful sea fishery does not extend to managing salmon farming. When the disease furunculosis, which causes boils on the flanks, hit Norwegian fish farms in 1985 it rampaged through the poorly coordinated industry, spreading to over 500 farms by 1992. Norwegian pen-cages are described by local critics as 'sieves'.

There are some respects in which the originator of salmon farming is still ahead. In Norway smolt production units are not allowed in floating cages in freshwater. They use recycled systems with control over both inputs and outputs, or bodies of water without migratory fish. Fallowing, which allows the benthos to recover, is at any rate officially approved of, though enactment of it is not properly enforced. Until 2009, when sea lice overcame the control systems, dosing in early spring and summer to coincide with when females had egg-trains had been suppressing the worst outbreaks. Chemical treatments have to be approved by fish-health biologists and each salmon farm is attached to a local fish-health service. Judgements about veterinary procedures are therefore in the hands of professionals, not local site managers. Norway's navy has revised its operational procedures in recognition of the sonar affects of some operations on fish in general, avoiding spawning grounds and intensely fish-filled areas and, uniquely amongst salmon aquaculture countries, it polices a 200-metre safety zone around all its salmon farms.

Mostly Norway is known as the home not only of the biggest salmon farming output but also as the domicile of the largest salmon farming companies, quoted on the Oslo stock exchange and remitting taxes to Norway. Marine Harvest, the industry leader, with a head office in Bergen, also has salmon farms in Scotland, Chile, Canada, the Faroe Islands and Ireland, and is the largest sea-farm operator in most places in which it operates. Including processing factories, Marine Harvest has operations in 21 countries.

Genetics is said to be a word that triggers instant sleep. People just switch off. Maybe they shouldn't. In Atlantic salmon, the gene is everything. Groups of genetic stocks are compatible, for sure. Peter Gray showed that the Tyne could accommodate strains from neighbouring rivers. The problem arises when a gene-type from a substantially different background barges into a new zone. The genetic stocks which today's biologists have shown to have developed singular characteristics, not only river by river but even in different branches of the same river, took thousands of years to differentiate. In evolutionary terms those altered profiles are vital. What they represent is detailed adaptation to survival on a micro-scale.

Evolved genetics of the salmon demonstrate evolution arming a particular fish from a particular river as best able to combat challenges which Nature may throw up. So it is that salmon are armoured with genetic resistance even to local diseases in their home rivers. Or minerals. If there is more or less aluminium, or iron, they adapt. As they have adapted body size, and rivers with awkward waterfalls have heavier-shouldered, stronger salmon able to make the jumps, so they have adapted genetically to water-quality issues, river by river. At a snail's pace challenges thrown up by Nature, happenstance or by human development, forge a response in the genes. The fish is bound on a wheel of adaptation for survival in the long timeframe.

This is where escaped salmon pose an unacceptable risk. Salmon scientists have coined the phrase 'extinction vortex' to describe what they believe could ultimately happen if genetically uncongenial salmon hybridise with steadily surviving stocks from a different location and a different latitude.

Take run timings. Scientists are fascinated by these. What makes a salmon in the north-east Atlantic, gaining weight and condition preparatory to the breeding migration, ready to go? What determines the decision either to stay on the winter feeding grounds and gain more weight to make a better chance of successful spawning a year later, or run now, maybe as a grilse, and replicate itself at the earliest opportunity? Some say that this decision is predetermined in the genes. Others say that individual fish have growth targets to meet before starting the long journey home. In any cohort of smolts it is known that more males return as grilse and more females as multi-sea winter breeders. Females grow slower. What determines these things?

Complicating matters are the historical records of cycles. The best of these were logged by salmon netsmen long ago. They sold salmon by weight and prices moved with the seasons. For one cycle salmon will mainly return as older fish. Then the timings switch – no one knows why – and they are coming back as grilse. In the main. No cycle is ever more than a switch by the majority. At some point a cycle of grilse turns into a cycle of older salmon. So something overcame the dictates of the genes to change the pattern, or that mutation was in the gene itself. Nobody can be sure which.

What sends the shivers up researchers is that the Atlantic salmon's supreme adaptability when faced with salmon farming, and a witches' brew of genetics swamping discrete and separate populations, may prove its undoing. The fish which has survived a panoply of mankind's attacks may be finally undermined by rogue elements in its own species.

Let us look closely at this. A fish from northern Norway is programmed to run in a six-week brief summer period when the river is physically accessible and when temperatures permit. It is a mere squeak of time. In parts of southern and central Europe, for example in the UK, wild salmon poke into rivers right through the year. The River Tay in Scotland is an example. The fish has evolved with as wide as possible a migration window to spread the risk of an inopportune arrival time. There could be a land-slide smothering the river-bed, and redds, with silt. There could be a drought which sucks life-giving oxygen from the water. There could be algae, de-oxygenating water. There could be a virus in the water. Long run-timings mean there is the maximum chance to beat Nature's googly, freak conditions. If all the fish in a river were farm descendants and they ran in six weeks instead of fifty, a huge chunk of the defence mechanism which the species had evolved would be gone. Rod anglers' opportunity to catch them would shrink too.

The elasticity of run-timing could involve new arrival patterns to avoid human threats, even salmon netting at sea or angling. It was shown in Canada, when studying the collapse of the northern cod, that 'fishing-induced selection' was a reality. Fish adapted to avoid being caught. It makes sense in two ways for salmon. The fish snared by nets set off Scotland at a particular time in a particular place continue to disappear as they are netted out; they leave no progeny. Rod-angling could plausibly work as another form of physical threat which the salmon genes could react to, even overcome, simply by running at a different time.

The mainstream scientific view is that run timings are determined, if not only by genetics then also by temperatures at sea – which in turn determine food supply – and by general climatic factors.

On every possible score when farmed fish invaded an environment occupied by wild salmon they did provable damage. That they can and do hybridise with wild fish is a fact.

The survival of escapees depends on circumstances. Autumn and winter escapes entail higher mortality and wider dispersal. Summer and spring jail-break fish disperse in the neighbourhood and survive better. Fish escaping anywhere near the breeding season tend to run the nearest rivers. At first loitering near their former prisons, and subsisting on the pellets filtering through the nets, they began to spread out after two weeks.

When escaped cultured females invaded rivers with wild populations in them they destroyed redds made by wild fish and cut their own in place. Fugitives were usually prone to spawning later than wild fish, then superimposing their own eggs. Farm fish actually destroy the egg-nests of successful wild hens. In a few cases they spawned earlier. Critically, the cultured fish progeny survive less well in the river because females do not cover the eggs as thoroughly as wild fish, and they make fewer nests. Their fins and tails, stubby from cage-rubbing, cannot dig good redds. They take up the space but fail to make it work for them. If they were in a fish farm they would be culled for inefficiency.

Tests done on the River Imsa in Norway demonstrated that survival efficiency of escapees was between a quarter (for males) and a third (for females) of that of wild stock. Offspring from the spawnings of escapees were then monitored the following autumn. The farm genetics failed to do well in the wild. Under a fifth of the population returning from the sea had farm genetic markers. Those that had survived, moreover, were hybrids, or half-wild. The pure farm offspring constituted only eight per cent of the first year parr. As smolts, the farm breed migrated down rivers to the sea earlier and at a younger age. Hybrids came next; wild fish ran last. All the timings were scrambled up.

When they matured, again, farm escapees came back at a different time. They matured after 3.4 years whereas wild ones waited until they were 4.2 years. Finally the researchers calculated the farm escapees' lifetime reproductive success. It was just 16 per cent of that of the native salmon. That comes on top of the population depression of wild smolts themselves from the effects of invading farm fish.

A ten-year experiment along similar lines done in western Ireland at Burrishoole showed the lifetime success of farmed escapees measuring only two per cent of wild fish. Researchers made the point that Burrishoole is a very long way from where the farm salmon genetics assembled in northern Norway. Survival at sea for these alien strains and their hybrids was close to non-existent.

Conversely, during the 1990s on the River Vosso in Norway in just eight years the proportion of wild fish in the run fell from 80 per cent to only 40 per cent. This river's native salmon was being replaced by an alien mix at frightening speed. But in the ensuing three years, with no reported escapement from cage systems at the mouth, the wild component of the run rose again, slightly.

The questions about recovery of wild salmon populations which have been impacted by escapees is very complex. Writing climate change into these wobbly predictions makes matters even more difficult and suppositional.

Much depends on how long the continued intrusions of farm fish into the native stock persist. Researchers have run several models to try to capture some definition. One model even showed hybrid fish replacing wild salmon completely over twenty generations. But the consensus was that if escaped fish become too numerous, there is real risk. Research scientists conclude that wild populations with farm salmon intrusions are likely to narrow their genetic variability, retain less survival fitness, and be more vulnerable to events thrown up by Nature.

It is resilience from adaptability which so critically risks being lost. The farm fish has not had the critical benefit of natural selection. Its programming is missing the continuous evolutionary adjustment which filters into the programming of wild fish. Protected in a hatchery for its early life it is also the subject of what they call 'directional selection'. That means breeding for specific characteristics. Shy of making grand statements which cannot be proven, biologists agree on one thing: escapes need stopping to protect wild salmon.

Look at it from the fish point of view and the survival challenge for farmed escapees is understandable. The fugitive salmon has left his confinement; an oceanic universe beckons. But tucked away in the fish's ticking time-clock is an atavistic instinct to breed. So ... find some fresh water. But this poor fish has no scent memory to guide him or her. He has no buried 'river experience', as scientists call early imprinting. He lacks any water chemistry route-finders, signals or environmental cues. So he explores the nearest freshwater he, or she, can smell.

Unlike the experience for the wild fish, he finds himself a stranger in a foreign country. That explains why responses to predators do not function properly for escapees. Redds have to be located in this strange territory. The wild fish merely returns to his own birthplace; electromagnetic fields, water chemistry and a host of geophysical factors help him. The escapee is an earthling on the moon. It is bad for him and it looks as though it is bad all-round.

Biologists conducting these research programmes were uniformly pessimistic about the overall species effect of farm escapees suddenly descending upon time-tested wild populations. They believe that future populations would have decreased survival fitness and less resistance to events. They envisaged the longer evolutionary term with fewer and fewer recruitment fish and populations tumbling down the slope to non-sustainability.

Particularly as farm escapement is repetitive, often an annual event, repeatedly attacking the integrity of progressively more vestigial wild stocks, they concluded that the Atlantic salmon species, in an invaded river, could die out.

The chilling phrase 'extinction vortex' expresses that ghastly contemplation.

Stressing the narrow genetic range of farm salmon in fish farms – up to 90 per cent of original stocks came from only four strains – they say that the heterogeneity found in wild Atlantic salmon and the phenomenal adaptive potential of the species will be gradually diminished and finally lost. It is an incredibly depressing picture.

The decrease of the wild strain reads like this. Farm fish colonists are larger as parr and more aggressive. But a river has a finite capacity for supporting young salmon. Punchy escapees hinder the breeding success of natives. The bigger Norwegian-origin escapees grow faster and can then compete with wild parr on the redds. Here is the crunch: farm escapees out-fight wild youngsters in rivers, but they survive much less well in the sea. So the loss of native strains in their nurseries is not compensated by marine survival of their competitors. It is a loss/loss situation. Less salmon of all types returns, full stop.

Farmed invaders can carry pathogens to which the native fish have less or no resistance. Furunculosis, infectious salmon anaemia, and infectious pancreatic necrosis (IPN) are salmon farm diseases that have spread into the wild. The latest assailant is amoebic gill disease, suffocating victims by blocking their gills, and supposedly originating in Tasmania. It is this horror that pushed the official number of farm deaths in the Scottish industry to 8.5 million in 2012. The greater the number and severity of environmental stresses, and overcrowding falls into this category, the more susceptible wild stocks become to diseases for which they lack immunity and which they are not programmed genetically to withstand.

I asked a blue-skies question to one of the leading scientists researching salmon farm impacts on wild stocks. Could the situation revert? If fish farms were removed from estuaries would the wild stock re-establish? I understand the scientists' predicament. Their entire training is not about speculation but about proving hypotheses by empirical test. Obviously, this question begs a situation which does not exist. But the reply, as a cautious guess, was that wild stocks might well recover, and if a river had lost its own genetic strain completely a neighbouring river could theoretically, over time, colonise the unoccupied territory. The hybrids which might at first be left occupying the river would breed out their alien genes and a new adapted genome of wild fish could appear. Maybe.

It is said when discussing species replacement and alien invaders that it took thousands of years to breed the wolf out of the dog, but it needs a mere flicker of time to breed the wolf back in again. What would happen in the case of salmon is a very interesting question.

For the time being we are left at the beginning of this cycle, not the end. The longer farm escapees had been on the loose prior to breeding the more they closed the gap in survival efficiency whilst the young fish were in rivers. The healthiest wild populations repelled and resisted farm invasions better than weaker under-number populations. That means that rivers already damaged because their outgoing smolts were attacked by swarms of lice were even less capable of withstanding an invasion of escapees than rivers without fish farms. If anyone takes these conclusions seriously, fish farm escapement should be stopped. Why isn't it?

Salmon have escaped from their cages from the beginning and without ceasing. One Norwegian salmon farm in August 2005 lost half a million salmon. Outbreaks go on and on unendingly. They get out in storms when nets collapse or tear but also when being moved about, dosed, vaccinated and dipped. Accidents can happen all too easily when moving large concentrations of big, fast fish in a fluid environment. They spot a hole in a net like water finds a hole in a bucket. When a cattle farmer shifts cows from field to field it takes a while to funnel pesky beasts through the right gate: try that when the ones that get away vanish with one tail-flip into a measureless environment, forever after invisible. Some escapees want to cut a good distance between themselves and their former confinement: farm salmon have been recovered 2,800 miles from their broken home-cages.

Industry assurances that security is improving have been shown to be misleading. As salmon production moves to wilder, more off-shore sites, partly to get round the waste-disposal issues of sea lochs, weather in open seas will be harder to handle. Directionless waifs will break into an open ocean. Until the world is devoid of storms, mountainous tidal surges and storm-driven swells, and also determined salmon predators, fish will get out. Whilst large active fish are moved around in vast numbers at sea, many will get free.

Escapes are meant to be reported. Who knows if they are? The official figure consists only of those reported. Observers believe it is a fraction of what really slips out. After all, they are untraceable. If government took escapement seriously, failure to report would be penalised. In the history of Scottish salmon farm industry there has never been a revocation of a license owing to failure to report escapes. Not one. Maybe to government, waif salmon are no more than seal-food.

One way of trying to remedy matters would be to have two layers of net. Some farms now double the net on and around the bottom to try to protect their stock, but doubling the nets doubles the weight to be lifted for cleaning. It doubles the investment cost. Attempts by regulators to force better security on salmon culturists are met with howls of protest about rising cost. The big international company owners threaten to move their operations to cheaper operating locations. After 50 years, farm salmon escapement is no closer to being solved. And while countries vie with each other to keep this ugly form of intensive production on their doorsteps, it never will be. As long ago as 1980 at two major scientific symposia there were clear warnings about the dire genetic and environmental consequences of the industry being allowed to continue as it was. Of regulatory or political reaction there was none.

They were not short of possible options. Regulators could have neutralised the risk of escapees at a stroke. Fish farmers could have been obliged to use triploids – fish which cannot breed. The process is simple, involving pressure-shocking the ova, and it is normal practice in carp, rainbow trout and oyster farming. Salmon farmers never liked the idea. Their quoted reason was that the public would be put off, that neutered fish would lose part of their healthful image. Truly? No one minds eating lamb or beef from castrated males. Even the question of minding is hard to conceptualise.

What actually deterred salmon farmers from wiping out threats to wild fish at a stroke was a simple inconvenience: in early trials triploids did not grow so well. There were some deformities, inadequate weight gains, more mortalities. Yet these were the sorts of problems the industry had solved in other areas. What really decided things was that regulators were asleep at the wheel, or condign in a conspiracy. No one insisted that this was the only acceptable route. In Scotland the research into better production of triploids was first reported 40 years down the line in 2011.

The report when it came stated that, despite low triploid knowledge levels, by using better ova, by altering diet, and by specific family selection programmes, the researchers had every hope of being able to produce salmon to compare well with conventional stocks. Which is what trout, oyster and carp farmers presumably did long ago. It seems amazing that the threat to wild salmon from escapees was never taken seriously enough at the outset to order from the industry a full-scale research effort into using sterile fish. As it is, we live surrounded by seas swarming with escaped feed-lot domestics capable of hybridising.

No one really understands what happens to the bulk of the fish that break free. Millions vanish into the North Atlantic every month. It is presumed many are eaten by seals or porpoises or fail to find food and die, to nourish crabs. Some, as is well attested, enter river systems introducing the threat of hybridisation and species-weakening. Fish flesh breaks down fast at sea. Despite the huge tonnages of fish which must die, seemingly many just vanish.

Salmon farmers' stock response to criticism about filling the sea with deceased domesticated animals is that escapes are not in their interests and therefore it is obvious that they do their best to stop them. This insults the intelligence. The industry has grown meteorically. The fact is that profit levels are sufficient to allow escapes to be absorbed financially. A form of farming which has no waste-disposal charges, either of food or excretions from the fish themselves or of chemical treatments, is saving an awful lot of cost.

Again, take in comparison a sheep farm. If stock die, the knacker is called and he disposes of them – for a charge. If sheep-dip is used, it is either pumped out and taken away, or drained or pumped into a licensed sump or disposal place. Dip disposal is charged and the licence to use your own land costs a fee. Animal feed is not wasted, it is too expensive. But if it did happen to be thrown around wastefully a farm inspector finding rodents can order the destruction of vermin, levy fines, and even close the farm down. If chemicals lapse out of date, they have to be collected by licensed agencies, and disposed of, at a high cost. The removal of a few gallons can cost hundreds of pounds.

A salmon farm in Scotland has one licence, a discharge consent from SEPA. The consent lays down the biomass, or number of tons of salmon, permitted on one site. That is the principal handle of official control. The consent, or licence, also lays down what medicines can be used. Fish farmers must tell SEPA before they intend using them.

The consents are site-specific. Each site has its own licence. Part of this consent is the obligation to do a sediment survey below or near the cage site. Just where the mechanised grab takes the benthic (bottom sediment) sample is imprecise. The aquaculturists commission this work themselves. At a literal level they manage the inspection of themselves. SEPA takes a few water samples, but the procedure is not laid down or methodical. Shellfish, which could potentially bio-accumulate wastes and chemicals, are not tested. The benthic surveys are the main source of information to government on the state of the site.

The consent costs fish farmers around £3,000. An interesting fact is that whatever the survey results, consents are never revoked. Recently, these surveys have become publicly available. Two things stand out: several sites and farm operations fail, and many cage farms remain untested. Still licences are not revoked. Providing the operator pays the fee, the license continues; in practice, fees are always paid and salmon farmers hang onto their discharge licenses. So as the industry expands, licences have proliferated. More and more by-products of salmon farming are accumulating in the sludge beneath cages.

Compare the situation in Scottish fresh waters. SEPA tests these rigorously. Some rivers are tested monthly. All are tested annually, regardless of whether there are consents for some form of aquaculture or not. In a contained body of water like a river the laboratory technicians say they can detect some chemicals present at one-millionth of the water volume. Some readings are in billionths. The European Union has introduced very tough directives on the health of fresh water. The days of polluting rivers with impunity are long gone.

Salmon farmers' relationship with a free saltwater environment represents a wonderful boon. Half a million fish lost need not result in the economic closure of the unit at all. Escapement and the disappearance of hundreds of thousands of the stock are regarded by the industry as part of routine costs.

Pen-cages cannot hold salmon effectively for reasons other than their physical inadequacy for the locations they occupy. One is that they attract predators. Seals in the northern Atlantic have probably never been more numerous. Before the days of industrial-scale commercial sea-fishing, seal populations are unrecorded. Seal harvests supplied leather for boots and clothes and all manner of useful things made of hide, and the fat for burning in oil-lamps and flesh for food had separate values, but the culls were not annotated.

When intensive sea fishing began in the nineteenth century, with modern trawls and seines, seals lost part of a fish food supply. More recently they gained protection in the aftermath of whaling. Finally, seals have feasted on a modern fisheries policy predicated on discarding fish for which skippers have no quota. Tons of good fish with burst swim-bladders are routinely tipped back in by trawlers, a cascade of free lunches for a resurgent seal population.

Salmon farmers have found voracious seals the worst marine enemies of several. Seals can act in a group and drive the fish to the corners of nets and then bite or slash through the entanglement. The enormous imprisoned food supply, a whisker away, is irresistible. They even damage fish by chomping through the net-pens when they fail to tear them open. Warm-blooded sea mammals move 'like greased lightning', as one salmon farmer said, and although they are usually pushed to capture wild salmon in open water, they can nail slower-moving cold-blooded fish entangled in netting with casual ease. Other creatures damage nets, including mink. The net-pen system in the estuary is akin to staking out a pen of goats in lion country. They are magnets for predators.

In most salmon farm countries seals can be controlled by shooting. Salmon farmers have tried acoustic methods of deterrence, but these last no longer than the crafty mammal's ability to detect their shortcomings. And seals are highly intelligent.

The problem with seals massing round salmon farms is that these places are where wild salmon are migrating. UK waters host 200,000 grey seals, according to ICES – over a third of the world's total number. Fishermen, who have to haul their nets with seals robbing them of fish right up to the side of the boat, say there are far more. It is reckoned seals take a big chomp out of wild salmon runs already. Bulky mammals, they eat around fifteen pounds of fish each per day. Seals and other sea mammals, like porpoises, of which there are 300,000–400,000 in the North Sea, and less numerous top-of-the-food-chain dolphins, frustrated by net-pen security deterrence then home in on the wild fish swimming past.

Another threat to the caged salmonids are jellyfish. They can sting salmon to death and asphyxiate them by clogging their gills. A million casualties have resulted from the worst invasions. Fish farmers are powerless to prevent this and live in dread of onshore winds twinned with sea conditions pushing jellyfish into their cages. Getting the slimy stingers out of the nets can be a testing experience. What happens to the corpses? The industry is disinclined to discuss this matter.

The estuary or fjord, long a place of relative innocence, has become a battleground for survival. One of the legacies of the battle lies on the sea floor and is present in the water. The most detailed work on this was done in New Brunswick by its Conservation Council.

In the Bay of Fundy over a hundred salmon farms, mostly owned by one company, are massed together. It is the densest concentration of salmon farms anywhere. Fundy is a suitable location for salmon farming in that it is a deeply indented, spacious inlet which is mostly ice-free in winter – its cold water is slow-growing but not too cold to grow fish – and its location enables road-transit to the market in Boston in under 24 hours. For government it was, like the north-west Highlands of Scotland, a desolate social scene, poor and devoid of employment options.

The fact that several dozen Atlantic salmon rivers debouched into the bay, when the industry first arrived, was not considered noteworthy. That many of these were suffering precipitous declines and the wild salmon was fast becoming endangered was an unconnected side-story. One river on the west of the bay had a spawning run which had collapsed from a thousand spawners to literally two pairs. That ranked as a side-story too. The fact that some Bay of Fundy salmon populations had a peculiarly restricted migratory pattern and barely left the bay, making them permanently vulnerable to coastal sea lice, was not understood then; it would have made no difference either. How do we know? Because when Bay of Fundy wild salmon runs contracted in the space of two decades from around 40,000 salmon to two hundred, that did not matter either.

One reason for the accommodating attitude of regulators was that the Atlantic Salmon Federation, speaking for wild salmon in rivers on the west side of the Atlantic, initially welcomed the arrival of salmon farming. The ASF saw low-cost farm salmon on the fishmonger's slab as taking the predatory pressure off wild salmon. If nets were being cut back and bought off all over Atlantic salmon range, river salmon would be under extreme pressure from poachers. Abundant supplies of this ersatz substitute would drag salmon prices down and eliminate poaching of precious stocks. It would help, also, to persuade the Greenland fishermen to stop netting offshore salmon in midwinter; if the price fell to the floor, it would not be worth their while. Atlantic salmon were becoming as chic as caviar; this would cheapen it and allow conservation to start its repairs.

It turned out that the ASF had made a pact with the devil.

The Conservation Council of New Brunswick now swivelled their probing searchlight on what was actually happening in this landmark bay. The quantity of ammonia urinated by fish raised ammonia levels measurably despite the dispersion effects of powerful tides and currents. Methane, carbon dioxide and hydrogen sulphide had cranked up what is termed the 'biological oxygen demand' in the water. Before 1997 not much was understood about the effects of persistent and continuing particulate and dissolved organic waste cascading onto an enclosed tongue of sea bed. By the millennium more was becoming clear. Researchers worked out that 1000 tons of salmon each day produce 566 kilos of faecal material, and in addition 90 kilos of nitrogen and 9 kilos of phosphorus. Salmon farms have hundreds of thousands of tons of salmon in their net-pens. All this effluent is squirted directly into the sea from open cages.

The human sewage comparison brings you up short. The Bay of Fundy was being dumped with the equivalent of 93,000 people's excreta, the nitrogen from 437,000 people and the phosphorus effluent from 63,000 people. In comparison, the nearby town of St John, which in 2007 discharged half of its human waste straight into the sea, has to handle a sewage burden of 68,000 people. So, the salmon farm industry's expulsion of wastes was on a different scale of contamination from that of the closest human settlement. The pollution equivalent was several towns without sewage treatment plants. The wastes matted the sea floor in a sticky grey sludge devoid of life.

What struck researchers was the rapidity of the fish farm impacts. After only two months of salmon farm use the numbers of a certain polychaete worm, which needs little oxygen and is used as an indicator of organic enrichment in marine environments, multiplied by six between summer and autumn. It was evident that the Bay of Fundy, deemed acceptable by regulators for fish farm use because of its well-known strong tides and refreshment capacities, was failing to cope with salmon farming wastes and suffering ecological dislocation.

The report reads like a sci-fi script. Impacts are described as 'moderate to heavy gas-bubbling, the absence of fish, invertebrates and sediment-dwelling organisms, the accumulation of fish faeces and fish feed on the bottom through a tidal cycle, or thick bacterial mats, and in severe cases, anoxia'. Anoxia is extreme water-quality depletion. On several sites bigger salmon nearer harvest, in their second grow-out year, caused manifestly more damage, eating and defecating more frequently.

The impression is of an ecosystem drowning in fish sewage. But this was not all the fish sewage; far from it. It was actually a fraction of the total. Strong flushing removed 90 per cent of wastes. This fouling up was emanating from a mere tenth of what splattered out of the cages! No monitoring at all was done of contaminants dissolved in the water.

Sometimes the state of the sea floor actually disrupted the condition of the water above in the pen-cages. It all makes you shudder.

Were regulators horrified into immediate action? Were they, hell! Administrators desperately juggled with definitions to permit salmon farming to continue. Companies were allowed to continue to degrade the seawaters, so long as they provided a fall-back plan to rectify the problems once standards had fallen! No recommendations were provided about how to improve things. Official documents appeared to expect fish farmers to repeat the same process again, dumbly awaiting the triumph of hope over experience. Companies were to undertake extra monitoring, present a remediation plan, and justify the continuation of existing fish harvest rates. In sum, write more papers. They had a month to act. No such thing, note, as urgent recovery attempts: the salmon industry had become the economic lifeblood of the area, an untouchable. Instead of habitat recovery, the opposite: from 2007 wider-scale impacts ceased to be measured. If the facts look bad, stop measuring them.

Abandonment of pollution measurements was to become a standard reaction across different governments drawing the wagon-circle around salmon farms. The cuckoo must not be allowed to fall from the nest it has soiled. What did the cuckoo do? Whenever regulatory measures of any sort have been proposed salmon farmers protest loudly that they are already regulated to the gills.

The determination to somehow justify the continuation of salmon farming despite the proven environmental costs was cleverly tracked and unravelled by the forensic efforts of the province's conservation consultants. They are owed a debt further afield than only in New Brunswick. Not everywhere was such a skilled team available to lay bare the ghastly secrets beneath pretty coastal vistas speckled with innocuous-looking pen-cage lids.

The Conservation Council of New Brunswick did not stop at the quantification of damage. They moved to research into the possibilities of recovery for the benthos. They found some recovery of sediment chemistry two years after the fish farm's departure. Marine organisms, though, revived more slowly. The researchers concluded that where sites were being temporarily closed, and so-called 'fallowing' was being enforced, the term should be long enough for creature recovery, not just that of sediment. A chorus of voices awakened by this alarming research called for controls on fish farming which would protect against further degradation of the coast.

By this time salmon farming had been conducted for twenty years. Some sites were refusing to improve despite having been vacated. The toxic sludge beneath cages in neighbouring Nova Scotia, composed of rotting feed, faeces and dead salmon, has been measured three feet deep.

Other environmental features of salmon farms were extra noise and extra light. Underwater lights are used to quicken production cycles. The effects of this on wild fish and other marine life is unknown and was never explored.

What was called the 'assimilative capacity' of sites was examined. In the densest areas of salmon farming it was reckoned that the licensed salmon capacity needed reduction by 90 per cent. Algal mats increased during fifteen years in one area from two per cent of the surface to over a third. Clams and their harvesters were seriously affected. Salmon farming degraded the coastal habitat and the livelihoods of its residents by any measure anyone chose.

After twenty years of its operation, concerns about the environmental consequences of salmon farming started to escalate. In 1994 seven countries with Atlantic salmon farming industries – being the USA, Canada, Norway, Scotland, Ireland, Iceland and the Faroe Islands (a dependency of Denmark) – ratified an agreement called, after the place it was signed, the Oslo Resolution. Chile, the industry's South American outpost, was not included. Under the resolution the signatories agreed to address ten categories of concern to the two programme instigators, the World Wildlife Fund (WWF) and the Atlantic Salmon Federation. There were criteria such as fish containment (net security and policies on escapes), standards of fish husbandry, maintaining benthos quality beneath cages, and the extent to which fish farmers tried to protect wild salmon runs by keeping net-pens away from migratory routes and leaving some of them industry free. Nine years after the resolution supposedly came into force an expert panel investigated what had been done.

Complacency does not adequately describe what they discovered. Marked on scores up to ten, Norway, the industry leader, scored highest with 3.4. Norwegian fish farmers' interest in the state of the benthos, though, appeared to be zero. Most of the disciplines were optional, not mandatory, and inspections were largely performed by the operating companies themselves. The only standard Norway met convincingly was its effort to limit areas open for salmon farming and thereby protect wild salmon in specified fjords and rivers. Its long coastline helped in meeting this concession. The measure itself implicitly concedes that the two uses of water are incompatible.

For the seven countries the average result was two out of ten. The progress report has an underlying theme: salmon farmers were being left to get on with it. Their theatre of operation was a free resource, out-of-sight, out-of-mind, there to absorb whatever the industry threw at it. On a visit to a salmon farm the site manager once described the location to me as 'prime agricultural land'. That was the truth. But regulators in these seven countries saw not only prime land unencumbered by the normal need for maintenance, but something extra: a cost-free disposal pit.

Degradation of coastal habitats has never ranked high as a worry amongst salmon farmers, even openly: in New Brunswick they went as far as saying the habitat was not their concern. What makes them stay awake at night is how to feed their fish.

Salmon feed is about half of all cost. That cost is rising. The reasons take one to the seas, commercial fishing fleet effort, and what constitutes feed for farmed salmon. This has been neatly called the industry's 'fishprint'.

A figure used in industry-speak is the conversion rate, or the amount of fish feed needed to cultivate farm salmon. Different figures are bandied about depending on what point is being proved. The WWF reckons the conversion is that to grow one kilo of farmed salmon requires four kilos of wild fish. The salmon farm industry has its own figures in which a kilo of feed nearly equates to a kilo of farm salmon. However, they bend their case at both statistical ends by using figures reflecting the processed weights of feed, not the 'wet' weight, and disregarding the off-cuts of the salmon as part of its weight. Oblivious to where the debate really lies they also claim that wild salmon need ten kilos of fish per kilo of their own weight to live on, introducing the sinister implication that wild salmon themselves use marine resources wastefully! Should we resume baleen whaling because the big mammals eat too much plankton?

The same number in Chile, a major farm salmon producer and beside where the so-called 'reduction fish' are netted, is ten kilos of fish to produce one kilo of farm salmon. In a world short of protein, this ratio is unacceptable, even grotesque; affordable edible fish for people in poor countries is being used to grow food for distant high-end markets, unsustainably. Intensive food production demand is depleting the local offshore food supply.

That imbalance became chronic when aquaculture's usage of the world's fishmeal output rose from a third to two-thirds in the nine years to 2009. Salmon feed producers had to do a health check, and fast. People were starting to ask, if we are what we eat, what do these caged salmon eat?

The salmon farming industry's ignorance about what was actually being fed to its fish was shocking. Site managers usually have little idea. They know the cost of feed, not the content. On a 2012 British television programme about sea fisheries a senior salmon farm industry figure confessed before the cameras that he had no notion what was in the fishmeal his salmon ate. Any idea that the industry might be worried about its wider ecological impacts, or its 'fishprint', was blown with one question.

When quizzed, fish farm managers protest lamely that fish-feed suppliers constantly change the balances of ingredients in feed and keep customers in the dark. Not a good excuse when you contrast conventional food industries which have to declare contents on the packet. You buy feed for sheep; the contents are itemised. Same for cattle. Same for everything else. Once more, salmon farming at sea had made a haven in a zone that was protected from scrutiny, where normal laws of operation, where environmental measurement, and where accountability were suspended.

The key component for salmon is fish oil. Salmon needs that for its Omega 3 constituent. Omega 3 is what is in the old nursery favourite, olive oil. It has a plenitude of health-giving properties, including stimulating the brain. Whilst about half the world's fishmeal is used by aquaculture, the sector takes 81 per cent of the worlds' fish oils.

Fish oil converts into salmon flesh more efficiently than either into chicken or pig meat. It is, after all, salmon's natural diet, not theirs. Also, salmon's bodies do not need to be heated as those of ruminants do; more of the feed goes into growth of the fish flesh than into elementary thermal defence.

Fish oil is the part of the 'fishprint' to focus on. Oils from rapeseed oil, sunflower, flaxseed and soya have become fish-oil substitutes, but they cannot be overdone as dietary components. Salmon do not respond well. In particular the 'finishing', preparation near the time for killing-out, needs real fish oil: rapeseed-flavoured salmon would sour off consumers. As to fishmeal, there has been a major turnaround: in 1990 sixty per cent of farm salmon diet was from wild fish; that has been pared down to as little as 15 per cent.

Just in time. The world's capture of 'industrial' or 'reduction' fish, sometimes misleadingly called 'trash-fish', was stable for many years but now it is falling, if not plummeting. Finding the fish oil, more than the meal, has become the limiting factor in the expansion of salmon farming.

In the 'reduction' process fish oil is pressed out of the bodies of oil-rich fish like anchovies. These extraordinary little fish constitute a hefty chunk of fishmeal and oil used on salmon farms. Mostly caught off the eastern edge of Chile and Peru in giant purse seines, anchovies live a short life and breed prolifically. They burst out of the cool, nutrient-rich upwellings of the Humbolt Current off South America in the largest concentrations of any fish species. Populations zoom up and down but in bumper years the catches, in millions of tons, exceed those of any other sort of fish. However, anchovies' numbers are climate-related; populations can crash too, almost nothing is caught, and then fishmeal manufacturers lack raw material.

Jack mackerel, the second-biggest 'industrial' fish species, is similar. A little heftier, it is found near the sea surface off Chile and Peru. Jack mackerel is one of the smaller fish which can aggregate into a spinning ball or gyre of thousands of individuals in what is thought to be a protective formation to deter predators, one of which is tuna. This dense consolidation of numbers makes it easier to seine-net entire shoals. Belying the term 'trash-fish', some jack mackerel is canned for human consumption. Its stocks have been over-fished since 1997. In recent years over-generous quotas could only be half-filled.

What makes the fishmeal and oil from this part of the world especially attractive to salmon farmers is that the southern oceans, devoid of industry, have no dioxins to be absorbed by small fish. The waters are uncontaminated. To north Europeans that is an almost impossible notion.

Dioxins were the dangerous substances found concentrated in sand eels off northern Europe. They are the persistent leaking chemical residues from a previous age of industry. Located in fridges and industrial machines they dribbled into watercourses, shifted with currents, and in due course wound up stranded on sandbanks in the North Sea. There they got into the oily bodies of sand eels, at one time a major component of the industrial fish catch in the North Atlantic. Sand eels were fodder for everything bigger than themselves, including cod, haddock and herring. Reduction fishmeal may no longer use so many sand eels, as the role of sand eels in the marine chain has become better understood and catches limited, but a major substitute is trimmings –

heads, tails, guts – from bigger, processed fish, which have eaten the same sand eels, containing the same dioxins.

The presence of dioxins obliged the World Health Organisation (WHO) to publish precautionary guidelines on the advised consumption of farm salmon, limiting it to two portions a week. No other food carried this sort of precautionary warning. For pregnant mothers two portions was dangerously overdoing it. Some prescriptions were a single portion a month. The more fastidious dietary programmes advise not eating farmed salmon produced from northern Europe at all on the basis that the half-life of the persistent pollutants found in feed is ten to fifteen years.

For the farm salmon industry to have set up and orchestrated a marque of excellence and awards schemes dutifully heralded by the press, whilst the food carried serious health warnings issued by the main international food standards body, represents a triumph of industry marketing. It is a lesson, perhaps, in how the creation of eye-catching and newsworthy awards and certification schemes, in actuality often self-promotions run by the industry itself, can circumvent or help sanitise some grim realities about the true nature of the actual product. In Scotland the Crown Estate distributes the honours in an annual gongfest. The landlord, in other words, anoints the tenants. The biggest tenant, surprise surprise, often picks up the trophies. In Ireland farm salmon marketeers tried to hijack the fashionable concept of Slow Food, though production processes were the opposite.

Conservation bodies, so spookily absent from the general debate about salmon farming, are in vigorous protest about 'reduction' fish. The overkill of reduction fish fits into their campaign against over-fishing at sea. They accuse all reduction fisheries of being outside any ecosystem-based management. Fish species such as pilchards, menhaden, capelin, sprats, blue whiting and horse mackerel are as cavalierly treated by the industrial fishery as South American anchovies and jack mackerel. Now salmon farming has had to act on the figures about reduction or factory fish partly because well-funded conservation bodies are making an issue of it. Certification is reserved for stocks it is acceptable to continue fishing; some retailers will only buy salmon fed from these approved stocks. The bar is getting higher.

Fishmeal manufacturers have every reason to worry. The fish used for meal and oil are running out. All the stocks which end up in fishmeal have been over-fished. Quotas for them have been ignored and exceeded. The fishmeal and fish-oil industry itself publishes the figures on these species, which are of scant interest to anyone else. In 2009 4.7 million tons of feed were manufactured from small bony fish like anchovies, jack mackerel and sprats, which constitute the base material for fishmeal. However, that was the lowest figure for over twenty years. The world had previously used nearly double this amount. That was as big a catch as stocks, now being monitored, would allow. Users say the quality has dropped along with the quantity.

Two things stand out in the figures about reduction fish and the fishmeal indsutry. The headline is falling catches, the other is that critical numbers are often mysteriously missing. Some numbers are years out of date. A dramatic example is cost. Industry publications give average costs of fishmeal which rise steadily starting in 1981. The table ends in 2002. But when I visited a Scottish fish farm in August 2011, the meal being fork-lifted off a lorry on the quay was priced at £1000 a ton, nearly treble the 2002 figure. That shrieks the word 'shortage'. For freshwater farms and smolt production feed is more refined and costs are higher, approximately double. Wherever I went on salmon farms that summer, managers bemoaned the cost of feed.

Salmon farming is generically different to shrimp, carp, tilapia, eel or catfish farming. Some fish are omnivores, but salmon's natural diet is amphipods, crustaceans and fish. They are more like tuna, trout, sea bass or sharks. For their unusual predatory acceleration they need more fuel-oil than other fish. Salmon's oil requirement is in a different league, it is up to a fifth of their whole diet. The world today produces five million tons of fishmeal and one million tons of fish-oil. If El Niño enters the play, as happened in 2008, average figures go haywire and catches from Peru and Chile, the jumbo producers, crash to almost nothing. A problem.

Resuming: to get one ton of oil, twenty tons of fish and trimmings are needed. Oil is expensive to procure and the source species are in short supply. The use of fish oil by aquaculture has vaulted. Once 17 per cent, it has now collared 85 per cent of all fish oils. And the main market for the oil is salmon.

The only novel source of fishmeal and fish oil is from factory trimmings of other fish like cod, haddock and mackerel, as they are processed and portioned for the display shelf at the retailer. Heads and offal and tails now constitute a quarter of all the raw materials used in producing fishmeal and oil.

One of the basic sources of raw material used to be tropical mixed-fish catches landed by artisinal fishermen. Nets were hauled containing a cornucopia of diverse species at different stages of growth. Better awareness of exactly what fish were in those hand-hauled nets showed they were often food-fish for poor and hungry local communities, or the juveniles of fish which would be critically important food supplies when they matured. This form of catch is now deemed non-sustainable and not included in accredited supplies for reduction.

From the organisations which make and market fishmeal and fish oil there is a jaunty official tone. Underneath lurks worry. Stocks of the feed-fish have been somewhere between falling and collapsing. Now regulators have stepped in, quotas have entered the frame, the different supplies have been separated out and subjected to accreditation, and there is better management control.

As wild-fish capture faltered, salmon-feed manufacturers have turned to new oil sources in plants. But salmon need still more oil and more meal sources; industry expansion is outpacing the discovery of new feed supplies.

The regulations which followed outbreaks of BSE, when ruminants were fed other ruminants, put a stop to the possibility of farmed salmon trimmings being processed and fed back to their own kind. Salmon do not possess prions, the rogue proteins which caused cerebral breakdown for cattle, but some risks persisted. It was a road no one wanted to tread: farm salmon trimmings took a side-turn into pig-feed.

Also, lifestyle concerns have reminded the west European public about the health-enhancing benefits of capsules of fish-oil. Expensive items, capsules. Salmon farmers were being outbid. The Marine Stewardship Council's approved fisheries list began to limit what went in the front end of fishmeal plants. Salmon feed was beginning to look very tricky.

Enter the vegetable growers. Cheaper, capable of being mass-produced, growable all over. But when does a carnivorous salmon fed on vegetables cease to be a salmon? BSE bored into cattle when they were fed meat-protein from other animals; herbivores were filled with carnivore material. Salmon do not eat vegetables naturally, yet fish farmers are feeding them with plants. Whether it is ultimately safe, or right, is a question, like so many others, passed by.

As canola has different oleaginous properties to soya there is talk of salmon being graded according to which type of oil it has been fed. Algae is one new food source in a succession of wide-ranging current ideas, another is ragworms. If the farm salmon industry cannot find the fish, and if the sector needs to go on growing to help solve a hungry world's protein needs, what exactly are they going to eat?

The question is given a twist by 'eating down the food web'. This means eating fish we have ignored before. This fashion has taken off in Britain and creatures formerly part of the industrial fish catch have replaced farm salmon as the lowest-cost fish on the slab. When pouting were first marketed by the supermarket chain Tesco in 2011, they were a runaway success, selling at just under the prices of other sea fish. Less pouting for salmon-feed, more competition from pouting at retail. Blue whiting, gurnard and dabs followed. Salmon farmers had to ratchet down their prices to try to get in competition again.

'Eating down the food web' was sparked by disgust at the ugly phenomenon of discards in the European Union's fishery and the need to develop markets and a taste for all sorts of new fish which, instead of being discarded as trash, could be relished as novel protein sources. Foodie television programmes widened the message. Already reduction fish like anchovies and sardines are perfectly good eaten as they come. So why macerate them down in an energy-intensive process to make pellets to be pumped down feed-pipes to slavishly-programmed farm salmon which do a bad job of turning them into decent food anyway? All this at the expense of the estuaries and bays where the industry disgorges its wastes unchronicled?

The farmed salmon as a product gets a little murky. We have drifted a long way from the image of a silver torpedo-shaped fish, a definitively pure and natural food from a pristine coastline in a beautiful and deserted hinterland.

It could all be different. A clean way of farming salmon may exist and it has several advantages, such as useful byproducts.

We need to look at the two phases in growing farm salmon. The first is the smolt stage. This is when small salmon are transferred from hatcheries to freshwater lochs to grow in nets until they smolt, or become ready for the sea. From the egg this takes up to a year or just over, accelerated maturation being possible through altering water temperatures. The smolts occupy nets, about a ton of fish in each one, maybe ten nets attached to a main raft. When their biological clock gives the signal, the small fish shoal and turn silver: saltwater beckons.

The smolt-cage phase is the little talked-of part of salmon farming and its physical scale is minor compared with the needs of the 'grow-out' phase when fish are adult. However, the smolt phase is critical for this reason: smolts escape just like adults, but being smaller, more get out. Smolt farmers cannot count small fish so easily and breakouts are less measurable. But they matter just as much from the gene-mixing angle. A farm smolt is the first harbinger of the foreign genes.

Smolt farms are not headline news material. But for Scotland in particular the kink is that many of the smolt farms are on the east coast. The main industry is on the west coast, but the juveniles are grown on the east and half of them, around 17 million, are in freshwater lochs. The east is the coast supposed to be protected from salmon farming, where the genetic stock is kept pure and uncontaminated. Tragically, smolt escapes mean that this is no longer the case. Salmon farming is genetically undermining natural stocks on a coast far from its fattening cages.

Salmon farmers hide behind a critical let-out clause in law. They are not obliged to reveal the genetics of their fish. Within the law, they can refuse to cooperate. The let-out is not historic; it was negotiated by the fish farmers when they saw that genetic analysis of escapees could nail them for polluting wild strains. Hard though it is to imagine how the case for secrecy was argued, they succeeded: the door was evidently ajar for their advocacy. If the smolt genetics were known, then an assortment of smolts could be netted and tested. The genetics of wild fish were already being logged. The farm ones and the wild ones could be told apart. But the farm businesses would have been open to charges of contamination, possible legal action and possible penalties.

One of the large smolt units is in a shallow long loch in the north Highlands called Loch Shin. It is supremely unsuitable for a porous system holding a foreign gene pool of salmon, issuing as it does into a bigger river feeding four separate salmon waters, but planners overlooked that. Planners are not versed in fish genetics and lobbying by the fish farmers is a well-oiled procedure. Following an escape, anglers on Loch Shin have sometimes caught smolts in dozens. Local people say there have been escapes again and again. Local fisheries trust biologists consider that the gene pool of smolts leaving Loch Shin for the sea has been diluted significantly. The smolt farmers refuse point-blank to disclose their genetics.

The escaped Norwegian smolt will of course try to relocate at maturity in the nursery water-source, in Loch Shin not in Norway. There it could mix with native River Shin salmon. Any diseases caught on the smolt farm could transfer to those highly valuable wild smolts, where treatments are impossible. The gene risk is in evolution's gift. Matthew Arnold's chilling phrase comes to mind: 'Nature forgives no debt.'

Smolt farming can be done on land, in contained re-circulation systems which are escape-proof. Already run-of-river smolt farms, where the water is diverted, used and then returned to the stream, go halfway to this. These streams may be near the sea and devoid of any wild salmon themselves the whole way to the brackish water. In a fully closed system the inputs, chemicals, feed and the rest, can be contained and sieved out from the water. No escapes, no trail of rogue chemicals, no risks.

To the sides of burns and rivers this has been happening for awhile. The lochs, though, allowed bigger-scale production. For a long time smolt farmers have privately known that the arguments against their continued stay in freshwater lochs, where brown trout lethargically patrol beneath the cages gluttonising on waste feed, and where escaped farm smolts compete with genetically valuable wild smolts, could in the end prevail. They also realised they could potentially save money by farming smolts in big contained systems. Control over light, growth rates, feed and wastes would be taken in hand. At a political level, they could toss a sop to the indignant wild fish lobbyists to whom the public were now listening. They had had a good run in freshwater, but time was being called, and they heard the bell.

Marine Harvest was one of three companies to build large-scale re-circulation smolt units in Scotland in 2012. Its west Highland smolt unit is at Lochailort, where commercial salmon culture started way back in 1965. If it is a symbolic gesture, or a lightning conductor diverting attention from bad news zones, it is on a considerable scale: the output will be five million smolts a year for moving to the sea-cages, and five to six million fry or parr for on-growing in the smolt units still in freshwater lochs.

The features of the new unit are typical of the concept as a whole. Circular tanks are half-buried and half above ground. The whole plant is roofed and contained. Filtration twinned with carbon dioxide stripping removes solid wastes from the recycled water. Ozone is converted to oxygen before being returned to the fish tanks. This shaves the new freshwater need down to almost nothing, cutting the plant's demand on the external environment.

The re-circulation model allows operators to sterilise and disinfect their water, control ammonia and destroy pathogens and infection risks. Water temperature, as Peter Gray found out long ago, dictates all with young fish. Managers at Lochailort can maintain a 15C degree temperature year-round to enhance growth rates. Overcoming low winter temperatures and winter's dim light means the unit can produce three instead of two batches of smolts a year ready for the grow-out phase. Imagine the luxury of it: weather is held at bay, no fish can escape.

So, if they can do it with smolts, why not with big fish? Why not move the whole industry on land, with complete control, no wider-scale environmental soiling, no escapes and ferocious genetic debates, no sea lice? Sure, there will be extra costs, one being pumping either seawater if the unit is to be near the sea or freshwater if it is fully inland, but there are possible byproducts, like fertiliser and manure for farming or aquaponics. This is the direction being taken by commercial producers of salmon in 2013. Adhering to their right to sea farms, moving into ever more open-sea situations, in part to more rapidly disseminate their fish-farm wastes, companies are also looking at operations on land. Stung by the gibe that they are 'One of the world's largest, wealthiest and most influential sources of licensed pollution', made by Allan Berry of the Society for the Protection of Salmon and Sea Trout, commercial salmon farmers are thinking outside the box. Some people are not thinking there, they are already operating there, and their success looks instructive.

The objections to on-land salmon farming using re-circulation systems focused at first on energy cost. To pump water from the sea would cost too much; even to pump water round the inland plant would add a severely burdensome energy cost. But what if the re-circulation operation was sited at the foot of a mountain stream, the pen-cages on the beach, and the energy from the stream was trapped for hydro-electric power? The power is used to pump. If seawater were pumped from deeper down it would be colder and not in the sea-lice layer. Any lice could be netted out with filtration. Problems were soluble. Reconsideration of the alternative ways of growing salmon were overdue. Our wild salmon may rely for their assured future on the new developments.

In West Virginia the Conservation Fund Freshwater Institute has been growing table-ready salmon for ten years. The key thing is the non-reliance on outside water. What the Institute's director, Dr Steven Summerfelt, calls 'minimal direct hydraulic connection with the environment', is in fact filtering and recycling up to 99.8

per cent of the water used to grow 3,000 tons of fresh salmon a year. The 0.02 per cent is sludge waste, also known as fertiliser. Dr Summerfelt identifies locations where electricity is cheap and markets are close as the target sites for a re-circulation salmon farm. The theoretical possibility exists of salmon-production plants, situated beside the towns which they will feed, using low-tariff power costs to pump their self-contained water supplies.

With larger fish generating vastly more wastes than smolt units, Dr Summerfelt has been using the phosphorous, nitrogen, carbon and waste nutrients from the fish for recycling into nutrients for vegetable and herb-growing and into aquaponics systems, or for methane production. The wastes pouring from salmon sea cages have been converted, with a new purpose and economic value.

Again, compare land farming. In intensive livestock production increasingly wastes are a quantifiable bonus. The slurry from dairy and pig units feeds biogas plants; chicken litter provides energy for biomass. Waste equals energy. Pen-cage aquaculture is both archaic and wasteful.

This evolution of intensive food production in West Virginia has arisen, note, not because of loose regulation but the opposite, because in the USA there are extreme constraints on the use of fresh water. Water is a treasured resource. Tough regulation has produced ingenious creative alternatives.

The methodology goes further. The Institute is exploring, in particular, salmon diet. It is investigating how to match nutrients in fish-feed to the precise requirements of the fish. Fish faeces are being studied to see if new diet compositions can alter the solidity of faeces, making it easier to separate it out with filtration. Mineral supplements may in future partially replace fishmeal.

Collected wastes from new diets will become positive assets, acquire a market value of their own and influence how the salmon are grown. The holistic production of salmon uses geo-thermal heating technology.

Most critically, the Institute's leaders believe that they can compete on price. Re-circulation salmon farming, even with the burden of managing its byproducts, can compete head to head with the primitive free-for-all at sea. That is the crux.

Britain has its own innovators who share the same philosophy. FishFrom is a 2012-registered company which intends to build the same sort of re-circulation units as in West Virgina. One focus is feed. The ghastly carbon footprint entailed in shipping South American anchovies across a hemisphere to feed domesticated salmon in Scotland is being shelved. Instead the fish will eat polychaete worms with the same nutrition qualities as fish. Oils from algae will be mixed in and amino acids will break down the constituents. When salmon eat too much vegetable their faeces is too loose to capture and use. The diet is unnatural. But polychaete worms live in burrows in brackish water and have the bromophenol properties of capelin and prawns. Potentially the worm diet will achieve the usual weight-gains and drop the disadvantages of fake and unreal diets. Farms will be near beaches and water will be pumped out of boreholes from 150 feet or less with low-energy pumps. If salmon are in brackish water they are apparently neither susceptible to pathogens which live in saltwater or those that thrive in freshwater. A win-win.

The unit will run a worm-farm too. It doesn't need much space, the worms live six inches down in sandy sediment. The operating company will own the whole production process and be independent of all external raw material costs and most running charges. Originators have done their sums and are sufficiently confident to be opening similar salmon units in four other countries. The future model in salmon farming had started to happen at the moment the present unreconstructed barbarism is coming unstuck. There is an appealing serendipity to the passage of events in 2013. All that is needed is a suitable level of investment.

My own hunch is that we will look back in a few years and say, what was going on here? How could an entire industry slip the leash to this extent? How could the paramount importance of our great natural strains of this fabulous fish count for so little?

The political class will reply: we established some jobs and built a major export industry. Maybe. For how long, at what cost? The concept of plonking labour-intensive industries in wild places, to spread the national effort and shake awake some of the dreamier outposts generally has a poor track record. Scotland is one fatality. The 'growth-point' concept of the 1960s saw old-fashioned metal-bashing types of industry set up like monuments on the fringe, and an indigent population from the cities exported to labour in them. Scotland had the aluminium smelters, the pulp-mills, the textile factories. All failed. The concept was abandoned. Displaced dependent communities were left drawing unemployment benefit. Maybe some of the cashiered workers wound up on salmon farms.

Unlike the growth-point concepts which have only economic and social downsides, the salmon farm industry harms the wider world. In the case of hybridisation the effects may show up for hundreds of years, or forever. What happens to the outwash from this industry, in the form of chemicals, antibiotics, morts, geographically befuddled swarms of escapees and persistent pesticides, no one has any idea. But then when they put dioxins in fridges the engineers can never have imagined that they would end up not immured in landfill but drifting at sea, then in the bodies of sand eels, and then in salmon feed, and then in human beings who ate the salmon. The chemicals in the backs of fridges ended up in human digestive tracts. For salmon farming, the precautionary approach was thrown to the winds. Thought-free policy triumphed and future generations are to pick up the tab.

Allan Berry, not one to mince words, has said: 'Proponents of a scientific approach have been intimidated and excluded, while some supposedly 'independent' bodies can be accused of operating a protection racket, protecting polluters for reward. Presenting the industry as the only way forward, industry promoters have denied the environmental damage, and deliberately suppressed attempts to bring the matter under proper scientific scrutiny'. He goes on: 'Policy is defended by a science establishment charged with harmonising science with policy … Control of funding, reinforced by intimidation, is the means of maintaining control.' It is hard to think of an industry which has been lambasted with such withering contempt. If right, politicians and policy makers have drifted a long way from the concept of public trust with which democratic society charges them.

Certainly, the grip salmon farming has exerted on policy makers has been extreme. On the west coast of Scotland native salmon are probably permanently compromised; in some rivers they are gone. In eastern Canada the prospects for the more fragile runs competing with a leviathan production industry of this size trampling their environment seem almost non-existent. Their fish have been sold down the river. When the Canadian Food Inspection Agency in January 2013 gave the green light for

240,000 Nova Scotia farm salmon dying from ISA to be processed for human consumption, letters pages, blogs and public commentaries erupted. The New Brunswick processing plant would have to be disinfected afterwards! What other diseased corpses would be foisted on passive Canadian consumers by the tone-deaf political henchmen of a cynical industry? In an epidemic six months earlier, 450,000 diseased fish from Newfoundland, after public disquiet, had been destroyed. Something somewhere in eastern Canada's representational democracy had got totally out of hand.

Even more extraordinary is the concept of Atlantic salmon farming on the west Canadian coast. Here were the fantastic primeval-sized runs of Pacific salmon, a stupendous resource. The last time I was in Vancouver the sockeye run was estimated at 24 million and the bays were full of boats with fishing rods projecting from the stern; sales of farm salmon in the shopping malls died.

Why would anyone risk harming that scale of resource? Yet refugee Atlantics are hard at it again, spawning in rivers on the wrong side of the continent, introducing sea-lice blizzards that the wild fish have never had to contend with before. The federal government was found muzzling the authors of inconveniently damning science published in top research journals, with senior fisheries scientists protesting about, 'an iron curtain' being 'draped over the communication of science'. Finally a law was proposed threatening to jail anyone pointing the finger at farms suspected of being diseased; in the end it was turned down. It is behaviour more reminiscent of fundamentalist zealotry in totalitarian states.

Meantime epidemics unleashed from the cages of the intruder species had decimated the bountiful native sockeye salmon in the

Fraser River and had even got into Chinooks, the iconic leviathans of the salmon tribe. In a legal commission investigating the effects of farming Atlantic salmon the court was told that salmon farms were a source of new diseases, produced novel mutant diseases, and increased the virulence of existing ones. Government was accused of favouring cultured salmon above wild native salmon, and ruthlessly muzzling evidence of environmental pollution from cage farming, even from its own employees. The lead voice against salmon farming, Alexandra Morton, said: 'If you are going to create an unnatural environment for animals, take them out of the natural environment.'

Feelings and anxieties mounted with the evidence of damage. For this was the world's surviving honey-pot zone for wild salmon. That is why public demonstrations numbering in thousands took to the streets in Vancouver.

The blind defence of a relatively new food production system, taking a lethal toll on the environment, begs the question: why? What induced national and provincial governments to bolster, underwrite and periodically sponsor an industry with a dubious reputation which progressively got dirtier.

In Scotland some government scientists attest that bad news about salmon farms and their effects, and warnings that the industry side-effects were dangerous, were deliberately buried to allow the industry's continuation. Why? The Scottish government is accused by wild salmon supporters of paving the way for salmon farms to colonise the west coast by sidestepping the critical coastline when recommendations were being lodged with the European Union in the 1980s for designated conservation areas. It is indeed eerily odd that the north-west, so famous for its wildlife and nature richness, was largely excluded from this designation process. Anyone might suppose the best wildernesses would attract more conservation, not less. In the few places designation was secured under EU law there are now legal challenges from locals whose ecology has been damaged. Wild fishery people have long believed selective conservation was no coincidence; the west coast from the north of Glasgow was to be sacrificed, its wild salmon to take their chances. How did such a bandwagon take control?

Salmon farmers provide part of the answer. Citing the 1980 figure of nine per cent of aquaculture fish in our diet compared to nearer half now, they claim that aquaculture is taking over our eating habits. They claim fish culture only can solve global seafood needs. It is the industry of the future. Politicians backing it could be identified as solving tomorrow's issues.

Then the producers are not like farmers of livestock. They are not family businesses with domestic-scale balance sheets. They are the big boys, large companies with operations spanning the continents, and promising solutions for places in which there are few people and fewer jobs. They could browbeat and steamroll governments, and they did.

Stock farmers, competing with farm salmon in the protein division, must maintain records for their animals. In Europe, every cow has an individual passport. If you eat the beef in a cut, it can be traced back in case of disease trouble. A sheep can be traced back to the flock electronically, and the flock's record book will show what treatments were administered to its members. Not so salmon. Salmon farmers did not take the time and trouble to identify their charges. They were marketed as a commodity. If thousands got out and vanished into the big beyond, that was a risk of doing business, an ordinary running cost. No leading politician challenged this point, or drew comparisons with other parts of the food industry.

Salmon farming was not unaware of the need for good press, hence its vigorous media division. Attempts to make good the industry's shortcomings have been sporadic. A theoretical system headily called 'integrated multi-trophic aquaculture' was trotted out as being able to address salmon farming's dirty legacies, but then it was showed that the ability of mussels, other bi-valves and seaweeds to absorb the vast volumes of wastes and blooms around the farms was in reality limited. Like with wrasse, the scale of the job was too much. More genuinely integrated, and in line with the 4,000-year-old freshwater aquaculture tradition of China, is the practice of using wastes as fertiliser and raw material for other purposes – which is where the re-circulation concept, situated on land, looks good. On land the wastes can be captured, at sea they can't.

The fish farmers voiced claims that hit a political nerve: they could solve the food problem. The first duty of leaders is to feed people. Grasping at this straw administrators looked the other way and gave salmon farming a dummy run, shut to detailed scrutiny, for close to fifty years. But times have changed. The public perception of salmon farming has dramatically altered over the last few years. Wherever salmon farmers have hung their cages wild fish have declined. People have latched on to that. In Chile the disease epidemics which virtually closed down the whole shebang in 2008 and 2009 cost 15,000 redundancies and perceptibly shook the regional economy.

In any case, industry credentials as a major employer weakened with mechanisation. A salmon farm worker who started on a Scottish fish farm in 1987 and ended up as a manager saw the sea-cage workforce drop from 35 to only four by the time he left the industry in 2004. The amount of salmon being produced remained the same. Jobs were anyway concentrated in processing, where migrant labour was the norm, in urban locations rather than on the actual sea-cages in the sea lochs. At the beginning, the creation of employment on the outer edge was a main reason why salmon farming was grasped by officialdom with both hands. Today, salmon farmers applying to open new sites portray themselves as resuscitating the withered communities on shore. They target thinly populated locations deliberately. Those living there have spotted this and look squint-eyed at new development proposals.

Too many stories floated home from divers describing the foetid reality of the loch bed beneath the cages. There were uncomplimentary television programmes, filming the densities in salmon cages. Irish wild salmon interests took its government to the European Court for their failure to protect wild smolts on passage to the wintering, as they headed instead into lethal blizzards of pen-cage sea lice.

From around 2011 new salmon farm applications in Scotland began to give birth overnight to local protest groups pleading that they valued their sea lochs. Despite salmon farm companies resorting to offers of cash sweeteners to communities along with their applications for extended licences, in the way supermarkets had refined the arts of 'planning gain' to sweet-talk their way to planning permission, planners got bold enough to turn down contentious expansions. There was a shift in sentiment: official grounds for refusal became more blunt – apprehensions about the environment. Most people know now that farm salmon are pink owing to in-feed dye and that without it they would be the same grey as the sludge underneath the places they were reared. Enough cashiered salmon farm workers are out and about saying they would never contemplate eating the stuff. Legislation introduced in 2013 offered the chance to address the salient issues, but the opportunity was ducked.

The salmon farm industry trumpeted its 'Freedom Food' accreditation from the Royal Society for the Prevention of Cruelty to Animals (RSPCA) in the UK, but when people realised that the production method was the epitome not of freedom but of incarceration such logos began to be seen as cynical ploys, taking consumers for dummies. The media turned on an industry which for so long had been a stream of unalloyed good-news stories. The term 'salmon farming' has taken on a new sour note.

Maybe the re-circulation closed containment systems will change all this. For the sake of the remaining wild salmon families, we had better hope so. At stake is the future of the most important wild fish of the lot.

Survive or be Damned

The special features of Atlantic salmon make it a key indicator of human management in Nature. Natural systems have not only declined in modern time, some have been recovered and got better. Often it has been the consciences of consumers, or those who cleave to this fish, more than the moral imperatives of governments that have forced the changes.

The media is key. In Britain the veal industry was virtually shut down overnight when a television presenter in the 1990s tore back the veil on how veal calves were reared in the dark, killed very young, and fed only milk to keep their flesh white. Veal as a commodity died an instant death. Slowly, slowly, veal is becoming acceptable again. New methods have been introduced to farm the calves humanely, mixing a commercial meat objective with sound rearing practices. It has taken a long time and the bulk of the industry remains unreconstructed, but acceptably reared veal is edging back into the market, heralded by the bellweather consciences of the consumer – celebrity chefs. A little corner in animal production is being turned.

The same can and will happen to salmon cultured in new ways. Take the firm Hebridean Smokehouse on the isle of North

Uist in the Scottish Hebrides. The stock on this salmon farm are from older salmon and they are native, from the island itself. This has several benefits. Firstly, they are acclimatised to local pathogens and diseases, so medication needs are minimal. Sea lice, happily, do not exist in the fast-flushing site; the islands are outcrops poking out of a wrap-around tidal race. Next, if any fish skip out of the few small cages, from a biological perspective it doesn't matter. They re-integrate with their own kind. To avoid injury or infection from handling, the fish egg-stripped for the hatchery are killed afterwards. The product is truly Scottish not only in place of culture but in genetic origin too.

Lastly, it is low-density farming using low-energy feeds. There are 400 fish in a nine cubic metre cage, so no crowding. The first thing that strikes you looking down into a cage on a typical commercial salmon farm, what the Canadians have dubbed 'feedlot' fish-farms, is that all the fish swim in the same direction, wide-eyed zombies on invisible circuits; the density of bodies means they have to. In the Smokehouse cages there is room to swim both ways. They glide about, as in an aquarium. When I visited, half the cages were empty; the focus was on the quality of individual salmon. The reason customers pay more for the salmon from the Smokehouse is that they taste better.

Byproducts? Yes, a win-win there too. The skins are cured – salmon skin is one of the toughest leathers, and vertebrae from the salmon skeletons are used in fashioning local jewellery. The Smokehouse maximises the salmon and leaves no footprint.

Its owner, as it happens, is a passionate rod-angler. The greatest champions of Atlantic salmon have consistently been anglers. The various bodies which exist to protect salmon are funded in almost every case by rod-fishermen. Hunter protects the hunted.

Maybe it is odd that the sportsman seeking to capture the fish of his dreams also develops a passionate feeling about his quarry, at a generic level. Unlike for the wing-shooter bringing down birds, or the deer stalker, or the rabbit-shooter, the salmon angler hooks his quarry, draws it into his grasp and then handles it whilst alive. There is an eyeballing moment.

Salmon conservation by anglers existed before catch and release, but ask anglers to get discursive about their sport and they often come back to the point of the release. Something about letting the fish go, with a tail-waggle, to scoot back to a hidden hole in the river, captures the imagination. You can see it in the fishing magazines. Anglers talking about the feeling they have on release. It is as if some spirit of their own was re-entering the mysterious depths, as if the preservation of the fish somehow related to the preservation of themselves. It is not an entirely straightforward emotion.

What it has produced, though, is a deep and complex attachment – man to his fish.

My son recently went to fish for salmon on a neighbouring river in the north Highlands of Scotland. He only fishes occasionally and is convivial. He and his 83-year-old ghillie, following the arc of the sun over the low hills of Caithness on a July afternoon, exchanged tales and fables. The ghillie came up with this story.

He had a customer who had been coming to fish the river every year for a long time. This man had reached the age of 90. The year before, the last time he ever came to the river, he arrived in a new Range Rover. The ghillie asked why he had brought such a fancy car along. The old man said, it is for you. The ghillie was stunned. The old man continued, explaining that he was single, all his friends were dead, he himself would soon be dead, and that the faithful ghillie was his only remaining friend. The car was for him – if he performed one last act. The old man wanted his ashes scattered on the river where he had caught so many salmon over time. He wanted his last bodily remains to drift with the swimming fish.

Consider the story more. Perhaps there is no other activity that would produce this sort of relationship. Ghillie and angler can get very close. The angler is away from work and worry and ties; his mind is free to rove. It is not only that ghillie and angler, or 'rod' as the fisherman is sometimes described, spend a lot of time in each other's company, in places where there is often no one else, in weather which may push individuals together, standing in water that has a soothing effect, but also the act of hooking a salmon is an emotional one. The angler is exposed at a moment when his self truly emerges. It is hard to pretend to be what you are not when a salmon is extracting from you a range of emotions: anxiety when he thrashes off to the other side of the pool, desperation when he goes further and begins to wallop down the turbulent waters at the tail of the pool, tension when he is at the net, mostly visible, his eye showing in the water, his great silver body twisting beneath your hand.

Then there is the landing. Everyone knows that salmon have a knack of getting off 'at the net'. As the battle climaxes, the atmosphere can get pretty tight. When the net slips underneath the fish and is lifted suddenly all the tension drains from the angler – and the ghillie too. The drama takes a new rhythm. There is the sweet moment when you look at the fish. Sometimes it is knocked on the head; fine. Consumption of the salmon is the follow-through to catching it; philosophers might say the fish becomes part of the captor. Other times it is held in the water facing the stream, and swished backwards and forwards to re-oxygenate the lungs after a tiring struggle, and to restore equilibrium. In that business of resuscitation of the fish the angler and the ghillie are bathed in the glow of the successful capture. The fish has been caught but not killed.

Whatever the psychology, the ghillie and his angler become well-acquainted in the course of fishing. They just do. Possibly starting from opposite sides of the street, here they are equals. It is, or can be, a very close relationship. This has been commented on since the earliest angling literature.

The Caithness ghillie, driving home in the spanking-fresh comfort of a new Range Rover after saying goodbye for the last time to his old client at the end of the fishing week, would have had a range of emotions swirling in his mind. That shadows the relationship, too, with the salmon. Not personal, it is symbolic. The salmon is the free spirit we feel we have lost. The British cardiovascular doctor Dorian Haskard put it this way: 'Salmon have an archetypal quality – and fishing is a link to the collective unconscious.'

Not everything in fishing reaches the record book, including what I saw from my office window one time late last autumn. The large-frame window in the isolated building which serves as my office and more resembles a cow-shed has a view down some of the choicest autumn pools on the River Helmsdale. One pool in particular this season had been consistently yielding fish to the extent that often when I glanced out I saw taut figures in the process of landing a salmon. This day I idly surveyed the scene. On the water-edge was a lissome figure, casting away energetically, the ghillie heavily encased in weatherproofs standing watching on the bank. Next time I looked up the angler was on the bank, rod bent back, and the ghillie was stooped, netting the fish. A squiggly shape was rapidly put back in the river, the two figures bent intently over the proceedings on a gusty day in poor light. All done and the lady angler danced a little jig and then threw her arms around the ghillie – who reared backwards in alarm – with a spontaneous embrace.

A few thoughts crossed my mind. The lasting one was, where else would a pair of strangers have this private celebration on a wild river on a bad day in a faraway place? Only the consequences of chasing the salmon occasioned a happy and outlandish scene. So much for the fish and the camaraderie.

There is another feature of salmon culture. There are stereotype actors in the fish drama. One such is the Scottish ghillie. But this is not the ghillie who finds ladies throwing their arms round him on bleak moorland. This is the dour, weather-beaten fellow, sparing with words, a country person in the bone, and someone who has spent time with a range of people and on whom a certain amount of their sangfroid has rubbed off. Ghillies can play up to the taciturn caricature.

One time I was to fish a famous gorge on a river in north-eastern Scotland called the Findhorn. My buddy was the angling legend of his day, Mark Birkbeck, with a sixth sense for sea trout and salmon, which it seemed he could extract from places they never occupied. He and I assigned to meet the ghillie, himself a known figure at the end of his career. We waited in a clearing on a fine day above the famous gorge which was roaring and gurgling below us. From the surrounding trees a tall man materialised like a genie from a bottle. His Highland dress was immaculate – full tweeds, deerstalker tight-down, wearing not waders but smart boots. He eyed us and placed his foot on a rock. Leaning on an elbow at his leisure he lit and drew from a battered pipe, and vanished in copious smoke. Agog, we waited for his benedictions. 'You're too late, gentlemen,' he announced. 'The fish have run through.' We blinked; he proceeded. Water temperature dictated on this beat how long the salmon wait before running a considerable falls. They had had great fishing last week, he said with satisfaction. Salmon followed salmon. The anglers were even happy to go home. The spring run had been holed up on the beat, packed in deep waters in the scenic gorge. Then, last night air pressure swung around and the temperature had risen. The fish had surged over the falls, leaving a pretty chasm and wonderful-looking water, and in it … not a fish-scale. With a parting remark about the fate of the salmon angler in thrall to weather, the old ghillie stepped into the trees and was gone.

Mark and I caught one or two, maybe back-of-the-class personalities too dozy to get the message and go. But I remember better the scene with the acclaimed ghillie. He had put in a virtuoso performance, just for the two of us. The Scottish ghillie incarnate.

What it all means is a subjective matter. The ghillie to many is the stanchion of the river, its defining manifestation. But surely the Japanese, who have developed rod-casting as an art form in itself, rows of people studiously throwing lines tipped with cotton wool instead of fishing flies, reducing fishing to a metronome abstraction or existential paraphrase, are missing out on chunks of the fun – no fish and no ghillie. Everyone to his own.

To the salmon-seeking holiday there is an aspect of symbolic odyssey, even a tribal reunion. Families on rivers far and wide re-convene to fish for salmon. They stay in the same houses, re-encounter the same people, fish the same pools and walk the same riverbanks. In some sense they look for a salmon they caught there before, seeking an experience which they remember and want to repeat. About these holidays there is a ritual aspect; the repetition is itself soothing; if we lived in a religious age there might be a faith metaphor to coin.

When the first flush of green brightens the tips of blades of grass around February, I start to get telephone calls. Are the salmon in? Who is fishing? Numbers of fish caught, lost? Big, small? The minds of fishermen are beginning to latch again onto what is happening in salmon rivers. They hone the steel of their hooks and slick the interiors of their reels with petroleum jelly. Even a glance in the fly-box, mentally noting spaces which need filling, fumbling to remember what fish at what place resulted in that space being there at all. Some have been tying flies over winter and have a box of dainty virgins competing to be floated on the first pool of the year. To others all that enters the affray is the thought of the tug on the end, the fierce savage pull of the first salmon, the release of emotions which that feeling brings. Other minds wander to the wanderer. The salmon is on the way, maybe, forging along an ancient pathway in the sea, governed by water temperature and the food supply which that entrains, guided by the instinct to pair and reproduce. Everyone thinks of the salmon at a different point, but think of them they start to.

I know one lady whose annual salmon-river excursion, from England to Scotland, entails hauling, in a large pick-up, her choice soft furnishings and lamps and fittings. For the week she and her tribe are on the banks of the salmon river, she re-creates a familiar home. But with a difference: a salmon fishing-themed home. The fishing week is several things at once, a retreat, a reunion, time in flowing water, a time pivoted on one fish.

Just before going to press with this book I went to a secluded north Highlands river in the evening in low water. Someone had built a sort of dolmen on the river-edge, a teetering monument of precariously balanced stones. In fact, a shrine. This is where an angler had encountered, or maybe just seen, a salmon. What other creature stirs humans to erect shrines? These reasons explain why salmon anglers have dug deep in their pockets to save their fish. They have mounted some of the more extraordinary rescue missions exerted for any species in the natural world. In Scotland in 1872 the Marquis of Huntly bought up the river-mouth nets on the River Dee where he owned fishing rights upstream so that rod-anglers, rather than those pulling curtains of twine, could benefit from better fishing. Around the same time it was said by a long-serving member of Parliament in London that he had never known a parliamentary session without a salmon bill. The money and time spent on the silver fish has been prodigious.

The efforts to bring back eastern America's salmon expended truly vast sums of money. Although in the first drawn-out phase, it failed, there may be a next phase and it will be better informed, and do better. Each dam that is dismantled on American rivers clears a free passage for anadromous creatures like salmon. Salmon anglers have funded hatchery programmes, scientific explorations, bailiff teams to protect salmon from human predators both in rivers and at sea, they have financed buy-outs of nets to allow their fish to breed, they have even funded vessels at sea to search for salmon-pathways, how water temperature and changing currents alter them, and how these relate to the salmon food chain.

Inevitably, salmon conservationists have had to become political. This has worked differently in different countries. In Iceland the dominance of Orri Vigfusson in salmon conservation, twinned with his ability to straddle the world stage, have meant that in some way he has added to national definition by virtue of his presence and influence. This role is not replicated anywhere else.

It is worth looking at. To effect conservation Vigfusson became a political force. Modern politicians have never espoused salmon; to do so is not in the self-help manual of how to get places. Politicians are remembered for what they have done not what they have prevented happening. Yet Vigfusson ended up with more clout than most of them. But he had a clear advantage; he was authentic, knew the sea, and came from a fishing family. His message never got scrambled because he acted alone, without intermediaries. Then, he was acting not for himself but for the fish. His commitment was entirely genuine. Using his contacts at sea he built a unique knowledge base about salmon in saltwater. Sundry people needed to access it. And he had persistence and passion, and no pre-conceptions. So he was listened to. He broke all the rules, a true one-off.

He has set the stage, too, for the next step in resource allocation of the salmon. Vigfusson has highlighted that the salmon's weight gain is laid on off the seas of Greenland, the Faroes and Iceland. The extent to which it does so also in international waters, and precisely where the feed is sourced, are unknowns, but the answer will be a movable feast: salmon will go where the food is, regardless of 200-mile sovereignty limits. Unlike with any other marine fish or any other fisheries debate, the angler is a stakeholder who, by and large, returns his fish to the wild. The angler does not reduce the salmon capital. Who, then, owns the salmon? Greenland is paid its grazing-fee. What about the sovereign owners of the other waters the salmon fattens in? Vigfusson is the person who has seen this long-range question from afar.

In Canada both east and west salmon anglers have been prominent conservationists, but also the pivotal ethos of the salmon has enjoined a wide constituency fighting for its survival as an uncontaminated wild creature. Indian tribes, coastal dwellers, boaters and wildlife generalists have coalesced to fight for the Atlantic salmon in a way which is not quite the same in Europe. For many east coasters salmon is in the psyche; when dams come down, it answers a deep call somewhere far inside. It restores the wild country that the early pioneers rejoiced in; it decontaminates the industrial era's excesses. A bandwagon developed which crossed many divides and was therefore harder for political forces to stigmatise.

In Britain salmon conservation is represented in several organisations with similar-themed aims. They might have had more leverage as one group. Complexities arose maybe because Britain was the spiritual home of rod-angling for salmon. Its conservationists have fought successfully for salmon on matters like water quality and healthy river-flows.

Dealing with salmon farming has proved an altogether tougher struggle. Anglers faced a unified front of government locked in partnership with large international companies. The fish farmers leaned heavily on their social and economic role in providing significant numbers of jobs, and servicing an export market. Therefore to hit at salmon farming could be portrayed as heartlessly shunning the issue of joblessness in sensitive areas, and disregarding trade. Knocking salmon farming looked whimsical, even effete.

There was a locality factor. On the west of Scotland seaboard where salmon farming occurred, river and fishing owners developed a different view. Some leased foreshore sites and buildings to fish farmers. Salmon farmers needed access points on land and fishery owners could benefit from these leases. Other landowners leased freshwater cage sites to hatcheries supplying salmon farmers.

Before salmon farming ever arrived west coast river owners anyway did less business from their fishing rivers than those on the east coast. West coast rivers were shorter and faster, owing to the high spine of Scotland being to the rainier west side. Western rivers tumbled precipitously to the sea when it rained. When it did not rain salmon either held station out at sea or holed up in deep river-holes and went doggo. Instead of angling seasons starting, as some east coast rivers did, shortly after New Year, western rivers started in early summer and had shorter fishing seasons. The west rivers had fewer salmon and counted for less.

When salmon farms arrived there was concern, but there was also a prickle of interest lest some of the business could be made to stick. Landowners on the west, often owners of fishing rights too, had less, if any, arable and productive land; fresh sources of income were welcomed. By the time it became clear that salmon farming and wild salmon could not share the same estuaries, the fish farmers were making big profits and were in expansion mode. Increasingly owned by punch-drunk international corporations, they had the ear of government. The angling community could be cast as old-fashioned and reactionary, a recognisable tabloid cliché. Some of the river owners on the west lived in England and turned up on their ravishingly pretty waters only in the summer; they felt they had a precarious foothold in the debate, even though they could see what effect the big intruder was having. Others, resident, loving their rivers, anguished by the expiring gene banks of their wild fish, writhed between a rock and a hard place.

Over turbulent years various accommodations and agreements between fish culturists and anglers were made, un-made, and cobbled together again. Salmon farmers maintained the appearance of cooperating. Concordats were announced. They never settled down well. There were fundamentally contrary aims. One was to utilise the sea lochs as intensive food production zones, the other was to leave them clean, natural and free for returning migratory salmonids.

Sea trout took the biggest hit. Their lifecycle, feeding near shore and shunting up and down the coastline, pushed them straight into the maw of the inshore-dwelling parasitic sea-lice swarms. It had already happened in Norway where some populations of sea trout have departed this earth. There was only ever one winner in this conflict. Famous sea-trout fisheries like Loch Maree in the north-west Scottish Highlands, known to fly anglers all over Europe, just sank, as the faithfully returning trout succumbed in their juvenile phase to rampant vampirism from parasites. Sea trout go to and from the sea more often than salmon, lethal for a fish whose whole lifecycle rubs against the Norwegian neighbours from hell.

Scotland's fishery boards, that for so long had protected the migratory fish which it was their statutory duty to conserve, tried to reach agreements. Sites would be fallowed, lice treatments would harmonise with sensitive times for outgoing smolts, cage expansion would be limited, and so on. From the salmon farmer's point of view they were designed not to work but to fail. Salmon farmers dissembled that the sea louse piggybacked into their zone on wild fish. Wild salmon and sea trout were the

Trojan horse for the nightmare parasite; they didn't need wild salmon.

Fishery boards accused salmon farmers of wanting to do away with their congeners in the wild. The fish farmers in reality were focused on output production and the salmon biomass reaching the marketplace; talks were window-dressing. Fishery boards were a nuisance, noises off to the proper business of keeping salmon processors busy. Any residual fidelity to the species which they had domesticated, which had succoured them, given their balloon its gas, was forgotten.

The see-saw of the protracted arguments is tedious. It shows what happens when neither side can really say what it believes, and there is a perceived need to keep talking. Timing lice treatments to allow smolts passage to the sea worked up to a point, as far as anyone could tell. But salmon farmers eventually wanted to treat lice when it suited them, not at any other time. They had epidemics to counter, money at stake, and the law on their side. All the agreements with fishery boards were voluntary and could be jettisoned at will. Their cynicism about communities, potential objectors to developments polluting their shorelines, became absolute when plans first made public were simply accompanied with promises of slugs of money. Inelegant, but it often worked.

To government, the anglers were shouting from the sidelines. Salmon angling could be re-directed to the river-rich east coast. The geographical cake had been bisected and that was that. Industry was preferred to leisure.

Government was guileful. By nodding approval for the talks between wild salmon interests and the fish farmers it slid out of its regulatory role. It devolved the issue to parties doomed only to have meetings, to achieve nothing. Government and government alone could tame this industry. It needed primary legislation. By brokering talks between irreconcilable opposites the government ducked its duty and the side it backed was assured of success.

Government also had a private iron in the fire. The Nationalists were loudly demanding that ownership of the sea-bed be transferred from the Crown Estate, or the United Kingdom Exchequer, to themselves. It was their sovereign property, and was an asset belonging with the newly devolved administration. The reasons given publicly never mentioned the main one: with the sea-bed came the salmon farm rents. The Scottish government saw the money, but it did not see the sea-bed, which was no longer clean. Say, for supposition, the salmon farmers were ever nailed for polluting the inshore environment. Many think that day is getting closer. The salmon farm companies might have faded into the fog by that time, or hived off tenancy issues to bust subsidiaries. It would be left to the landlords to tackle the restoration work and pay reparations. The EU could demand a clean up. The Scottish government would have seized the lucrative freehold only to discover a poisoned chalice. For someone, someday, may have to clean up.

The salmon fishery boards, anyway behind the curve with salmon farming, never focused on this. They had their own fish to fry. In an effort to appear to impatient stakeholders to be logging progress in protecting salmon, the boards got too close to their natural enemy. A pinch-point came when attempting to control the cage industry turned into acting as facilitators in net-pen expansion.

This process started in 2011 when Norway displeased China, the largest expanding market for western food, by championing a Chinese dissident artist. China retaliated by cutting Norwegian farm salmon imports. A new supplier was needed and Scotland's devolved government's First Minister jumped gleefully into line. Bagpiping a leased Chinese panda to its Edinburgh zoo, he welcomed a Chinese delegation to Caledonia, airily promising a salmon farming expansion in Scotland to help solve China's food supply problem. Scotland was to go for a 40 per cent output increase. No one had been asked how; it was a triumphalist decree.

This is where the boards entered the scene. Where were all these extra salmon to be grown? On open-sea sites? The sea lochs were full. Boards were persuaded that playing a part in positioning this expansion was part of their brief. Or fish farmers, brandishing planning gain community bribes, would just spread anywhere. Without consulting the fishery owners boards and their colleagues on fishery trusts drew up a list of rivers on the west coast which were more or less suitable – or expendable, as some of the fishing owners of those rivers saw it. And the fishery owners were paying levies to finance activities of those boards. Some owners protested that they were financing their own execution.

Participation in this re-mapping of the aquaculture sector was being done in the full knowledge of all the new understandings: the knowledge that sea lice were out of control, that many rivers had genetically unique stocks of salmon, that farm escapees damage them, that escapement was inevitable, that some river salmon stocks were hanging on a thread – or were already history. There are two views: that fishery boards had walked into a trap, or that refusal to cooperate would have led to results that were even worse.

River owners on the east were relieved the expansion was on the other coast; some of the volunteer salmon farm expansion draughtsmen had blatant conflicts of interest; various scientists on fishery trusts backed off, saying there were critical unknowns, such as what paths young salmon used migrating northwards. It was a mess. The sport fishing sector began an internecine argument, as should have been foreseen. Salmon farmers must have looked on with satisfaction.

Their ire against wild fish supporters had in any case been rising because river boards had initiated legal actions against salmon farms, citing their reckless damage to the environment and to migrating runs of salmon and sea trout. Auto-reflexive aggression from salmon farmers called for river owners to assess stocks, throw open their policy-making to the public, and finished with the contribution that angling was doomed. Warming to the attack, salmon farmers said that angling caused pain to fish, constituted an animal welfare abuse, and that anglers needed to be brought to book. The argument and mud-slinging got increasingly heated. The politicised fate of the fish was bringing it increasingly into the public arena.

One benefit of the arguments was that salmon became a news story. Herrings were not so controversial. Familiarity breeds interest and the profile of the fish was reinvigorated.

Up to this time it has been managed at different points in its lifecycle. One such point was the juvenile phase, little fish darting out from behind rocks and shade and nipping away at morsels as they bide their time for growth and for migration. Headwater streams have been cleaned and titivated to favour the survival of young salmonids in many places.

There were resounding triumphs like on the Tweed, with the largest salmon population in Europe. Here the problems of salmon-friendly habitat were vigorously addressed. The hundreds of miles of miniature streams feeding the bigger branches and the hundred-mile main river were protected from trampling cattle and over-numerous sheep with fencing. Riparian zones were brought back into a condition they would not have seen since before Man started serious farming, grasses flopping over the flows, scrub and bushy cover affording protection and shade. Banks grew in, flows which had braided out in slow oxygen-deficient dribbles were concentrated again, and there was cover and food for young salmon. The whole effort was vindicated not only in wonderfully recuperated young salmon densities but dizzying catches by anglers, peaking in 2011. Directed human effort could redress history and generate salmon-bonanza results all in a short time, given a fair wind.

Fishery boffins talk of 'straddling stocks' being those marine fish which span several fishing zones. More stakeholders have to reach more involved agreements to protect them. Salmon is the ultimate straddling stock. That is why control of salmon netting has been such a great achievement in contemporary time. Dam removal and modification is making habitat for salmon in easy sweeping gestures by opening up miles of river to renascent pioneers relocating ancient breeding territories. It is the equivalent of planting a garden of luxuriating shrubs on former waste-land and watching the nesting birds arrive. The carrying capacity of these beckoning water-zones for fish is ratcheted up dramatically.

Still lacking, though, is an overview protection of the salmon in its complete life-phase. The biology says it needs watchful protection all the way from egg, through its sea odysseys, to physical entropy as a rotting kelt washed out by spates onto floodplains in the aftermaths of winter storms.

European and American salmon people know that the weak point in the cycle is at sea. Where fifty years ago as many as one in three smolts which swam out of rivers in the spring managed to come back in enlarged form as adults, today the figure is usually between two and five in a hundred. Growing salmon are disappearing out at sea, nipped in the bud; out there somewhere is a Bermuda Triangle. It is not the first time this has occurred. Around 1900 the same hiccup in salmon returns was noted and similar anxieties were ventilated.

Angler organisations have rallied as ever with funded research. The Atlantic Salmon Federation is sponsoring wave-glider robotic tracking instruments which can detect a salmon at sea 800 yards away, to try to shed light on the black hole of the salmon migration. On rivers in Maine biologists have been blowing salmon eggs, at eyed ova stage, down long pipes which fashion redds using hydraulic pressure, gently burying them in gravel to re-awaken in early spring. In four Maine rivers they deposited over a million eggs this way. People are acting as spawning salmon. Some say these are messages in a bottle, daft whimsicalities, others hold up the example of native North Americans long ago who, it is said, pioneered transplanting eggs of spawning salmon on the Pacific coast.

Around the northern hemisphere there are many of these people, bright-eyed enthusiasts smitten by the salmon bug, nudging its continuation along with ingenious encouragements, nurturing ova and fingerlings, repairing habitat and expanding the salmon occupation zone, peeping from behind the bushes at the torrid scenes of egg-fertilisation, as fixated by the fish as the early cave dwellers who scraped its image into the rocks of their homes. There are schoolchildren all over salmon country adopting delightfully pink eggs, watching for the development of the little black eye, the tadpole tails emerging, and then returning personalised fry to streams in spring. Maidens, mothers and misses are inspired by the salmon story to render our part of their territory more hospitable, spending their time and energy and money. There are salmon festivals – I am thinking of one on the Miramichi River in Canada – where inflated salmon float surreally over the lampposts, salmon in the sky, celestial salmon. Salmon top polls of people's star fish.

If salmon do disappear off the radar, anglers cannot be accused of a lack of fibre in trying to prevent it. The survival test will be sharpest in the marine, a hard place to find anything out and a hard place to put anything right.

Findings are anyway often alarming rather than reassuring. Work by the prestigious science research body the Royal Society traced the dramatic spread of our old friend the louse *Leoptherius salmonis.* They concluded that a stupefying thirty-nine per cent of wild salmon in the north-east Atlantic are dying from the effects of lice. A third of the marine population is succumbing to one parasite.

One of the authors of this report, Dr Martin Krkosek, has confirmed that it was common to find samples of wild salmon in which every individual had attached lice sucking the host. Mortalities include lice-kills on young fish caught at sea. A difference in the louse on salmon and a tick on a sheep is that a sheep tick fills its belly and drops off, but the salmon louse feeds and stays on. However, the salmon louse has another arrow in its survival quiver: it can swim amongst hosts, discard a dying one and batten onto a fresh victim. New parasite studies show that multiplying the family members can be preferred to eating the host to death. Instead of abandoning a dying host they lay more eggs. The salmon louse turns out to be an altogether formidable operator.

Questions abound. Was salmon farming responsible for the proliferation of the sea lice? Or were they always there? Before salmon farming, did a third of salmon at sea die like this? No one knows. Recent increases in sea temperatures in the North Atlantic suit sea-lice proliferation as they replicate quicker in warmer water. The estuaries, where they mass, are warmer too. Is this a factor? No known answers. Salmon farmers have battened onto the paper and attempted to invalidate it. There is the familiar Punch and Judy show in the trade press. What is indisputable is that salmon farming has produced its own parasite onslaught in its own region; the parasites are found far and wide, and their proliferation threatens wild salmon. It may be a coincidence that wild salmon are being throttled this way, it may not. It gives one a creepy feel.

Not as creepy perhaps as transgenic salmon. Yes, you read right. Not content with faster-grown fish accelerated by telescoped light-cycles, fed more on vegetables than fish, an ingenious biotechnology company has been splicing genes from other fish into salmon to make them perform better, do a higher dance. This search for a super salmon started in the 1990s when an American biotechnology firm inserted a Chinook or king salmon gene into an Atlantic salmon to make it grow faster. A Pacific salmon was blended with the Atlantic one. New-wave salmon will be harvested at the same size, but they will have got there twice as fast.

But it is not destined only to be a crossed Atlantic-Pacific salmon. Hidden away in the genetic brew is another insertion, this time from a completely different fish – the big-headed, thin-tailed ocean pout, deep-down dweller in the North Atlantic. The gene being selected here is an anti-freeze one; if you recognise the gene flavour, it is already present in ice cream! Its contribution to the newly engineered salmon creature-creation is to help survival in colder waters, thus opening up aquaculture sites further north than are currently used. Further north, but no loss of growth-velocity: two hits in one.

Any downsides? Although they live less long they will need about the same amount of food. No feed-saving there. Then, to cope with bionic growth rates the new transgenics may get sick and need more medicines. The industry has never blanched at buying more medicines before, so why do so now? The crop, after all, will be grown from the smolt phase nearly as fast as a vegetable itself. The super salmon will be a veritable piscine mushroom.

The biotech research to create this bionic novelty was done in Canada but the grow-out is scheduled to occur in Panamanian high-altitude lakes. Some say this is to make escapes irrelevant, as the new hybrid will be far from any possible home, and others say it is to circumvent the licensing requirements of the USA's Food and Drug Administration. But the FDA recently pre-empted speculations by making encouraging remarks, stating that it is likely to be unworried by transgenic salmon as they will be from triploids and therefore neutered.

This is despite the fact that this laboratory fish would be the first GM animal ever approved for human consumption.

The company which has created the first transgenic salmon has been quietly persistent and spent seventeen years getting to the point of applying for a production license. Let's posit a scenario. They are permitted to sell the stuff simply as Atlantic salmon, as being requested, with no mention of genetic fiddling and splicing. Grown at great speed, suddenly huge volumes of extra salmon flood the market. Overnight the fjord magnates, the Chileans and the Scottish Vikings are undercut. Their lumbering old-style Norwegian salmon are too slow. They need these new fish too. What administration, faced with soaring food costs and more and more consumers, would deny them a faster-growing salmon?

Gene manipulation between animals is not allowed in some countries, one being Norway. However, times change; salmon history shows that. Laws adapt. The new transgenics will be in the sea lochs and fjords and minches, getting out, mixing, as ever, with the remnants of the wild fellows clinging to their time-worn and evolution-tested pathways and timescales, stealing their rations. Not a bonny prospect.

At some point the question jumps at one: what is the survival chance for this almost lethally romantic fish? We know that as a partner with us in freshwaters and lakes, spawning maybe in the mountains behind where we live, the salmon is in our backyard. The silver fish also flashes its glinting colours out at sea in front. Residents overlooking bays where salmon congregate before running rivers detect the waiting shoals from water-shimmer. If the wild salmon ever disappeared that shimmer would be no more. The rivers would lack their most life-giving denizens.

That would not be the sum of all loss. In its gills the salmon carries the larvae of freshwater pearl mussels, opalescent beauties which the Romans noticed and harvested and took home. It was thought, until recently, that freshwater pearl mussels colonised the gills of trout or salmon equally. But studies in Norway show that some populations of these heavily protected crustaceans deposit their larvae only on salmon and not on brown trout; other populations in the same river select only the trout and not the salmon. If salmon ever faded from our biosphere, those specialised salmon mussels would go too. Pearls thrown before swine.

River trout and other river-fish would lack salmon fry as their whitebait; gulls, ravens, sawbill ducks and otters, bears and raccoons in the Americas, would all miss out; river-life would be a pale imitation of the past. The colour silver itself would lose a champion. When you stop to consider, very few fish are silver. Look on the fishmonger's slab anywhere in the world. Silver is the presiding pigment of some of the big billfish like swordfish, the tuna clan, herrings, steelhead and some other trout. The silver soldiers are always pelagics, inhabiting surface layers. But the great bulk of piscivorous life is dull in hue.

This proximity to humankind hugely compromises the salmon existence. It is a thought: no non-dinosaur sea-fish has ever become extinct that we know of. They are all out there somewhere, if we needed to find them. But if the salmon does not come home, passing by the bottom of the garden, to occupy his natal tenements in the home stream, then he is gone. If not gone right away, he is doomed to be gone before long.

Consider the sturgeon. This extraordinary prehistoric-looking fish which can live longer than humans and measure twenty-five feet, which has barbels resembling gaucho moustaches hanging from its mouth, and ridges on its back and sides, has all but disappeared in many places. It once slithered into the Thames to breed. No more. The salmon has come back and swims past the Houses of Parliament, but the sturgeon, despite once having the status of a royal fish reserved to the Crown, is gone. In most of Europe it is extinct. It is gone, too, from most of the Danube up which it once travelled 1500 miles from the Black Sea. Damming reduced surface water areas by as much as half in some Danube basins, side-channels were filled in, and the mighty river was engineered, cinched into functional channels, and whipped into shape to accommodate human needs, regardless of sturgeon needs.

The Danube, interlacing eighteen countries, is Europe's signature river. Long ago six species of sturgeon savoured its waters. All types are extinct in the Upper and Middle sections and only four species still breed in the Lower Danube. Treasured for their eggs called caviar, sturgeon were trapped from the beginning of time. Damming stopped species survival in its tracks. Romania was still constructing sturgeon-throttling mega-dams in the 1980s.

The history of wanton sturgeon destruction is no better across the Atlantic where there are still seven species. Almost devoid of financial value until the 1860s in Canada, their bodies were tossed back into the river when caught. Then someone thought of using them as fertiliser and feeding them to livestock. There are reports of the huge bodies of lake sturgeon being stacked 'like cordwood' on the timber dock at Amherstburg, Ontario, from where they were retrieved from total waste by serving as fuel-stock for steamboats plying the Detroit River. The status of North American sturgeon species is between secure and declining.

Sturgeon in Russia met a sticky end by a different route. Pollution from industry and fall-out from nuclear accidents poisoned rivers on an epic scale. Salmon do not eat in rivers, an advantage for them. But as sturgeon slowly glide along the river bed vacuuming up organisms on the bottom they can quickly saturate themselves with chemical benthic horrors. Their purpose in these places is, like salmon, to breed. They deposit their sticky eggs on the stream bed in summer. Over half of the sad specimens from Russia's Lena River autopsied in the 1980s had lost much of their reproductive ability owing to pollution. The few faithfully returning survivors were therefore often unable to breed. Filth had simply overwhelmed their defences. These ancient long-lived fish, which originated in Europe around two hundred million years ago and then spread to Asia, are now endangered in most of the places in which they cling to our planetary existence. It is not a good omen.

Survival is not always backwards and one-way: recently a small fish called the Danube streber, like the sturgeon a river-bottom feeder, has reappeared after a century spent incommunicado. Cleaning up the Danube produced its little miracle. But sturgeon is charismatic, a creature to send the imagination spinning. I saw a picture of one long ago, a formative memory. There were four smiling men standing in a row, not very close together. They held in their extended arms a sturgeon. Its head and its tail were touching the ground at each end of the row. There was something disturbing about the image, as though the men and the fish were phenomena that should never have met. Also, it was bedded in the past: this just couldn't have been now.

Take a step back. The salmon has a strategic advantage. It lives in the North Atlantic. A bookmaker would give better odds for survival in that zone than, say, for the rhinos in central Africa. Two reasons: the North Atlantic is a politicised zone meshed with controls, fishing zones and international agreements; and cash-rich Chinese do not rank salmon alongside rhino-horn.

Salmon has no scarcity-value ... yet; one reason salmon propagation in cages, done right, has to continue. The nations bordering the North Atlantic may not be mind-bendingly enlightened about species survival but the technology they possess has the capacity not only to destroy the creatures in its domain, but also to protect them. Indeed, there is a huge public constituency for salmon survival on both sides of this ocean. Time has shown that efforts to save salmon can be mounted with amazing élan and intensity.

Say for example that the flotilla of plastic rubbish which has been dubbed the North Pacific Gyre, which could be as big as Texas and which is presently adrift on the skin of the ocean, was actually in the Atlantic instead, it is possible to imagine consensus for its removal. The nations which have Atlantic salmon ascending their rivers in the autumn would gird their loins and act in such a situation. They just would: embarrassment would do the trick.

The North Atlantic is a reasonably promising place for a migratory fish to be making its stand in the face of what is coming.

There is the talking point about humanity balanced with natural creatures in the present prospectus for our civilisation. History suggests it is the pressure of human development which has narrowed down the survival zone of salmon. The fact that we can now see that clearly is good. Whether we can go on altering natural systems, and freshwater rivers, in order to make space for those hungry human populations and do it in sync with fish needs, the requirements of amphipods and tiny grubs and larvae we cannot see, is the issue. The pressure of human development is the issue. More people, or more salmon? Over to you.

Further Reading

Salmon: The World's Most Harassed Fish; Anthony Netboy, Andrew Deutsch, 1980.

The Atlantic Salmon: A Vanishing Species?; Anthony Netboy, Faber and Faber, 1968.

To the Sea and Back: The Heroic Life of the Atlantic Salmon; Richard Shelton, Atlantic Books, 2009.

Salmon; Peter Coates, Reaktion Books, 2006.

Memories of the Months; Sir Herbert Maxwell.

The Longest Silence; Thomas McGuane, Yellow Jersey Press, 2000.

Indian Fishing: Early Methods on the Northwest Coast; Hilary Stewart, University of Washington Press, 1977.

Silenced Rivers: The Ecology and Politics of Large Dams; Patrick McCully, Zed Books, 1996.

American Forests: A History of Resilience and Recovery; Douglas W. MacCleery, Forest History Society pamphlet, 1992.

The River Alta and Its Salmon Fishery; Jens Petter Nielsen, Kjell Roger Eikeset and Kari Heitmann, published by the Alta Salmon Fishery Partnership, 2009.

Vermont River; W. D. Wetherell, Lyons and Burford, 1984.

A World of Rivers; Ellen Wohl, University of Chicago Press, 2011.
King Of Fish: The Thousand Year Run of Salmon; David R. Montgomery, Westview Press, 2003.
Life History and Habits of the Salmon, Sea Trout, Trout and other Freshwater Fishes; P. D. Malloch, Mallochs of Perth and London, 1910.

Acknowledgements

The salmon bug is a culture not an epiphany. As the Canadian writer Frederick H. Wooding summarised it: 'This species has a mysterious influence on human hearts and minds.' You get hooked up over time. Therefore those to be acknowledged have played a part often unwittingly. Two stand out: Andrew Tennant and John Hardy Sutherland. Both are passionate rod-anglers and both learnt what they know from observation and an inordinate time spent in water shared with salmon. One time Andrew Tennant caught twenty-eight salmon on one pool on the River Deveron during a thunderstorm flashing on and off over twenty-four hours, when fish are meant to lie low. Helmsdale ghillie Johnny Hardy notched up a reputation as the canniest reader of salmon-water and an inspiration to anglers, standing head and shoulders above the pack. Both have huge practical knowledge. My grandmother, Ina Wigan, was apt to read weather and the passage of time in terms of the opportunity to engage fruitfully with salmon and caught six thousand of them to her own rod in twenty years. Wildfowl punt-gunner in his spare time, Dick Shelton is the scientist most able to communicate salmon life-science. Master caster Mark Birkbeck has a sixth sense for fish of which he has caught a huge number; his piscine fascination now sends him down onto the reefs armed with a primitive fishing-sling. Eila Grahame, my cousin and my fishing companion when I was a small boy, was the same: she drilled down on what she was doing and had the ability to conjure even from the slack times a form of drama merely from being in the same place as the silver fish. With all of them, something is always about to happen. They all have abnormal powers of concentration.

My knowledge and enthusiasm for salmon has also been added to by the following individuals: fishing camp manager Walter Faetz in British Columbia, Eddie McCarthy from the River Thurso, Peter Quail and Glen MacDonald from the Helmsdale, Rick Warren on the Restigouche, Padraig Fallon for his radiant enthusiasm, the late Robert Biddulph who unfurled during one week's boat-fishing the secrets of the Grimersta salmon, and the well-known neurologist and healer Peter Behan. Peter Power was the creator of the astonishing camps on the Kharlovka, Rhynda and Litsa in Russia's Arctic north, galvanised by infectious enthusiasm for the great fish. Vanya Hackel, with his wide contacts range, has helped with this book unstintingly. Scottish writer Bruce Sandison apprised what was going on with salmon farming long ago; his long crusade to expose it approximates to the heroic. Nathaniel Reed, Assistant Secretary of the Interior for Fish Wildlife and National Parks in two US government administrations, has introduced me to select rivers and saltwaters and the intricacies of practical conservation with astonishing generosity. Orri Vigfusson knows more about the salmon than almost anyone, reads the future, and has a knack of understanding the position of salmon in our culture and in our history; he has devoted his life to its preservation. Andy Russell, outback writer and one-time grizzly bear hunting guide, took me on my first steelhead fishing trip in British Columbia and made me understand that articulating conservation needs is not an option, it is an obligation. Lastly, thanks to my publisher Myles Archibald, to whom nothing needed to be explained.

The writers who have addressed the salmon matter are crowned by Antony Netboy, who accumulated a vast body of knowledge and evidence in a series of books. Not many have written better about the act of fishing than Sir Herbert Maxwell. Tom McGuane and David Profumo use adroit prose to communicate the thrills of contact with fish on trembling threads almost alarmingly sharply. The mercurial American writer, W. D. Wetherell, author of the low-key, laid-back fishing classic *Vermont River*, is funnier than any of those who try to tell jokes. West Canadian angler-judge Roderick Haig-Brown plumbed the depths of salmon mystery with a superb lucidity. In my pantheon, the South Africa trout angler Tom Sutcliffe and Chris Yates, who wrote *The Secret Carp*, add to our understanding of why people hold fishing rods. In impressive research work, Inka Milewski's forensic investigations on the effects of salmon farming in New Brunswick are brutally logical and make any slippery refutations unimaginable. Ray Humber in Newfoundland is an inspiring salmon fishing-camp manager, having more energy, brio and general thrust in pursuit of keeping his anglers happy than anyone I encountered.

Hilary Stewart's 1977 book *Indian Fishing* is in a special class. This lady actually constructed herself the fishing devices she describes, as used by the Pacific coast Indians securing their salmon harvest. She procured the plant, timber, gut, bone and other ingredients, manufactured the ingenious contraptions and made sure that they did what folklore said they did. Her own drawings of these devices are models of clarity. The whole study is deliciously detailed, one of the most attractive books I know. It makes you want to shed your clothes, run off and live in a cave and intercept salmon to stay alive.

Telling legends, stories, myths and fables often grow in fishing-huts and fishing-camps. The salmon binds together the unlikeliest assortment of sometimes wayward individualists. The spirit of camaraderie which can develop over breaks in some rattling hut perched in the gale-swept tundra of the north rivers is one of the enduring reference points of my own magnetic field. When February days are bleak and rough I think of the tails developing on the eggs of the salmon ova buried in the stream-gravels and the promise of what is to come. Many others living on or near rivers have the same thought process and in this odd linkage the salmon world is a distinct fraternity. The many contributors to my approximate understanding of the Atlantic salmon go back to childhood and not all of them can be recollected as individuals.

So my dedication is to all those who understand the poetry of salmon, those who feel their pulses racing when they experience the fish, whether through a vibrating fishing-rod, or at a waterfall when they are jumping, by a placid pool where a salmon unexpectedly leaps, on a narrow stream at spawning when the great hen fish leans sideways expelling eggs, or even in the feelings of a farmer in a flooded field cradling a marooned fish in his arms for return to a nearby river. Call them a brotherhood of souls, or what you like.

The late aviator Alan Mann once fished a late week on the Helmsdale with his fishing buddy and they landed over eighty salmon. But Alan had only half a dozen – and they were a mistake. He had been fishing minute dry flies on long light-weight leaders and casting square. He said: 'I had a wonderful time. I only wanted to see them rise.' That is the spirit of appreciation to which this book is dedicated.

Index

Index

Index

Index

Index